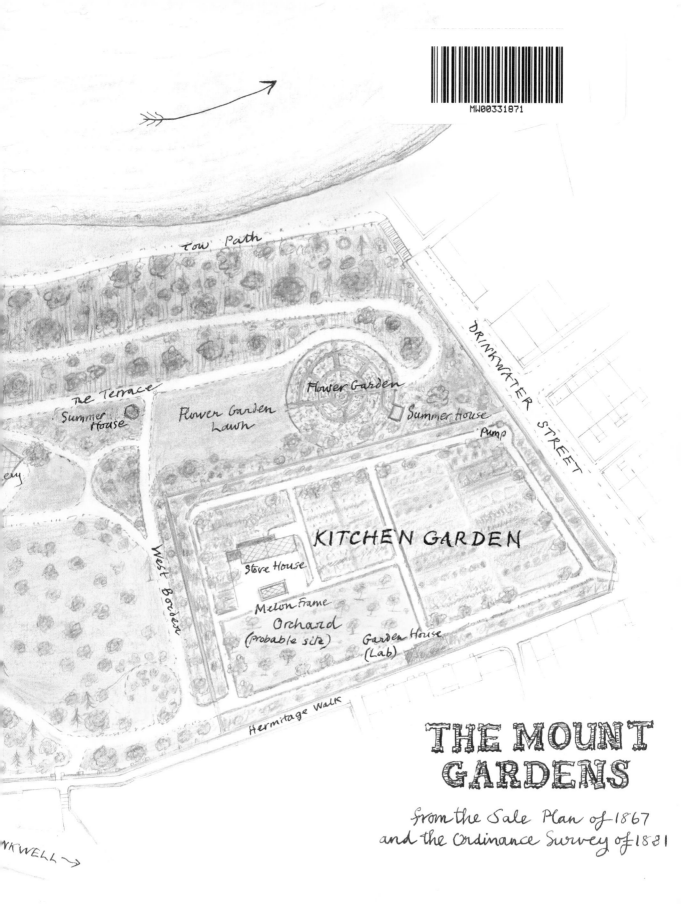

Tow Path

DRINKWATER STREET

The Terrace

Summer House

Flower Garden Lawn

Flower Garden

Summer House

Pump

West Border

KITCHEN GARDEN

Stove House

Melon Frame

Orchard
(probable site)

Garden House
(Lab)

Hermitage Walk

NKWELL →

THE MOUNT GARDENS

from the Sale Plan of 1867
and the Ordinance Survey of 1881

THE

GARDEN DIARY

OF

DOCTOR DARWIN

1838 – 1865

A Garden History

researched, written and illustrated

by

Susan Campbell

UNICORN

Contents

1839 Hay making

1840 Flower garden mowed. Beans first time for Family.

1841 Lettuce and Knight Broccoli planted.

1842 making Hay.

1843 first Carrots got in garden

1844 tomatoes planted by Stove last asparagus cut. (2652 head cut this y

1845 Sunday

1849 Raspberries & Strawberries gathered for Preserving

1850 Brussels Sprouts planted

1851 Guinea fowl began to sit on Terrace.

1852

1853 Turnips sown on S. border.

1854 ~~Sunday~~ Thursday. planting Brussels Sprouts.

1855 sowed Hollyhock seed - layed Rose de Meaux in F. Garden.

1856 Sunday.

1857 gathered Raspberries for preserving - planted Lettuce out. & Geranium bed.

1858 sowed Spinach & Lettuce - 1st Artichokes gathered

Sunday

Endive and Broccoli sowed. Letter D made a press by Peach tree with nitrate of soda. applied also ~~in other places~~

Black currants for preserving. a cow attacked with the distemper. the one they call Silly.

Lime tree made from a cutting reported

making Hay.

4 Sunday Blue water Lily open.

5 making Hay.

9 pruning Vine on front of house

5 Rose budding for M.r Harding's King of Battles

1

2 Currant & Raspberries for Tart

3 Thinning Grapes in 2.d Hothouse.

4 Florence Cherries gathered.

5 cleaning out Wheelbarrow place cutting dead Laurels. very hot weather

6 digging trench for Hollies

7 mowed Flower Garden — with Mowing Machine — transplanted Pomme de Merano — No not yet

8 rainy weather

62 Ruby had her 1.st Calf

5 Ruby calved 4.th time

Charles Darwin as a child, drawn by Ellen Sharples

FOREWORD

James A. Secord, FBA

Director, Darwin Correspondence Project, University of Cambridge

Charles Darwin, whose explorations of nature helped to change the way we think about the living world, was first inspired by the garden of his child-hood home. High above the River Severn at Shrewsbury, the 7 acres at The Mount House occupied an enduring place in his life. This is where his earliest adventures took place, where he climbed trees and learned to observe animals and plants. It is here that the young Darwin watched his mother keep doves and where he and his older brother set up a chemistry laboratory in the tool-shed.

The real hero of this remarkable book, however, is not the naturalist later famous as the author of *On the Origin of Species* but the Darwin family garden itself. The garden at The Mount was designed by Charles's parents, Susannah Darwin (born into the Wedgwood family) and her physician husband Robert Darwin. It began to take shape soon after their marriage in 1796, along with the house itself, into which they moved in 1800. The garden included many striking features, including a 680-ft-long terrace walk, a steep river cliff, a large circular flower garden, and facilities for supplying the house with seasonable fruit and vegetables, as well as specialities like winter cucumbers and hothouse delicacies such as pineapples and bananas.

The great virtue of *The Garden Diary of Doctor Darwin* is the way in which it brings the garden at The Mount vividly to life. The author, Susan Campbell, is internationally acknowledged as a garden historian and illustrator, known for her writings on walled kitchen gardens; she is thus particularly qualified to reveal the broader context and unusual features of this very special domestic garden. Campbell is the leading expert on the garden at The Mount, having published several articles about it in *Garden History*, the journal of the Garden History Society (now the Gardens Trust). Best of all, her account is based on a unique source–a diary covering the later years of the garden's development from 1838 to 1865.

Susan Campbell's knowledge of garden history and horticulture enables her to uncover deeper patterns of change and stability behind the diary's often brief and cryptic daily jottings. The book evokes the constant routines of planning, planting, pruning, mowing and harvesting–a world of physical work and aesthetic enjoyment, of traffic between the kitchen and the garden, between servants, family and friends. Cosmic events, such as the sight of Donati's Comet across the sky in 1858, are witnessed, but what really matters is the passing of the seasons.

If the garden is to reveal something new about the man who once called it 'Paradise', it is that small, everyday things are of great significance–and not only for our understanding of Darwin but also of the natural world of which we are a part. Charles Darwin, like his sister Susan, who followed her father in maintaining the garden and keeping the diary, would have appreciated the meticulous attention to detail that is apparent throughout this work, its careful accounting and historical specificity. This is nicely evoked in the book with a comprehensive list of every plant known to have been in the garden and an almanac bringing together observations from the different months of the year.

This beautifully designed volume has many of the pleasures of a garden. The text is complemented by the author's exquisite line drawings: a basket of apples, the turn of leaves on a tree, a common frog, a measuring tape, prospects of fields and of the house. These images are simultaneously transitory and unforgettable, like the long-lost garden that this book enables us to visit in our imagination.

INTRODUCTION

Susan Campbell

Today, Wednesday 13 November 2019, we picked apples here in Hampshire and sent them to the family in London. And tomorrow our gardener will continue to move our tender plants into the greenhouse.

170 years ago to the day, on Tuesday 13 November 1849, and nearly 300 miles away as the crow flies, my namesake Susan wrote in her father's Garden Diary 'Camelias taken to Hothouse–Basket of Apples sent to Charles 10 Dozen.'

It was the idea of comparing a mid-nineteenth-century garden with our own twenty-first-century gardens that first attracted me to this Garden Diary, but I was also aware that the date of that entry and the identity of the diarist were of equal, if not more, interest.

Susan's apples were to be sent from her garden in Shrewsbury to Down House, in Kent. 'Charles' was her brother, then busily occupied with his monograph on cirripedes and the father of six children, three of whom were suffering at the time from scarlet fever.[1]

Ten years later, again to the day, Charles was modestly sending the first copies of his book, *On the Origin of Species*, to a few of his friends but, since Susan's Diary relates only to her garden and livestock, there is no mention of that momentous event.

13 November also happens to be the anniversary of the death, in 1848, of Charles and Susan's father, Dr Robert Waring Darwin, at the age of eighty-three. The Doctor was the original diarist. He began to keep it on 1 September 1838 ('sowed ribes sanguinea. Took up Miss Darwins iris roots. Planted out Broccoli'). He kept the Diary going until 10 May 1846 ('Sunday. Large aloes taken out of Back shed'), when, in his eighty-first year, he appears to have lost interest in it. There are one or two entries later in that year, in a hand which is different from both the Doctor's and Susan's. When compared to a letter written to Charles in 1841, it proves to be that of the Darwins' gardener, John Abberley.[2]

Again, there is no reference in the Diary to the Doctor's death, but only a week after his funeral, Susan, then in her mid-forties, unmarried and therefore still living at home, opened the Diary, and entered, in pencil: 'Bacon pig killed 14 score short of 1 pound this is', with the weight overwritten in ink. She kept the Diary going until 17 October 1865 when she, too, ceased writing, and there it ends. She died on 3 October the following year.

The Diary therefore runs from 1 September 1838 to 17 October 1865. The only significant omissions occur between 1846 and 1848, with very few entries by Susan after 1860. As can be seen from the few entries already quoted, its subjects include fruit, flowers and vegetables as well as pigs, to which can be added weather conditions, trees, shrubs, cows, guinea fowl, hedging, ditching and manuring, as well as the names of numerous places, neighbours, gardeners, servants, friends and family.

The format is unusual: technically known as a perpetual diary, each day of the year occupies a single page, with annual, one-line entries. These start at the top with 1838 and end at the bottom with 1865. Large quarto, it is bound in leather, with marbled endpapers, just like the Doctor's hefty account books, which can be seen in the Cambridge University Library.

The garden in the Diary was at The Mount, a large brick house on the northern edge of Shrewsbury, built by Dr Darwin in the last years of the eighteenth century, shortly after his marriage. Several entries refer to events preceding 1838, which indicate that a diary previous to this one was also kept, but so far it has not come to light.

The first question I am always asked, when I talk about the Diary, is 'How did you come by it?' The brief answer is 'Somewhat nefariously to begin with.' Some thirty-five years ago I sent some letters by a famous writer to a well-known auction house for sale. The night before the auction my son was flicking through the catalogue when a full-page entry for this Diary caught his eye. I was immediately intrigued, having just embarked on a career as a garden historian specialising in walled kitchen gardens. However, the sale was to take place the next morning! I immediately phoned a friend who worked at the auction house, and he promised to break the strictest rules by letting me see the Diary an hour before the sale began. On arriving there I found him in a rage: 'The bugger has withdrawn it!' To me that could only mean one thing; the owner had decided to make a book out of it. So, the next question was 'Who is he?' Again, my friend was prepared to bend the rules; a letter from me was passed on to a natural historian living in Folkestone, Peter Dance.

To cut a long story short, Dance contacted me; he told me he had bought the Diary from a bookseller with connections in Norfolk and Bedford, who had simply told him that 'a little old lady just brought it in one day'. He confirmed my hunch that he was indeed proposing to make a book from the Diary, and being a conchologist at the Natural History Museum, as well as a natural history historian and an already established author, he was well placed to do so. However, he knew nothing about gardens, so he agreed that we should combine our knowledge and act as co-authors.

Peter Dance was generous with what he already knew about the Diary. He sent me a Xerox of the whole thing, which I transcribed on to my brand new computer. Moreover, since the Diary revealed that the Doctor was making horticultural experiments for Charles, and growing plants to help him with his earliest theories (something that had hitherto been unknown), he put me in touch with a Darwinian professor and a Darwinian descendant. He sent me Darwinian books and we both sought publishers, in vain.

Time trickled by. Peter retired and moved to Carlisle, to write more books on shells. I was already working on a book about a kitchen garden in Northamptonshire and researching my next book, on the history of kitchen gardens. It was only in 2000, when I read of floods in Carlisle and learned that the Diary was in the vaults of a bank there, that I thought perhaps I should offer to buy it from Peter, who had long since given up any thoughts of working on it. And so, eventually, it took its place on my bookshelves.

Even so, although I had been familiar with the Diary since the 1980s, it was some time before I felt properly equipped to write the book. I needed to diagnose each entry and apart from writing something that would be of interest for garden history enthusiasts, I needed to find out much more about Dr Darwin and his daughter Susan, not to mention the Diary's *éminence grise*, Charles Darwin himself. I have therefore divided the book into three parts. Part One is for the general garden and Darwinian enthusiast. Part Two is intended to be of more interest to keen garden historians, being in the form of an old-fashioned garden almanac. Part Three is intended for even more serious garden historians, cataloguing almost every plant mentioned in the Diary.

Both the Darwins' Diary and their Correspondence have a fair quota of literary errors. Throughout my own text I have avoided using the family's frequent misspelling of plant names in particular but, rather than litter quotations from those original sources with bracketed 'sics', I have kept their erratic spellings as well as their occasionally idiosyncratic punctuation.

Although it was the gardening side of the Diary that I was originally concerned with, writing the biographical material was a challenge. There is a mass of information available on Darwin's life and work, but there is relatively little about his birthplace and his father, and even less about his sister Susan. Moreover, Shrewsbury, especially in the 1990s, was more concerned with contemporary matters (such as being the TV setting for the adventures of a fictitious detective-monk named Cadfael) than being the birthplace of Charles Darwin. However, I did have material that was good enough for a start; I had contacts with a handful of Darwinian experts in that town, and the publication, year by year, of Darwin's *Correspondence* had just been launched. I also had a large-scale Sale Map of The Mount and its gardens dated 1867, with its accompanying Sale Catalogue, and above all, although it consisted, at most, of three brief, terse sentences a day, I had a diary recording the activities of nearly thirty years in The Mount's garden.

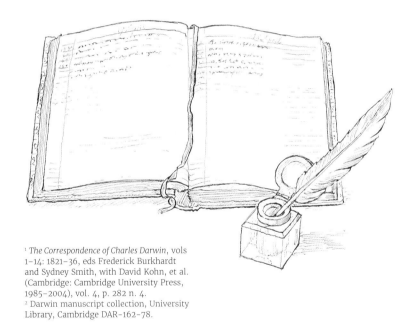

[1] *The Correspondence of Charles Darwin*, vols 1–14: 1821–36, eds Frederick Burkhardt and Sydney Smith, with David Kohn, et al. (Cambridge: Cambridge University Press, 1985–2004), vol. 4, p. 282 n. 4.
[2] Darwin manuscript collection, University Library, Cambridge DAR-162-78.

Fig. 22.—Placing the fumigator in a frame.

THE ATHENÆUM DARWIN DINNER

14ᵗʰ OCTOBER 2009

PART ONE

The History

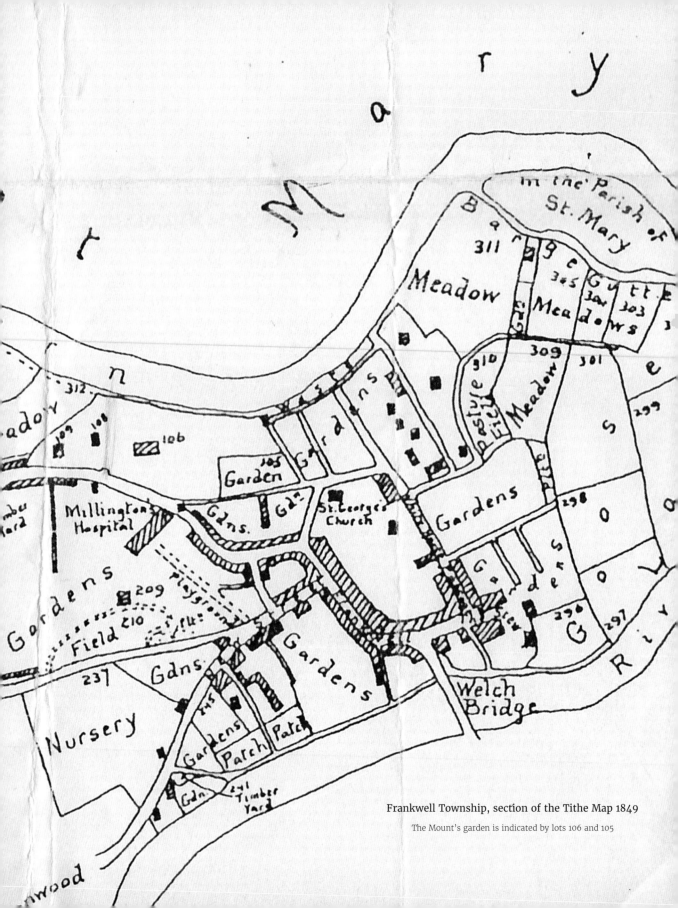

Frankwell Township, section of the Tithe Map 1849

The Mount's garden is indicated by lots 106 and 105

ONE

The Beginnings of The Mount and its Gardens

Although the residence of the Darwins was officially called 'The Mount House', none of the closest or even the most extended members of the family ever referred to it as such. To them it was always simply 'Shrewsbury'. Now locally known as 'Darwin House', The Mount House and some of its gardens still exist. The site is on top of a 100-ft-high cliff above the River Severn, where it flows eastwards along the northern limits of the town of Shrewsbury. The old mail coach road from Shrewsbury to Holyhead (now the A458 leading to the A5) and the district of Frankwell form the southern boundary of the property. To the east and west there are clusters of suburban villas.

Scarcely a mile from the centre of the town, the site was originally a bare 5-acre field known as Upper Whitehorse Field, after a nearby pub named the White Horse. There had once been a proposal to build Shrewsbury's new prison there; at the time of its purchase by Dr Robert Darwin (1766–1848), in 1796, it was being used as the municipal rubbish tip, where 'fire was said to burn all the time'.[1]

THE MOUNT AND ITS MEADOWS

By 1796, only ten years after he came to Shrewsbury as a newly qualified, twenty-year-old physician, Robert's medical practice was thriving and lucrative. 1796 was also the year of his marriage to Susannah Wedgwood (1765–1817), daughter of the famous potter Josiah Wedgwood, who had provided her with a very generous marriage settlement. 'Brick and slated',[2] large and imposing, The Mount House was built for the Darwins the following year. As well as a dining room, drawing room, morning room and library, with the usual kitchens, still rooms and cellars, it had fourteen bedrooms 'with suitable dressing rooms',[3] as well as a yard surrounded by stables, a saddle room, a coach house, a dairy, a piggery, a coal store, work sheds and a poultry house. When Dr Darwin was asked why he had built such a big house, his practical but somewhat pompous reply was: 'Had I built a small one nobody would have enquired about me and would not suppose a person of eminence could live in such a one ...'.[4]

Robert Darwin also bought, in 1798, Hill Head Bank, a 2-acre meadow lying to the west of his new house, as pasture for his house-cows. The

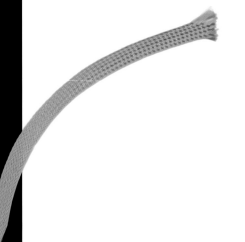

meadow, which gradually slopes down to the river from a continuation of the high bank below the mansion, is now in public ownership and forms part of a larger meadow known as 'the Doctor's Field'. However, the family always referred to it as 'Bank Field'. The Diary rather ambiguously relates, in August 1844: 'Alderney cow killed in consequence of a fall in Bank field.' In the winter of 1820–21, Dr Darwin bought (from 'Mad Jack' Mytton who owned land in Shrewsbury) three more fields: Sparkes Field, Bishops Land and Far Bishops Land.[5] All these fields adjoined one another and lay about half a mile to the west of the mansion. Work in every one of them is included in the Diary. After the death of his daughter Susan, the three latter fields were sold, to become the site of Copthorne Barracks in the 1870s.

The newlyweds did not move into The Mount until 1800, possibly because the house they were currently living in still had some of the lease to run or possibly because Susannah, never in the best of health, had given birth to her first child (Marianne) in April 1798 and was pregnant again with her second, Caroline (born in September 1800). The new house was meanwhile let.

The space around it, which had hitherto been nothing but pasture and wasteland, had yet to be laid out as a garden in the late Georgian style – a garden which was to become renowned as one of the most beautiful in Shrewsbury.

By including the river cliff below the mansion, the garden would cover almost 7 acres. Views across the Severn and the vast, open countryside beyond were provided from the top of this cliff (always referred to in the Diary as 'the Bank'), by a 680-ft-long Terrace Walk running along its top.[6] There was a lower path, allowing access to an ice house, which led to steps down to the river's towpath and a boat which was used for carrying, rather than pleasure. On the south side of the house, trees, lawns, walks and a sweeping drive, shrubberies and a glade lay between it and the busy town beyond. On the one-and-a-half acres at the eastern end of the site, Dr Darwin had a walled kitchen garden and orchard created. A circular flower garden, summer houses, herbaceous borders and various glasshouses followed in due course. The late-Georgian/Regency character of the garden remained essentially the same until the 1860s; apart from the two summerhouses there were no fussy artifices such as parterres, grottoes, rockeries, pools, fountains, columns or sculptures. This garden would be described as *gardenesque*, that is to say, relying on its beauty for its dramatic setting, well-kept lawns and walks, flower beds, specimen trees and shrubs. It also had rare exotics in its glasshouses and an abundance of fruit and vegetables in its kitchen garden.

The Diary reveals that Robert Darwin lost no time in creating this garden. His entry for 18 November 1844, 'Oak tree north side the house cut down (from Halston 45 years ago)', indicates that he had planted that tree in 1799, and that it came from Halston Hall, Jack Mytton's nearby family seat, famous for its oaks. Two more entries, the first dated 13 November and the second 14 November 1842, refer to trees planted in 1800 and the Doctor's habit of measuring. The first says: 'Sunday. The willow planted a slip the size of a quill in 1800 is 8 feet 10 inches round 3 feet from the ground & is 32 feet 6 inches to the fork.' The second says: 'The Naples oak planted in 1800 is 3 feet from the ground 62 inches round. From an acorn gathered by the Earl of Powis in the Kings garden at Naples.'

The reference to 'the Kings garden at Naples' can only mean the garden of Ferdinand IV at the Palace of Caserta, which was one of the high spots for Englishmen on their Grand Tour in the eighteenth century. George Herbert (1755–1801), the second Earl of Powis, made this trip in 1775–6. Whilst in Italy he collected marble sculptures for Powis Castle and, clearly, pocketed a few acorns for his own garden from the oaks at Caserta as he went along. He had no children. Edward Clive, his brother-in-law, who succeeded him as the third earl, was, like Mytton, one of the Doctor's many debtors, and very probably also one of his patients. The oak in question could be either the Italian oak *Quercus frainetto* or the more familiar evergreen oak, *Quercus ilex*. Sadly, it lived only fifty-one years. In February 1851, Susan writes: 'Cut down Naples oak.'

GARDENING CONTEMPORARIES

Robert inherited his enthusiasm for gardening from his father Erasmus Darwin (1731–1802). This enthusiasm was also nurtured by two of his contemporaries, his brother-in-law John Wedgwood (1766–1844) and the distinguished botanist, experimental horticulturalist and plant breeder Thomas Andrew Knight (1759–1838). In the February of 1803 Darwin was planting fruit trees, not only in his brand new kitchen garden, but also against any other suitable wall. A letter from Knight, postmarked Ludlow, describes four new varieties of apple which Knight had raised and was sending to Darwin.[7]

T.A. Knight was, with John Wedgwood, Joseph Banks and William Forsyth (King George III's gardener), a founder member (and later president)

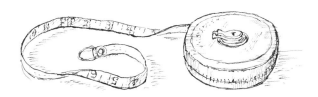

of the Horticultural Society of London.[8] It was John Wedgwood who first thought of forming the society and it is doubtless that through him Darwin made Knight's acquaintance. Knight, seven years older than Darwin, was also his patient; another letter to Darwin, dated 25 December 1802, describes Knight's reactions to the drops and liniment prescribed by the Doctor for his 'endless pains and discomfort'.[9]

Knight was to publish countless papers on his horticultural experiments on fruits and vegetables in the *Transactions of the Horticultural Society*. His topics included the construction of hot-bed frames and forcing houses, the grafting, inarching and budding of fruit trees and new varieties of fruits other than apples, such as peaches, cherries and grapes. There is no evidence that these papers were read by the Doctor, but it is difficult to imagine that he was unaware of them. What is certain is that Knight's papers in the *Transactions*, on cross-breeding, were read, many years later, by Charles Darwin.[10]

There are dozens of references in the Diary to the sowing, planting and harvesting of 'Mr Knight's' gooseberry, 'Mr Knight's' nectarine, 'Mr Knight's' cherry, 'Mr Knight's' marrow pea and 'Mr Knight's' 'protecting brocoli', which indicates that Knight was the source of other fruit and vegetable varieties at The Mount beside apples.

John Wedgwood, the eldest son of Josiah Wedgwood I, was an exact contemporary of Robert Darwin and was Susannah's brother. Their respective fathers – Josiah Wedgwood and Erasmus Darwin – were close friends and the youngsters had all known each other from childhood, sharing, in 1778, a home tutor at what old Wedgwood called his 'Etruscan

School'.[11] John was not cut out for running his father's pottery business (or any business at all, come to that), preferring the life of a gentleman farmer and gardener. Like so many others in Robert's circle, Wedgwood was one of his patients and was generously subsidised by him with huge sums of money. He was also a close friend and correspondent of William Forsyth, discussing, among other horticultural matters, the best shape for a kitchen garden. One of his innovations was to create the north wall in the shape of a semicircle. This he did at Cote House near Bristol, where he lived from 1797 to 1805; he also kept a Garden Diary.[12]

Wedgwood's diary is laid out in a more conventional style than The Mount Diary. It is in the form of a small notebook, the entries follow one day after another and are more detailed; the only unconventional aspect about it is that the flower garden starts from the front and, when you have turned it completely over and upside down, the vegetable garden starts at the back. Many pages consist solely of lists of the varieties and grafts of plants that Wedgwood was growing. These lists are astounding – sixty-two kinds of pear, one hundred kinds of apple, thirty-three of plum, sixty of peach and thirty-one of strawberry.

The flower garden entries run from 1825 to 1841. After selling Cote House and returning to run the pottery at Etruria, its restless author and his family lived in London, Exeter and Betley before moving, in 1825, to Kingscote in Gloucestershire for three years. The Wedgwoods then spent a year wandering abroad. In 1829 they moved to Hill House in Abergavenny and lived there until 1835, when they moved again, to a house about 4 miles from Maer, the Wedgwoods' family home in Staffordshire. Thus, the flower garden entries cover three different

gardens. The vegetable section covers only one garden. It starts in 1829 and continues until 1835. It was between these dates that Wedgwood lived at 'The Hill' in Abergavenny, which, like his old garden in Bristol, also had a semi-circular north wall.

'Mr J.W.' appears in Robert Darwin's Diary four times, always as the provider of plants. It was a 'Poppy Paeony tree' in 1839, a 'Courge a la Moelle' (vegetable marrow, then a horticultural novelty), sown and 'put into small pots' from 'seeds from J. Wedgwood who had them from Paris' in 1840, and rhubarb '3 Scarlet Giant Goliath', also in 1840. There were no doubt other gifts and exchanges of plants before these dates, as the two families made many visits to each other in the years before 1838, when the Doctor's Diary begins.

An account of the Darwins and the garden at The Mount is included in a memoir published in 1871 by the novelist and biographer Eliza Meteyard (1816–1897).[13] Eliza's father was a surgeon to the Shropshire Militia. He was posted to Shrewsbury in 1818, where he and his wife became friends with other medics in the town, including Robert Darwin. Darwin had recently become a widower, as Susannah had died in 1817, leaving him with six children. Eliza would therefore have best known him, his offspring and The Mount when she was a child, aged between two and thirteen, as the Meteyards moved on eleven years later, in 1829, to Norfolk. Nevertheless, Eliza's memoir is vivid, based on a collection of papers relating to the Wedgwoods,[14] as well as her own 'verbal portraiture' which, in respect of 'the old Shrewsbury doctors is drawn from life… . I recollect them as distinctly as if they now stood before me.'[15]

Because of its extensive views across the river to the north and the 'beautiful assemblage of clustered castle, bridge, free schools and church spires' to the south, Eliza's opinion of The Mount's situation was that 'it was exquisite in the extreme', apart, that is, 'from the wretched suburb of Frankwell that led to it'. This 'wretched suburb' was known to Meteyard as 'a mere narrow, ill-paved defile of mean and tottering tenements interspersed here and there with an old timbered house of more pretensions; and where some newer hand had tried his skill in building, the result was so utterly mean, wretched, and unworthy, as to add to the general air of squalor and indigence'. With most of Shrewsbury's gentry housed in 'beautiful old garden houses with stately courtways and precincts' on the other side of town, 'it evinced no ordinary courage', says Eliza, for the Doctor 'to choose this site for his house'. The young Eliza was equally impressed by the sight of the Severn, which rolled in front of the house 'in swift, pellucid and magnificent volume', and the road leading from Frankwell to North Wales, along which 'nightly dashed the picturesque Holyhead mail, with two thirds of the correspondence of Ireland sealed up in its great leathern sacks'.[16]

SUSANNAH DARWIN

As for Mrs Darwin, who brought with her on her marriage a fortune of £25,000, 'her higher fortune was a gentle, sympathising nature. She entered zealously into all her husband's pursuits; and as he took almost as much interest in botany and zoology as his father, Erasmus Darwin, their gardens and grounds became noted for the choicest shrubs and flowers. They petted and reared birds and animals; and the beauty, variety, and tameness of "the Mount pigeons" were well known in the town and far beyond.'[17] The 'pigeons' were more likely to have been doves, as it is 'doves' to which Susannah refers in a letter to her brother Jos (Josiah II), in August 1807.[18] Some thirty years later the Diary makes no mention whatsoever of either pigeons or doves; their presence at The Mount ceased, perhaps, with the death of Susannah, but the breeding of pigeons was to become, for her son Charles, one of the many sources of his research into heredity in his later life.

Another letter from Susannah to her brother Jos, written in February 1808, refers to some rooted 'suckers of the white Poplar' which has 'become so fashionable a tree that Lady Bromley has sent for some cuttings for Baroness Howe, to decorate Pope's Villa at Twickenham, as all his favourite trees have been cut down'.[19] Again, the Diary, which mentions a huge variety of trees, has no record of white poplars. Nor are there any to be seen today in the area surrounding Alexander Pope's villa.

Susannah's home, until her marriage, had been Etruria Hall, near Stoke-on-Trent. There too, the site had originally been bare fields; it was to be designed as a park and gardens for the Wedgwoods by the then fashionable landscape gardener William Emes.[20] Meanwhile, in 1807, Susannah's younger brother, Jos, was to make his married home at Maer Hall, a comfortable Elizabethan mansion set in a 1,000-acre estate, with woods and rides, hills, a park and a lake, as well as an established garden, some 7 miles from Etruria. Here, Jos employed John Webb, formerly Emes's foreman, to redesign the park. Thus, the latest schemes for landscape, parks, gardens and gardening were well appreciated by both the Wedgwoods and the Darwins.

CHARLES DARWIN'S CHILDHOOD

Charles's own childhood memories of the gardens at The Mount are recorded in his autobiography. Born in 1809, he was seven years older than Eliza Meteyard, who would have initially encountered him when he was at his first day school. At the time of his mother's death he was eight; his older sisters, Marianne and Caroline, were nineteen and seventeen, respectively. Susan was fourteen. The household was amply looked after by servants, but at first it was the responsibility of the two older girls and later, as she grew older, of Susan as well, to comfort and act as aides to their grieving father and as governesses and mothers to their younger siblings, namely Charles, his older brother Erasmus Alvey (then thirteen), and his younger sister Emily Catherine, then aged seven.

By his own accounts, Charles was 'in many ways a naughty boy', passionate and quarrelsome, with a tendency to tell fibs and a liking for reading, solitary walks, birdwatching, collecting 'all sorts of things', climbing trees, fast running and fishing. The Mount's enormous garden, with adjacent fields, woods and river, was free for him to enjoy.

On one occasion, for 'the sake of causing excitement I gathered much fruit from my Father's trees and hid them in the shrubbery, and then ran in breathless haste to spread the news that I had discovered a hoard of stolen fruit'. He also relates how he 'sometimes stole fruit for the sake of eating it; and one of my schemes was ingenious. The kitchen garden was generally kept locked in the evening and was surrounded by a high wall, but by the aid of neighbouring trees I could easily get on the coping, I then fixed a long stick into the hole at the bottom of a rather large flower-pot, and by dragging this upwards pulled off peaches and plums, which fell into the pot and the prizes were thus secured.'[21]

Years later, in an introduction by Francis Darwin to 'an abbreviation' of his father Charles Darwin's life and letters (published in 1902), there is a description of a Spanish chestnut tree growing by the Terrace Walk ('the Doctor's Walk') that runs along the top of the river bank: 'the branches of [this tree] … bend back parallel to themselves in a curious manner, and this was Charles Darwin's favourite tree as a boy, where he and his sister Catherine had each their special seat'.[22]

A drawing of a large tree on the bank, made by Charles when he was about thirteen, shows a crossbeam attached to a pin driven into the trunk, with strings, pulleys, weights and coloured rags at either end. He marks the spot in the branches above 'where I sit' and includes the following instructions: 'when the red rag is pulled up come to me, when the other lie still'. This scheme, which forms part of a letter to a friend, dated 12 January 1822, is preceded by the reminder 'next summer to make two cave one for warlike instruments, the other for relicks. Note spoon, old spear knife squirt if it can be found, and the name cut on the ash tree over the seat in the bank.'[23]

It is not clear if the signalling tree is the same as the chestnut tree mentioned by Francis Darwin; it is possibly an ash tree, but a blot on the original letter makes it hard to decipher. There are numerous references to ash trees and even chestnut trees in the Diary, but none to a Spanish chestnut. What is clear is that the bank made a wonderful place for boyish adventures.

In the February of the same year, Charles's brother, Erasmus Alvey, was admitted to Christ's College, Cambridge. Erasmus was five years older than Charles, with a passion for chemistry. However, before going up to Cambridge the two of them had set up 'a fair laboratory with proper apparatus in the tool-house in the garden', where Charles 'was allowed to aid him [Erasmus] as a servant in most of his experiments'.[24] The tool-house in the garden was a brick shed measuring about 8 x 20 ft, attached to the south wall of the kitchen garden with a window on the north face, looking into the kitchen garden. It is frequently referred to in the Diary as 'the Garden House' and still exists.[25] It is often assumed to be the only laboratory referred to in the autobiography, but subsequent letters from Erasmus prove this not to be the case.

In October 1822, Erasmus writes from Cambridge to 'Bobby' (the family nickname for Charles, whose second name was Robert) about a splendid shop there, which can supply him with every kind of glass and instrument needed for chemical experiments. A month later, Erasmus is asking him to make improvements to the laboratory, in the form of shelves over the window and over the door. This is accompanied by a rough drawing of a window with shutters and a row of bottles on a shelf above it.[26] Four months after that, Erasmus asks Bobby, 'How does ye old fireplace get on?' (He had a plan to replace it with a little stove 'with a moveable top so as to have a sand bath or a kettle or any thing else to fit on ye top'.)[27]

The next letter from Erasmus to Bobby, with reference to the laboratory, appears nearly two years later. Headed 'Cambridge, January 1825', it contains more requests for alterations and improvements, with a careful plan of what Erasmus wants. However, this laboratory was clearly not the same as the tool-house in the kitchen garden which, 'as we know to our cost, wants a dry place to keep our apparatus in'. For one thing it apparently had no window. Erasmus marked a place for one to be made, facing south 'looking into the drying yard ... and being South would do very well for any experiments with the Sun's rays, which is also a desideratum in our Lab'.[28] The drying yard forms part of the stable-yard. Apart from being conveniently close to the kitchens, and less damp, this outbuilding was a little larger than the tool-house, and more solidly built.

Another consideration for the move might have been that, in order to satisfy the need for his master's boys to mess about with chemical experiments, the gardener would have had to relinquish his tool-house-cum-potting shed, with its cosy fireplace and situation in the kitchen garden, and make do with something inferior.[29] The Diary refers to at least three other sheds in the gardens which served as storage places for root crops, onions and the over-wintering of aloes, one being behind the glasshouse in the kitchen garden, one behind the stove-house just to the east of the mansion and another in the backyard.

The laboratory was to stay in the drying yard until, nine years later, Susan wrote to Charles, now in the third year of his voyage on the *Beagle*, to tell him that 'the Laboratory is turned into a Laundry… . Erasmus when he came home in the summer found everything turned topsy turvy people ironing in his Lab, & a baby in his bedroom.'[30] The Sale Map of 1867 confirms this alteration, showing a laundry next to the dairy in the stable-yard and a tool-house in the kitchen garden.

Charles's helpfulness extended to gardening. When he was only ten, his father set him to counting the number of flowers on the peony plants. 'Papa asked me to do this. Ther was in year 1819, 160 flower on the Poenies. In the year 1820, 384 flower. In the year 1821, 363 flower.'[31]

Apart from admiring the diligence with which Papa's request was executed, for anyone interested in gardening this task raises a few questions. The counts of flowers, buds, asparagus spears, pounds of butter, quinces, guinea fowl eggs, baking apples, loads of ice, plums and shaddocks are frequently recorded in the Diary, both by the Doctor and by Susan. One might say it was a family trait. Is that why the Doctor asked his young son to do this? The Doctor's plan for Charles was that he, too, should become a doctor. Was it a kind of advance training in observation? And why peonies?

There are two main types; the tree or Moutan peony (*Paeonia suffruticosa*), which sheds its leaves, but not its stems, in winter, and the hardier, more shrubby, herbaceous or 'common' peony, which dies down completely in winter. Tree peonies, which were introduced to English gardens from China and Japan relatively recently, in 1787, are the most likely suspects. Moreover, being somewhat showy, they would have been among the

Doctor's pet plants. According to the Diary they were grown in pots at The Mount and taken into a hothouse in November, December and January, to force them into flowering. They would then be taken into the conservatory attached to the mansion. They were taken out again in May, either to stand outdoors for the next few years before they could be forced again, or to be planted in the peony bed in the flower garden.[32] Up to three peony trees would be forced at a time, but after forcing they would be useless for flowering for at least two or three years. The quantity of flowers in Charles's notes reveals that a fairly large number of peony trees must have been under cultivation.

When he was sixteen, Charles had left his detested boarding school in Shrewsbury and in 1825 joined Erasmus at medical school in Edinburgh. A letter from his sister, Caroline, written in February 1826, reminds him how the girls used to press him into watering their flower garden. However, now 'We are going to have pipes laid to have a supply of water in the flower garden, so next summer your goodnature will not be taxed with "Charles it is very hot." ("very hot indeed" you unthinkingly answer). "Dear Bobby, the ground is so dry that the pans [cans?] of water you brought half an hour ago did hardly any good, would you bring some more?"'[33]

Another letter from Caroline, written a month later, reveals that Charles had his own share of the garden: 'It made me feel quite melancholy the other day looking at your old garden, & the flowers, just coming up when you would be so happy watching. I think the time when you and Catherine were little children was the happiest part of my life & I dare say always will be.'[34] Caroline's 'melancholy' may have been, in part, due to the fact that not only were both Charles and Erasmus away, but her elder sister, Marianne, had married Dr Parker only four months previously, and was now living at Overton-on-Dee, some 22 miles north of Shrewsbury.

Both Charles and Erasmus rejected any hopes their father might have had regarding medicine, and in December 1827 Charles went to Cambridge, with his father's wish that he would become a clergyman. The many histories of Charles's life relate how the naturalist in him, rather than the parson, was fostered here and how, in 1831, the invitation to join Captain FitzRoy on his expedition on HMS *Beagle* was issued.

'PAPA'S HOTHOUSE'

Events in the garden at The Mount, in the years before the commencement of the Diary, are occasionally described in the letters sent by his sisters to Charles during his five-year voyage on the *Beagle*. They took turns to write to him, one letter a month. In late October 1831, Charles left home for Plymouth and waited there until the end of December for the voyage to begin. Meanwhile, at The Mount, a hothouse was being built, just to the east of the mansion, next to where no. 9 Darwin Gardens now stands. According to the Doctor's account books,[35] it cost £746 3s 9d (nearly £53,000 in today's money). The preparations for the voyage and the constant postponements of its commencement obscure all mention of this building, which measured about 20 x 12 ft. However, a letter from all three sisters, posted from Shrewsbury on 31 December 1831, three days after the *Beagle* had at last set sail, mentions 'the Hothouse'. Susan writes first: 'Papa is very well & I think every day gets more interest in the Hothouse which he is constantly going to see & I expect he will find a very nice amusement and little occupation – our days pass much as usual, cards in the evening & after Papa is gone to bed Eras, Charlotte & we draw round the fire & have an hours cosy talk together … generally about you.'[36]

The hothouse was finished by the beginning of February 1832; a letter from Catherine to Charles tells him it is 'very perfect, and [has] some plants in it'.[37] This is followed by a letter from Susan: 'Our Hothouse is quite finished & we have got several Pines [pineapples] & plants in it. Papa sits there a great deal & it answers well as a hobby for him.' (The Doctor was by now aged sixty-six and beginning to see fewer of his patients.)

She then adds: 'We have had pipes laid down in the Greenhouse & the regular warmth of the hot water makes the morning room very comfortable as it is apt to get very cold at night.'[38] The 'Greenhouse' referred to here is an extension of the morning room. It is labelled 'Conservatory' on the Sale Map of 1867 and, because it forms an extension to the house, that is what it would be called today, but the words 'Green House', 'Greenhouse', 'G. House' and 'G.H.' rather than 'Conservatory' are consistent throughout the Darwin correspondence and the Diary. Furthermore, there is a difference because, according to a contemporary writer and gardener, Charles M'Intosh (1794–1864): 'The green-house is distinguished from the conservatory, by having all the plants portable, and generally placed on stages: whereas, in the conservatory, the major part are usually planted out permanently in beds or borders prepared for them.'[39] That this was the case at The Mount is verified by the next monthly letter to Charles, this time from Caroline: 'My Father is very well & takes great pleasure in the Hot house which answers very well & the green house is filled with pretty gay flowers from it.'[40]

Letters to and from Shrewsbury to the *Beagle* could take anything from two to six months to reach their destinations,[41] but Charles was probably aware of his father's plans for a hothouse before he left England. He can't resist a little bragging: on 10 February 1832, as he writes from St Jago, Cape Verde, his eyes 'have already feasted on the exquisite form & colours of Cocoa Nuts, Bananas & the beautiful orange trees. Hot houses give no idea of these forms, especially orange trees, which in their appearance are as widely different & superior to the English ones, as their fresh fruit is to the imported.'[42] Three months later, in May 1832, he wrote: 'I am very glad to hear the hot–house is going well; how when I return I shall enjoy seeing some of my old friends again. Do get a Banana plant, they are easily reared & the foliage is wonderfully beautiful.'[43]

In September, Caroline tells Charles that a banana tree is being sent for 'principally from your advice'.[44] However, a banana tree had in fact been ordered by the Doctor before the arrival, in August, of that letter from Charles. By October 'Papa is ... more occupied than ever with his pet, the Hot house: his Banana tree is sent for, and a deep hole dug for it in the highest part of the Hot house, that it may have room.' Moreover, 'Papa means to call it the Don Carlos tree, in compliment to you.'[45]

Once it has arrived and been planted, in the March of 1833 the Doctor himself wrote to Charles, to tell him, 'In consequence of the recommendation in your first letter I got a Banana tree, it flourishes so as to promise to fill the hothouse. I sit under it, and think of you in similar shade.'[46] The tropical theme was increased even further by Susan's news, in November 1832, that 'The two great Palm trees are arrived & touch the top of the Hothouse now so I don't see how they can ever flourish.'[47]

The banana tree's arrival at The Mount does seem to have taken some time. The delay may have been caused by the choice of a *Musa cavendishii*, which, in 1832, was a rare, new variety and harder to obtain than the then larger and more common *Musa sapientum.* The former is smaller, but both can attain at least 16 ft in height. By the end of 1833, the Doctor's banana tree 'has grown so tall that the glass prevents even the few leaves it has from appearing in their natural shape'.[48] Growing a banana tree, at that date, was still quite a novelty for English gardeners, but it was not unheard of. Sir Watkyn Williams-Wynn, who lived at Wynnstay, only 28 miles north of Shrewsbury, and whom the Doctor would have known, had sent banana fruit from his own tree to the Horticultural Society of London as long ago as 1819. 'The plant is now sixteen feet high, and measures three feet round the bottom.'[49] Height rather than its cultivation was the problem. Where hothouses like the Doctor's were not high enough, tall narrow 'banana houses' were built specially for them.[50]

In the meantime, the Darwins' gardener, Joseph Phipps, managed to produce a pineapple in the hothouse: 'we eat our first Pine from the hothouse on Monday last Uncle John being with us who pronounced it very good. Joseph's head is quite turned by this first production.'[51]

By the time Charles had been away from home for three years, the sisters were telling him less and less about the garden. There are two garden-related references to Fanny Owen, the former love of his young life, when, in July 1833 Susan was staying at Woodhouse, the home of the Owens. On the first occasion: 'It was high strawberry season & Caroline Owen [Fanny's sister] said that always put in her mind, of when you [Charles] and Fanny used to lie full length upon the Strawberry beds grazing by the hour.'[52] Two years later, when Fanny was visiting Susan at The Mount: 'Whilst we were walking round the Kitchen Garden she burst out laughing saying she could not help thinking how you & she in former times had stuffed yourselves over the strawberry beds.'[53]

A letter to Charles from Susan, written four years later, when Charles was home from his voyage and living in London, makes a reference to the terrace being made in 1835: 'My father says soon after this house was built in 1798 he has a vague recollection of sowing a quantity of Broom seeds on the bank, which never came up – the Terrace was made

in 1835, and there was a good deal of moving of soil: & then all those Broom plants sprung up. He is sure there were none formerly on this place.'[54]

The voyage in the Beagle lasted nearly two years longer than originally expected, and Charles was homesick. In one letter of 1833 he reminisced, 'I often think of the garden at home as a Paradise: on a fine summer's evening, when the birds are singing, how I should like to appear like a Ghost amongst you.' He wrote to Susan from Valparaiso in Chile, in the spring of 1836: 'Everything about Shrewsbury is growing in my mind bigger & more beautiful; I am certain the Acacia and Copper Beech are two superb trees: I shall know every bush and I will trouble you young ladies, when each of you cut down your tree, to spare a few. As for the view behind the house I have seen nothing like it... . Snowden, to my mind, looks much higher & much more beautiful than any peak in the Cordilleras...'.[55]

At last, on 2 October 1836, the *Beagle* anchored at Falmouth, and two days later Charles wrote in his diary, 'Reached Shrewsbury after absence of 5 years & 2 days.'[56]

1 Henri Quinn, *Charles Darwin, Shrewsbury's Man of the Millennium*, 1999 (Henri Andrew Quinn), p. 25.

2 The Salop Fire Office Policy Book No. 3, 21 October 1797.

3 Sale Particulars, 1867, Shrewsbury Record Office, SC/4/36.

4 Quinn, *op. cit.*, p. 25.

5 Deposits paid at auction on 28 November 1820 and finalised in May 1821. DAR 227. 5: 82, p. 61. A famous English eccentric, 'Mad Jack' Mytton (1796–1834) was so named because of his crazy, extravagant way of life. He was heir to a fortune but died in the debtors' prison at the age of thirty-eight.

6 This walk was later commonly referred to as 'the Doctor's Walk', Charles Darwin and Thomas Henry Huxley, *Autobiographies*, ed. Gavin de Beer (Oxford: Oxford University Press, 1983), p. 2. It was not actually created until 1835, according to a letter from Susan to Charles, written in December 1837 (CCD vol. 2, p. 80).

7 DAR 227. 6: 94.

8 Now known as the Royal Horticultural Society.

9 DAR 227. 6: 90.

10 *Charles Darwin's Notebooks, 1836–1844: Geology, Transmutation of Species, Metaphysical Enquiries*, transcr. and ed. Paul H. Barrett, Peter J. Gautry, Sandra Herbert, David Kohn and Sydney Smith. British Museum (Natural History), (Cambridge University Press, 1987), p. 491, n. 1ᵛ–2.

11 Named after Wedgwood's Etruria works, which opened in 1769, and the village which he created for his employees.

12 The original can be seen in the Royal Horticultural Society's Lindley Library 999 (4B) KIN.

13 Eliza Meteyard, *A Group of Englishmen (1795–1815) being records of the younger Wedgwoods and their Friends* (London: Longman, Green, and Co., 1871).

14 The Meyer MSS.

15 Meteyard, *op. cit.*, p. xv.

16 *Ibid.*, pp. 258–60. The section of this road, which passes the southern side of The Mount's gardens, runs along a deep cutting. It was designed by Thomas Telford to ease the gradient for coaches, such as those carrying the Royal Mail and was executed in the 1830s.

17 *Ibid.*, p. 260.

18 *Ibid.*, p. 357.

19 *Ibid.*, p. 358, it being none other than Baroness Howe who had demolished both Pope's villa and all his trees and gardens only the year before.

20 William Emes (1729–1803), landscape gardener, friend of Erasmus Darwin via the Lunar Society, designed parks at Halston, Powis, Chirk and many others in the West Midlands, later moving to Hampshire.

21 Darwin and Huxley, *op. cit.*, p. 9.

22 *Charles Darwin: His Life told in an Autobiographical Chapter, and in a Selected Series of his Published Letters.* ed. by his son, Francis Darwin (London: John Murray, 2nd edn, 1902), p. 2.

23 Box C, D. 1, *Memorandum Book in form of letters to a friend, and other early fragments*, 1822. (Ursula Mommens Archive, Darwin Archive, CUL).

24 Darwin and Huxley, *op. cit.*, p. 24.

25 In 1931 the kitchen garden was developed for housing. It now consists of a road with semi-detached houses on either side. The old tool-house is divided in two by the garden wall that runs between nos 16 and 17 Darwin Gardens.

26 *The Correspondence of Charles Darwin*, Vol. 1: *1821–1836*, eds Frederick Burkhardt and Sydney Smith, with David Kohn (Cambridge:

Cambridge University Press, 1985), p. 3.

[27] CCD vol. 1, p. 6.

[28] CCD vol. 1, p. 12.

[29] The Doctor's willingness to provide his sons with a laboratory may well have been due to his own childhood enthusiasm for the chemistry lessons and experiments at 'the Etruscan School' which, as described by Meteyard, *op. cit.*, pp. 12-13, he shared with John Wedgwood in 1779.

[30] CCD vol. 1, p. 409.

[31] Quoted, without giving the source, by Janet Browne, *Charles Darwin: Voyaging* (London: Jonathan Cape, 1995), p. 15.

[32] If sufficiently well protected outdoors, they will flower in May.

[33] CCD vol. 1, pp. 31-2.

[34] CCD vol. 1, p. 36.

[35] The Account Books of Robert Waring Darwin, Darwin Manuscript Collection, Cambridge University Library. DAR 227.5.82.

[36] CCD vol. 1, p. 188. 'Charlotte' is a Wedgwood cousin. 'We' would have been Susan herself, Catherine and Caroline, Marianne having married in 1824.

[37] CCD vol. 1, p. 194, letter to Charles from Catherine.

[38] CCD vol. 1, p. 209.

[39] Charles M'Intosh, *The New and Improved Practical Gardener* (London: Thomas Kelly, 1847), p. 886.

[40] CCD vol. 1, p. 217.

[41] And even longer once the *Beagle* had reached the other side of the globe. Once Charles had reached Mauritius he wrote to his sisters to say that there was a possibility that he would have had no letters from them for eighteen months.

[42] CCD vol. 1, p. 206.

[43] CCD vol. 1, p. 230.

[44] CCD vol. 1, p. 269.

[45] CCD vol. 1, p. 273, letter from Catherine to Charles.

[46] CCD vol. 1, p. 301.

[47] CCD vol. 1, p. 283.

[48] CCD vol. 1, p. 361.

[49] *Transactions of the Society*, 1819. vol. vi, p. 138.

[50] Two such examples can still be seen, at Nostell Priory in Yorkshire and Heligan in Cornwall.

[51] CCD vol. 1, p. 255. Letter from Susan to Charles. 'Uncle John' is John Wedgwood.

[52] CCD vol. 1, p. 325.

[53] CCD vol. 1, p. 430.

[54] CCD vol. 2, p. 60.

[55] CCD vol. 1, p. 448.

[56] CCD vol. 1. Chron. p. 542.

TWO

After the Voyage:
Charles and his Father

Once back in England Charles, now aged twenty-eight and a confirmed naturalist, spent time in Cambridge and London, and was occupied for all of 1837 in sorting his boxes and bags of specimens, arranging his collections, meeting the scientists who had been his friends and advisers before the voyage, discussing his future and writing up *The Zoology of the Voyage of the Beagle*. He made a few brief dashes home (which he always referred to as 'Shrewsbury' rather than 'The Mount') and to Maer, to visit his Wedgwood aunts, uncles and cousins. There had been numerous marriages, births and deaths among his friends and family, so there was much catching-up to do.

His brother Erasmus, now aged thirty-three, had (like Charles) given up all intentions of becoming a doctor and was enjoying the idle life of an unmarried, intellectual gentleman in London, with his interest in chemistry undimmed. According to Susan he moved into his present lodgings (at 43 Great Marlborough Street) with '13 Cab loads of Glass bottles &c from his

Lab'.[1] In March 1837, after three months in Cambridge, Charles moved as well to Great Marlborough Street, to no. 36, just a few doors down from Erasmus. He somewhat disparaged his 'good dear old brother's' lazy way of life; '[he] lives the same life of tranquillity as usual. Going to Shrewsbury he considers a terrible journey, only to be undertaken once a-year, and as far as anything further, he considers impossible ...'[2]

Unlike Erasmus, Charles hated London: 'What a waste of life to stop all summer in this ugly Marlborough Street & see nothing but the same odious house on the opposite side, as often as one looks out. I long to pay Shrewsbury a visit.'[3]

That very same year (in July 1837), he had begun his first notebook on the *Transmutation of Species*, shortly after a visit to 'Shrewsbury'. He made another, longer, visit in September, and then began to write *The Geology of the Voyage of The Beagle*.

One year later, after much work on his *Geology*, and eight days at Glen Roy, in Scotland, he spent a further couple of weeks at Shrewsbury, where he noted in his *Journal*: 'Very idle at Shrewsbury, some notes from my Father. Opened notebook connected with metaphysical enquiries.'[4] He then spent a few days at Maer, where he came to realise that his feelings for his cousin, Emma, might lead to marriage, but at that point he lacked the confidence to propose. At the same time, he had embarked on a frenzied amount of reading and theorising about the origin of species. He was now the secretary of the Geological Society and a member of the Athenæum Club, where he dined with fellow men of science and letters, luxuriated in its fine rooms and read and wrote in its magnificent library.

THE DIARY BEGINS

On 1 September 1838, one year and ten weeks after Queen Victoria acceded to the throne, and one month after Charles's romantic visit to Maer, Dr Darwin began the Garden Diary, which is the basis for this book. His eldest daughter, Marianne, was now Mrs Henry Parker, and mother of five children. His second daughter, Caroline (soon to be thirty-eight), was newly married to her cousin Josiah Wedgwood III and had set up home at Clayton, near Etruria. At this point, therefore, apart from some dozen servants, the Darwin household consisted only of the Doctor and his two younger, unmarried daughters: Susan, just turned thirty-five, and Catherine, aged twenty-eight. Thus, the first entry in the Diary reads: 'sowed ribes sanguinea.[5] Took up Miss Darwins iris roots. Planted out Broccoli' – Miss Darwin being Susan.

It may seem odd that the Diary begins on 1 September rather than 1 January, but if indeed a previous volume existed – and there is every indication that it did – then 31 August 1838 must be the date when that first volume ended. Furthermore, as there are twenty-nine lines to each page, and each line is devoted to a succession of years, it follows that if the previous Diary was of the same size and format as this one, it would have started in 1809. There was possibly a Diary even before that, since the planting of both ornamental and fruit trees (as already mentioned) began almost as soon as the house had been built, in 1800.

I like to picture the Doctor opening his new, leatherbound diary on 1 September 1838. The page he wants is already inscribed '1. September' at the top, in red ink and by hand, presumably by the stationer. He looks at the rest of the book – blank, except that each page has the next day and the month handwritten in red ink at the top, with twenty-nine neat blue lines below, and a margin marked in red on the left, for the years to come. It is a hefty object, weighing exactly 4½ lb. It measures 9 x 11 in and is 2 in thick. The paper is sturdy, with the watermark of Edward Smith, 1837.

THE DOCTOR

The diarist himself is now seventy-two, gouty, often breathless and concentrating on his gardens, greenhouses and books, 'for,' according to Eliza Meteyard, 'all which was new and progressive in literary thought found its way to The Mount'. He had spent some fifty years as a physician, often driving to see his patients, if urgently needed, night or day, near and far in all weathers, always travelling in 'his small yellow chaise, within which, so exactly did it fit him, there was not an inch to spare; with its two sleek horses … and his steady coachman'. His consultations were given in the mornings, but now his practice was virtually given up, though he still dispensed medical advice to his family and friends.

His patients had ranged in society from the local aristocracy to the poorest of the poor. His son, Charles, noted his 'intuitive perception of character' and 'that it was his sympathy which gave him unbounded power of winning confidence, and as a consequence made him highly successful as a physician'.[6] This success is all the more remarkable as, like Charles, Robert had had no desire to become a doctor in his youth. However, his father, Dr Erasmus Darwin, had given him no choice. It was possibly this factor that made Robert so tolerant of the unwillingness of both his sons to follow him into the profession. This indulgence was also possibly shaped by the fact that he had had a not entirely happy life as a child and a youth. His mother had died in 1770, when he was just a month under four years of age, leaving him with two older brothers whom he adored: Charles (1758–78) and Erasmus (1759–99). That Robert and Susannah Darwin were to call their own two sons Charles and Erasmus had, therefore, some significance. The first Charles had died as a young medical student, from an infection after performing a dissection on a child. His brother Erasmus went on to become a lawyer but was to commit suicide aged nearly forty. And Robert Darwin was never to compensate for the later loss of his own wife, Susannah, in the ways that his own, libertine father had done. Old Erasmus Darwin went on to have two illegitimate daughters by Robert's 'governess' and seven more children by his second wife.

Robert's early success with his more well-to-do patients enabled him to treat his poorer ones with charity and generosity, but rather than cause offence by not charging them, he would ask them to pay for the bottle which contained the medication rather than the medicine itself.[7] Many of these grateful and loving patients would have been living just down the road, in the slums of Frankwell or elsewhere in the town of Shrewsbury. One of these was a Mr Cook, who dealt in earthenware. Darwin made him one of the dealers in a nursery lamp which he had invented. After Cook's death, in 1803, Mrs Cook described how the Doctor had not only attended her husband *gratis* for five months, but 'wine, fruit, peas, artichokes, &c [were] sent frequently from his house'.[8] This proves that even in those early days, the kitchen garden at The Mount was in full production.

Besides his success as a physician, Robert was a shrewd investor, putting his money into the then up-and-coming industries, such as canals, railways, property and his brother-in-law's potteries. He also lent huge sums (with interest) to the local gentry, his relations and his own servants, and made smaller loans to local tradesmen. He supported his children throughout their lifetimes as well. Charles's voyage on the *Beagle* was totally subsidised by him. (When Charles protested, before his voyage began, that he would be 'deuced clever to spend more than my allowance whilst on board the *Beagle*', his father is said to have replied, 'But they all tell me you are very clever.')[9] When Dr Darwin died, he was possibly the richest man in Shropshire.

Apart from being enormously wealthy, he was an enormous size at 6 ft 2 in tall and weighing, in later years, 24 stone, with an enormous appetite to match. Although he was a teetotaller, 'He could eat a goose for dinner as easily as other men do a partridge,' Eliza Meteyard noted. Moreover, in his latter days as a physician 'it was impossible for him to ascend or risk narrow staircases and rotten floors; and as both were common in the more ancient parts of the town, a confidential servant was sent to make a survey beforehand'.

As can be seen from his portraits, Eliza's description of Dr Darwin's 'powerful, mild, and thoughtful face'[10] is exactly right but, although he was known for his unbounded kindness and was widely and deeply loved, he was prone to terrible fits of depression, irritability and anger, a condition which might be described today as bipolar. Visitors, especially young people, ladies and the Wedgwood girls, in particular, never felt entirely at ease with him, for he was doubtless bored by their girlish tittle-tattle. He had a habit, too, of holding the floor and talking very rapidly for two whole hours at a time in a strangely high-pitched voice. As Emma Darwin (née Wedgwood) was to write years later: 'There was a want of liberty at Shrewsbury whenever Dr Darwin was in the room; but then he was genial and sympathetic, only nobody must go on about their own talk.'[11] And 'no one must speak so that he did not hear.'[12]

His love for both his sons was perhaps not that apparent; his famous outburst, directed at Charles when a boy ('You care for nothing but shooting, dogs and rat-catching, and you will be a disgrace to yourself and all your family') was no doubt made in a fit of anger, but to Charles his father was 'the kindest man I ever knew'.[13]

[1] CCD vol. 2, p. 489.
[2] CCD vol. 2, p. 11. Letter from CD to his cousin W.D. Fox. In 1837 the journey between London and Shrewsbury, if made by stagecoach, took about sixteen hours. It went via Birmingham, and it was possible, by then, to travel from London to Birmingham on the new railway which, in spite of many changes, would have made the journey considerably faster.
[3] CCD vol. 2, p. 40, letter from CD to his cousin, Elizabeth Wedgwood.
[4] *Darwin's Journal*, ed. Sir Gavin de Beer (Bulletin of the British Museum [Natural History] Historical Series vol. 2, no. 1, London, 1959), p. 8. This notebook was labelled 'Notebook M' (for metaphysics) and ran from July to October 1838.
[5] The flowering currant, commonly seen today, especially in suburban gardens, but introduced here only in 1826 from northwest America.

[6] Charles Darwin and T.H. Huxley, *Autobiographies*, ed. Gavin de Beer (Oxford: Oxford University Press, 1983), p. 13.
[7] Cyril Aydon, *Charles Darwin* (London: Constable & Robinson Ltd, 2002), p. 16. This custom had the added advantage, to the patient, of a refund on the bottle and the satisfaction for the Doctor of knowing (or supposing) that the patient had taken the medicine.
[8] Eliza Meteyard, *A Group of Englishmen (1795– 1815) being records of the younger Wedgwoods and their Friends* (London: Longman, Green, and Co., 1871), p. 264, n. 2.
[9] Charles Darwin and Thomas Henry Huxley, *Autobiographies*, ed. Gavin de Beer (Oxford: Oxford University Press, 1983), p. 41.
[10] Meteyard, *op. cit.*, p. 263.
[11] *Emma Darwin: a Century of Family Letters, 1792–1896*, ed. Henrietta Litchfield (London: John Murray, 1915), vol. 1, p. 60.
[12] *Ibid.*, p. 140.
[13] Darwin and Huxley, *op. cit.*, p. 12.

THREE

Horticultural Experiments 'for C.D.'

Charles claimed that his father's mind was 'not scientific',[1] but the Doctor was definitely a person with whom Charles could discuss what were then regarded as highly provocative ideas. He certainly discussed medical matters relating to his own health, as well as psychological and physiological questions. For example, in another of his notebooks under *'Questions and Experiments'*, he asks: 'Does my father know any case of quick or slow pulse being hereditary.'[2]

One month after his father had begun keeping his new Diary, on 28 September 1838 Charles began reading 'for amusement' (and at great speed) the Rev. Thomas Robert Malthus's *Essay on the Principle of Population*, with the result that he had 'at last, a theory by which to work'.[3] Malthus held that human

populations were governed by food, shelter and disease, and that only the most successful would survive and continue to breed. In a flash, Charles saw that this theory could also be applied to the natural world and that it could be the answer to the feverish questions that were multiplying in his notebooks about the evolution, nature and existence of everything – not only animals, birds, fishes, molluscs, insects and plants, but landforms, rocks, corals and fossils as well.

Moreover, as he had, at that time, no garden of his own, trials and experiments on some plants could be provided with certainty by his father and his father's gardener. They were in an ideal position to do this for him.

SENSITIVE PLANTS

The first of Charles's requests was granted in the December of 1838, when the Doctor recorded sowing a sensitive plant in the stove in the kitchen garden. A month later Charles was at Shrewsbury making preparations for his impending marriage to Emma Wedgwood. He had proposed to her, and been accepted, the previous November. Needless to say the Diary, concerned solely with matters relating to its gardens and livestock, makes no mention of this happy event; the nearest we get to it is the entry for 29 January, the very day of the wedding, which reads, 'scarlet passion flower potted for Mr Salt'. 'Mr Salt' was Thomas Salt, the Darwins' solicitor in Shrewsbury. He would have been engaged in the days previous to this with legal matters relating to the forthcoming marriage, but he was also a keen gardener and a tour of The Mount's hothouse obviously ended with the gift of a rooted passionflower.

More significantly, on 16 January 1839, the Doctor records the sowing of more *Mimosa sensitiva* seeds in the beloved hothouse, followed on 21 January by: '2 sensitive plants come up.' Two more seedlings appeared on the 26th and two more the following day. On the 28th (the very day before the wedding at Maer), the entry reads: '3 of the sensitive plants put into Pots for Mr Charles.'

Charles was at The Mount twice that month, from the 11th to the 14th, and from the 25th to the 27th. The chief reason, no doubt, for two visits so close together in the depths of winter was the impending wedding. However, as the *Mimosa sensitiva* is a native of tropical South America, it very much looks as if the seeds sown by his father had been collected there by Charles and that he had brought them to Shrewsbury with him in the previous November.

As it happens, the species commonly known as the 'Sensitive Plant' is *Mimosa pudica*. It is so-called because it folds its leaves not only when touched, but also when deprived of light. *M. sensitiva* also reacts in this way, though, paradoxically, less sensitively. Whichever of the two leguminous species those seedlings were, Charles wanted to discover the mechanism behind the sensitivity.

His *Questions and Experiments* notebook shows that he planned to test his theory on the 'sleeping' ability, not only on the mimosas, but also on two other plants: 'the *Leptosiphon densifolium*[4] an annual closes flowers on all gloomy days & the garden *Coronella*[5] also sleeps on ditto – cover them up periodically and see effect'. The notebook reference is undated and listed under *Remote Experiments – Plants*.

Neither of these last two flowering plants is mentioned in the Diary, but the tendency of some plants to close their leaves or flowers when touched and of others to do so when the light fails was still of interest to Charles more than fifteen years later. In 1855 he asked his friend Joseph Dalton Hooker, who had just been appointed Assistant Director at Kew's Botanic Gardens, if he could help him 'to try one of my very most foolish experiments' by sending him another leguminous plant with this characteristic, the *Hedysarum gyrans*.

This is an even more intriguing plant. It is a greenhouse plant (synonyms *Codariocalyx motorius*, formerly *Desmodium gyrans*), popularly known today as the Moving, Telegraph or Semaphore plant, or Dancing Grass. It moves its leaves in reaction to bright daylight, to touch and also to music (or rather, to certain sounds). Although Charles by then had his own garden at Downe, in Kent, he was worried that the plant might need a hothouse, which he did not yet have.[6] Still protesting that he needed the plant 'for probably a <u>most</u> foolish purpose', he explains in a later letter to Hooker: 'I read somewhere that no plant closes its leaves so promptly in darkness, & I want to cover it up daily for 1/2 hour, & see if I can teach it to close by itself, or more easily than at first in darkness.'[7]

DARWIN'S POTATO

Following the sowing of the mimosa seeds in January and Charles's marriage at Maer, his next horticultural request came in April. He had discovered two distinct forms of potato growing wild in South America: one in the Cordilleras of Chile and the other on the island of Chiloé, in the Chonos Archipelago. It was the latter that he believed to be the true wild potato.

In his *Journal of Researches* he wrote:

> These potatoes grow near the sea-beach, in thick beds, on a sandy, shelly soil, wherever the trees are not too close together. In the middle of January they were in flower, but the tubers were small, and few in number; especially in those plants which grew in the shade, and had the most luxuriant foliage. Nevertheless, I found one which was of an oval form, with one diameter two inches in length. The raw bulbs had precisely the smell of the common potato of England, but when cooked they shrunk, and became watery and insipid. They had not a bitter taste, as ... is the case with the Chilian kind; and they could be eaten with safety. Some plants measured from the ground to the tip of the upper leaf, not less than four feet.[8]

Charles had written to his friend John Henslow about these potatoes: 'Amongst the Chonos dryed plants you will see a fine specimen of the wild Potatoe, growing under a most opposite climate & unquestionably a true wild Potatoe. – It must be a distinct species from that of the lower Cordilleras one.'[9]

It is the Chiloéan (Chonos) variety that is now known as the Darwin Potato.[10] Charles was clearly anxious about its continued propagation, once it had been delivered to Cambridge, for in April 1837 he wrote again to Henslow from London: 'Pray take in hand as soon as your lectures are over, the potato from the Chonos Islds.'[11]

This letter is of some significance, as in another letter to his cousin and close friend William Darwin Fox, he says that in the spring of 1836 Professor Henslow had sown the seeds of the other wild potato collected by Darwin in the Cordilleras of central Chile.[12] Henslow had then sent a tuber grown from this seed to Fox, who was being urged by Darwin as late as February 1845 to send him some time 'a few of my potatoes, & chiefly to get true seed from them, & see whether they will sport or not readily'.[13]

The reason for this request was that the Irish Potato Famine had set in, and the search was on for a disease-resistant potato. Charles was still interested in this problem at the very end of his life, corresponding with a Mr Torbitt of Belfast from 1876–87 on the feasibility of producing a fungus-proof variety of potato by cross-fertilisation.

However, before all this had happened the Doctor had once again been pressed into service. On 11 April 1839 he wrote in his Garden Diary: 'South American Potatoes planted. From those brought by Mr C. Darwin.' It is not clear if these were the original specimens, i.e. Chiloéan or Cordilleran tubers, or potatoes grown from either of them by Henslow, but in due course, on 17 October 1839, the Doctor wrote: 'Mr Charles Potato got up. The whole one 13 pound, the one cut 39 3/4 pound.' This implies that only two specimens were planted at The Mount in 1839.

Charles described the potatoes he found on Chiloé as small, so the weights as given by his father (a most pedantic weigher and measurer) must refer to the total weight of all the potatoes on each plant. The following year a 'South American potato' was planted again on 4 April 1840: 'Mr Charles Potato planted.' There is no record of this crop being lifted, its weight or of

it being eaten by the family, but it was most likely to have been grown again at Charles's request to provide more specimens for research.

YEW TREES

Charles and Emma had begun their married life living in their own house in London, at 12 Upper Gower Street. By 1841 they were the parents of two very young children and spent much of the time between April and August 1840, and slightly less in the summer of 1841, either with Emma's family at Maer or with Charles's at Shrewsbury. His *Notes on the Fertilisation of Flowers, 1840–1843*, show that at this time Charles was almost obsessively investigating all factors affecting variation. His observations included the manner in which the weather affected the secretion of nectar, and how the structure of a flower and its pollen (whether shaken, carried by insects or winds) affected free crossing, reversion, fruiting and seed-forming. 'My present ultimatum about intermarriage,' he notes in July 1841, whilst at The Mount, 'possible in all flowers – but self-impregnation the common order of events.'[14] He spent many hours in the gardens at Shrewsbury and Maer watching the activities of bees and other insects, and comparing the size, shape and position of the anthers, stamens, pistils and stigmas of different flowering plants, vegetables and shrubs.

In The Mount's kitchen garden, Charles studied the flowers and seeds of cucumbers, rhubarb, cabbages, peas and beans; in the hothouse he examined his father's passionflowers, the flowers of the tropical Rhododendron *arboreum*, orchids and the coral tree (*Erythrina crista-galli*); the herbaceous beds and his sisters' flower garden provided him with phlox, heartsease, pansies and violets, salvias, linums, geums, euphorbias, mimulus, foxglove and many more. One of his ideas was to: 'spread sheets of Paper, covered with some sticky stuff in flat places & see whether wind, on <<dry>> windy day << flower garden on gravel walk >> will drift many seeds ... have paper ruled in squares to facilitate investigation.'[15]

On the terrace he found *Linaria cymbalaria* (toadflax, also known as Mother of Thousands) 'in plenty', but noted that it was only visited by bees on a very hot day; clumps of *Silene inflata* (bladder campion) grew there too, some seeming never to shed pollen, others bursting with it.

Charles compared the structure of the flowers of the common thyme growing in the herb bed with that of wild thyme and lemon thyme. The Diary does not mention all the flowers he investigated, but two entries in November 1840 relate to his interest at the time in cross-fertilisation. They concern the sowing of yew seeds especially for him.

Yews grew at The Mount in various places, including the bank and the Terrace Walk. No varieties are named, other than a weeping yew which was planted by Susan below the hothouse in 1849, the year after Dr Darwin died. The Doctor himself recorded that some yew trees were planted, with laurels, on 9 November 1840, at the top of the garden to hide the new cottage that he had built for his butler Edward Evans and his family. The following day the Doctor wrote: 'yew seeds sent by Charles put into a pot in Hot House', and on 23 December 1840: 'yew seeds fr Miss Wedgwood of Maer[16] sowed for Mr C.D'.

Again, there are clues to the reason for these sowings in Charles's notebook containing *Questions and Experiments*. The first relates to the questions of how, and if, hybrids are produced among different species growing close together: 'pollen of own kind is much more effective than that of foreign', followed by: 'Would Yew fruit without impregnation.' In another proposed experiment he plans to: 'Place pin's heads with Bird lime near male yew tree & see whether they catch pollen.'[17] A few pages later, under 'Maer', a note reads: 'Yew Trees near Boat House any male branch. – Number of seeds in beginning of November 1841. – Trees above male?'[18] On the next page of his notebook, under 'Shrewsbury', he asks: 'Yew Berries germinate? – Yew trees sexes.'[19]

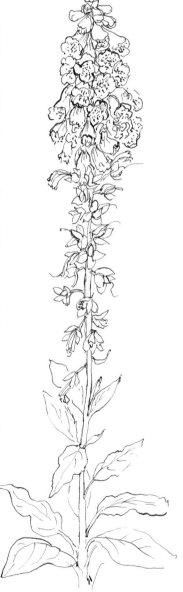

Two questions were crucial to Charles's emerging theories of evolution and natural selection. One was how variability arose, and the other concerned reversion to parent forms, both in plants and animals. Yews were of particular interest as, like holly, the trees are either male or female. It is not clear what the sex or the variety was of the yew by the boathouse at Maer, but four years later, in 1844, Darwin was still working on questions relating to yews and was in correspondence with Philip de Malpas Grey-Egerton and Joseph Dalton Hooker about the origins of the Irish yew (*Taxus fastigiata*) and the differences between those reproduced from it by cuttings and seeds, which in one case resulted in the variety known as the weeping yew.[20]

TASKS FOR ABBERLEY

Between 1840 and 1843, Charles makes several references in his notebooks to his father's gardener Abberley. The Doctor's previous gardener, Joseph Phipps, whose head was so turned by the production of a pineapple in 1833, had died two years later aged only forty-six, and no other gardener appears in records or letters relating to The Mount until 1840 when, according to the Diary, 'Abberly' (the spelling is variable) was keeping bees and working in the kitchen garden.[21]

Charles has clearly given Abberley instructions on various tasks, observing, in particular, the behaviour of bees, as well as ants, butterflies and thrips; reporting on the pollination of cucumbers both within frames and on open beds; growing peas and beans in a specific manner, and raising 'abortive' thyme, 'a pale green *cynoglossum*' (a hound's-tongue), and 'a *Geranium pyranaicum*' (a hardy cranesbill) '… with abortive stamens from seed'.

On 28 August 1839, the Doctor had written: 'Geranium seeds sowed.' This is the only reference in the Diary to geraniums being grown from seed. Among *Questions and Experiments* under the heading 'Shrewsbury', Charles remarks that Abberley 'has planted seeds of *Geranium pyrenaicum*, small white-flowered var. with abortive stamens. – show crossing &? hereditary?'[22]

On 18 July 1840, shortly after a visit from Charles to The Mount, the Doctor records that two of Abberley's beehives had been placed in the kitchen garden, doubtless to assist with Charles's investigations.

In November 1841, the Doctor forwarded a letter to Charles from Abberley, giving his observations, as requested, on The Mount's cucumbers: 'The Cucumber that the insects carred Pollen tou i have cut oppen but not one seed was in it the Horther that I dusted with Pollen had plenty of seeds in it... . I have tow moore furit which the insects have dust with Pollen as soon Sir that the are Redy i will Let you hear about them.'[23]

The Diary bears no reference to this experiment except for the entry 'cucumber seed saved' on 14 November 1841. As this is the only reference to the saving of cucumber seed in the entire Diary, it has some significance. Of equal significance is the entry, on 9 October in the same year: 'Sweet Pea seeds gathered.' Charles wanted to know if bees visited sweet peas, 'for if so, as they can be raised true, there is no crossing by bees'.[24]

In the same letter of November 1841 Abberley reported:

> Sir: I have gather the seed Peas but i dount see heney new kinds at all in them as the came up true to the sorts the Woodford Peas is Mildew i have all the sorts by themselves

> Beans
> I have not gather all the seed of the Beans & I think the /fan/ bean is in Clind to be a Mule for some of the seeds are tinge with green on the Edges

> Thyme
> I gather a Little thyme seed but it is verrey Poor the wet as been against it ripeing But i have cut some of the flowers to dry & verrey Liklea thear might be some seeds in it.

Charles had asked Abberley 'to plant SINGLE Peas, Kidney Bean & Bean, intertwined without sticks – in reference to what Mr Herbert observe on this subject', adding, in March 1842, that last year and the year before last 'peas

& beans were planted in rows adjoining & seeds gathered there were planted last year pell mell, without sticks & seeds gathered & these are now to be planted this year'.[25]

In July 1841, in his *Notes on Fertilisation*, Charles specifically writes the names of the peas that were sown in 1840; they were Woodford's 'Marrowfat', 'Early Frame' and Grooms 'Dwarf', all 'planted in rows close to each other & seeds gathered all came up in 1840 true. Shrewsbury. – Abberley'. He continues with notes on the beans sown: 'Early Magazine [Magazan] – &c. double-blossomed & dwarf-fan Bean, were planted in rows, & seeds gathered same year came up true in 1840: All in together blossomed together – The seeds of these plants will be collected and resown.'[26]

The Doctor makes no special reference to these plantings, but the sowing of Woodford's Marrowfat peas, Marrow peas or Woodford peas is recorded almost every year throughout the Diary. Early Frame is sown only in 1842; Groom's Dwarf is not mentioned, though Miller's Dwarf is (sown 1839). Of beans, all three mentioned by Charles are what are called today broad beans. The Diary simply calls them 'long podded beans or dwarf beans', differentiating them as such from kidney, cranberry, French, and white and scarlet runners.

NITRATE OF SODA

Another horticultural trial, which took place at The Mount in the summer of 1840, involved the effect on plants of nitrate of soda as a soil improver. HMS *Beagle* had allowed Charles to visit Tarapacá in the deserts of northern Chile five years previously, where he had seen the enormous natural deposits of saltpetre and nitrate of soda for which the district is famed. These were being mined and exported to Lima, Peru, mainly for use in making gunpowder. Nitrate of soda is now recognised as a quick-acting fertiliser, which is readily taken up by plants; however, although the known constituents of plants included nitrogen, John Claudius Loudon, in his third (1830) edition of *An*

Encyclopaedia of Gardening, displayed the then current doubtfulness about the use of manures of 'earthy and saline' or 'mineral origin', rather than manures of 'animal or vegetable origin'. His view was that 'The conversion of matter that has belonged to living structures into organised forms, is a process that can be easily understood; but it is more difficult to follow those operations by which earthy and saline matters are consolidated in the fibre of plants, and by which they are made subservient to their functions.'[27]

Even as late as 1847, Charles M'Intosh observed in *The New and Improved Practical Gardener*: 'the use of mineral manures is comparatively modern, and their effects uncertain'.[28] It is rather pleasing to note that Dr Darwin's and Charles's experiments into these effects were taking place at The Mount seven years before these words were published. Between July 1840 and June 1842, the Doctor recorded the application of nitrate of soda on eleven occasions, in both his kitchen and flower gardens, on his pots of *Cypripediums* and orange trees, and on his fields.

On 7 July 1840, he recorded that 'a 'letter "D" was made on grass by Peach tree with nitrate of soda. Applied also in other places.' As a result, the grass bearing the Darwin family's initial became a darker green. Charles was at The Mount at the time and recorded in his Notebooks of 1836–44: 'effects of Nitrate of soda under Beech – *Lychnis dioica* [campion or catchfly] answers this question'.[29] (Dr Darwin appears to have mistaken 'Beech' for 'Peach' in his entry. The question answered by the *Lychnis* is obscure.)

Sometimes, as on the lawns and fields, nitre was 'sown' or spread as a powder; at other times, it was diluted in water. The ratio of nitre to water is given as 2 lb to 3 gallons for potted plants (2:3); 4 lb to 14 gallons (2:7) for the carrot bed, and 1 lb to 3 gallons (1:3) for the asparagus bed. The effects of these applications are not recorded, but nitre would have had a beneficial effect when mixed with manure (as on 18 July 1840: 'Nitre of soda & manure on south part of Sparks field'). Whatever the case, it is not mentioned after 1842, which implies that it was used purely to help with Charles's experiments.

On the same visit at which the experimental letter 'D' was made, Charles wrote to his friend and mentor John Stevens Henslow, asking another question, this time regarding metamorphosis in plants, and in particular about one of his father's orange trees.

I remember in your lecture you said monsters were sometimes curious. – We have a largish orange tree, covered with oranges & nearly all these are annually horned, that is they have two or four projections, covered with the yellow rind, like cows horns in shape. – Many of the oranges are deeply ribbed, the number of ribs being generally seven, sometimes six or five. – It is evident the horns are segments more perfectly separated. – I send a minute ribbed one, with one cow's horn. – These horns branch off sometime near the footstalk, sometimes near apex. – The little one does not look odd the big oranges with two good large horns look very curious. – The tree has long been without manure. – If these are curious & exemplify the metamorphoses of some organ into the fruit orange, I will get a series. – If not curious do not answer this note.[30]

CHARCOAL AND CITRUS TREES

In his notebooks Charles asks again if the fruiting parts of a plant could metamorphose into leaves, and if the cause could be a lack of nutrition. This is answered by a note saying: 'Yes, my Father lost this character in grt degree from charcoal and good treatment.'[31] About eighteen months later, on 9 March 1843, some horned orange seeds were sown at The Mount and noted in the Diary, but their progress and progeny, if any, are not recorded. However, the Diary does frequently refer to charcoal being put to orange trees, and on two occasions its application occurred when Charles was at The Mount – in May 1841 and March 1844.

The type of charcoal used is not entirely clear; most references are simply to 'charcoal', but the Diary twice specifically refers to 'animal charcoal', which is just possibly the 'animalized carbon' described by J.C. Loudon in *The Suburban Horticulturalist* (1842). This, he says, 'consists of nightsoil of great age; it is sent to different parts of Europe from Copenhagen, where it has accumulated during ages in immense pits and heaps, which some years ago were purchased from the city by an Englishman. It is an exceedingly rich manure.'[32]

Alternatively, it could be the 'Bone-black or animal charcoal' listed many years later under 'Manures rich in phosphoric acid (seed-formers)' in the 1893 edition of *Cassell's Popular Gardening*.[33] Scott's *Orchardist*, published in 1872, states that charcoal 'forms a valuable auxiliary to manures and indeed, when applied to the soil without the admixture of manuring substances, it has great fertilising properties'.[34] In what looks like another experiment on the manuring value of charcoal and bones, four different rows of raspberry canes were dressed in October 1843: one with bones alone, one with charcoal alone, one with mixed bones and charcoal, and one with nothing at all. Charles was again at The Mount on this occasion, but the Diary does not record the result of this experiment.

The Doctor had an impressive collection of citrus trees, mainly as an object of interest and beauty, rather than as a supply of fruit. As such, they were grown in tubs and pots so that they could be taken from the hothouse to the greenhouse (conservatory) in order to display their dark, shiny leaves, brightly coloured fruits and beautifully scented flowers. On Boxing Day 1843, for example, the Doctor recorded 'orange & shaddock flowers gathered'. When all fear of frost was gone, The Mount's citrus trees were placed out of doors. Susan noted that the temperature was 72°F when she put her oranges out of doors on 11 July 1864. The more tender ones were left out between July and September, and the hardier ones from May to October.

Whilst the trees were outside, the glasshouses could be cleaned and painted. There is no indication of where the trees were placed when outdoors other than 'by the Cedar tree' (Susan, 1859).

Apart from the constant moving from hothouse to greenhouse and from indoors to outside, the cultivation of Dr Darwin's citruses followed the usual routine: propagating by seed and by cuttings, repotting in midsummer (sometimes with charcoal), cutting down when they became too tall, and washing or syringing them in midwinter. This would have got rid of some of the bugs and cobwebs on the plants; a dusting of powdered sulphur in August 1841 is the only insecticide mentioned. See Part 3:2 for citrus trees in detail.

 The Doctor's citrus collection included (as well as the aforementioned horned orange) lemons, limes and a shaddock (a pomelo), the blood-red orange, the box-leaved orange, the Mandarin orange, the sweet orange, the Tangier orange and the myrtle-leaved orange. Charles was to describe this last orange many years later: 'The myrtle-leaved orange is ranked by all authors as a variety but is very distinct in general aspect: in my father's greenhouse, during many years, it rarely yielded any seed, but at last produced one; and a tree thus raised was identical with the parent-form.'[35]

Following a request from Charles, on 22 November 1842 the Doctor wrote: 'wild oranges seeds from Mr Charles sowed. Came from America.' Charles had last seen America on his voyage in August 1836, and although he noted plantations of oranges several times in his notebooks, I have not so far found any reference to his collecting a 'wild orange'.

It is known that the naturalist Alexander von Humboldt had discovered a plantation of wild oranges on the tropical banks of the Cedeño River in the northernmost region of Venezuela some forty years previously, but he presumed that these were probably cultivated oranges that had been abandoned.[36] Charles so greatly admired Humboldt that his *Personal Narrative*, a gift from Henslow, was one of the few books he took with him on his voyage. He had, moreover, met his hero in London on 29 January 1842.[37] If there was any connection between Humboldt and the seeds that his father was to sow later the same year, they would have had a great significance for him.

On 14 September 1842, Charles and Emma left London and moved into their own house at Downe. Apart from the sowing of the wild orange seeds in November 1842 and the experiment with the raspberry canes in October 1843, there appear to have been no more horticultural or botanical trials at The Mount. However, on 14 and 15 March 1843, the Doctor recorded that a Wine Sour plum and a Coe's Golden Drop plum had been grafted 'for Mr. C.D.', doubtless for the new orchard at Down House, and two *Berberis darwinii* were planted in Susan Darwin's own bed in April 1854. *B. darwinii*, or Darwin's berberis, was collected by Darwin during the voyage of HMS *Beagle*, in Tierra del Fuego, and was named in his honour by Joseph Dalton Hooker. Hooker called it the 'pretty little Barberry of your Chiloean collection' and had it engraved in the *Icones Plantarum* (1844). Charles was interested in the pollination mechanism of the berberis, and it is possible that he had asked his sister to grow these two specimens especially for him.

One other entry in the Diary in connection with Charles is of interest. It occurs on 19 March 1842: 'Sir John Seabrights Melon and Manchester cucumber sowed.' Charles had been staying at The Mount for two weeks prior to this event. Quite how the melon seeds came to Shrewsbury is not known, but Charles was at this time aware of Sir John Sebright's writings and skill in selective breeding, both of birds and of domestic animals.[38]

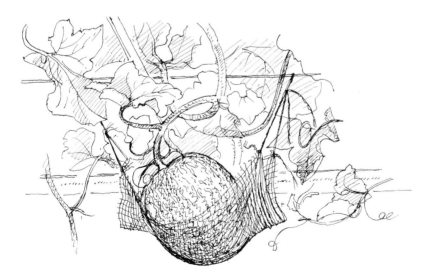

[1] Charles Darwin and Thomas Henry Huxley, *Autobiographies*, ed. Gavin de Beer (Oxford: Oxford University Press, 1983), p. 21.

[2] Notebooks, *'Questions and Experiments'*, op. cit., p. 494.

[3] *Charles Darwin: His Life told in an Autobiographical Chapter, and in a Selected Series of his Published Letters.* ed. by his son, Francis Darwin (London: John Murray, 2nd edn, 1902), p. 40. The reading of Malthus is recorded in Notebook 'D', which is the third of his four notebooks on 'the transmutation of species'.

[4] *Notebooks, Questions and Experiments, op. cit.*, p. 495. *L. densiflorus*, also known as *Gilia densiflora*, is perhaps what Darwin meant by *L. densifolium*, which does not appear to exist.

[5] *Coronilla*; another leguminous plant, species not given.

[6] CCD vol. 5, p. 339.

[7] *Ibid.*, 5, p. 345.

[8] Charles Darwin, *Journal of Researches*, vol. 3 (London, 1839), pp. 347–8.

[9] CCD vol. 1, p. 443, i.e. the 'Chilian' kind.

[10] D.S. Correll, *The Potato and Its Wild Relatives* (Renner, 1962). The specimens sent to the Herbarium at Kew were originally named *Solanum maglia*, but they were renamed *S. tuberosum* var. *quaytercarum*. A more recent synonym is *S. ochranthum* after a naturalist who 'rediscovered' them.

[11] CCD vol. 2, p. 14.

[12] *Ibid.*, vol. 3, p. 347.

[13] *Ibid.*, vol. 3, p. 142.

[14] From a draft transcription of *Charles Darwin's Notes on the Fertilisation of Flowers, 1840–1843*, ed. David Kohn.

[15] *Notebooks, Questions and Experiments, op. cit.*, p. 495.

[16] This would be Sarah Elizabeth (1793–1880), Emma Darwin's elder sister.

[17] *Ibid.*, pp. 498–9.

[18] *Ibid.*, p. 503.

[19] *Ibid.*, p. 504.

[20] CCD vol. 3, pp. 34–5, 218, 224, 226. It is, perhaps, significant that the weeping yew sometimes bears both male and female flowers on the same tree.

[21] Garden Diary MS (18 July and 7 September 1840). John Abberley is described as a servant at The Mount in the Census of 1841, but in the Parish Register for October of the same year, when he marries Ann Munslow, another servant at The Mount, his occupation is given as 'gardener'.

[22] *Notebooks, Questions and Experiments, op. cit.*, p. 505. The handwriting in this letter, in spite of its misspelling, is perfect.

[23] CCD vol. 2, p. 306.

[24] *Notebooks, Questions and Experiments, op. cit.*, p. 497.

[25] *Ibid.*, p. 501. 'Mr Herbert' is the Hon. and Rev. William Herbert (1778–1847), botanist. His observation 'on this subject' is that 'the closely allied genera Faba, pisym, vicia and ervum cannot be held as distinct'. See Herbert's *Amaryllidaceae: Preceded by an Attempt to Arrange the Monocotyledonous Orders, and Followed by a Treatise on Cross-bred Vegetables, and Supplement* (London, Ridgeway, 1837), pp. 352–3.

[26] David Kohn, in Charles Darwin's *Notes on Fertilisation 1840–1843*, notes that at one time this note was pinned together with Abberley's letter.

[27] John Claudius Loudon, *An Encyclopaedia of Gardening* (London, 1830), p. 243.

[28] Charles M'Intosh, *The New and Improved Practical Gardener* (London: Thomas Kelly, 1847), p. 67.

[29] *Notebooks, Questions and Experiments, op. cit.*, p. 505.

[30] CCD vol. 2, p. 271.

[31] *Notebooks, Questions and Experiments, op. cit.*, p. 498.

[32] Loudon, *op. cit.*, p. 243. The Englishman is not named.

[33] *Cassell's Popular Gardening* (London, 1893), vol. 3, p. 348.

[34] *Scott's Orchardist* (London, 1872), p. 598.

[35] Charles Darwin, *The Variation of Animals and Plants Under Domestication*, Vol. 1 (London, 1868), pp. 335-6.

[36] According to Humboldt: 'In the midst of the forest, on the banks of the Rio Cedeño, as well as on the southern declivity of the Cocollar, we find, in their wild state, papaw and orange-trees, bearing large and sweet fruit. These are probably the remains of some conucos, or Indian plantations; for in those countries the orange-tree cannot be counted among the indigenous plants, any more than the banana-tree, the papaw-tree, maize, cassava, and many other useful plants, with the true country of which we are unacquainted, though they have accompanied man in his migrations from the remotest times'; Alexander von Humboldt, *Personal Narrative of Travels to the Equinoctial Regions of The New Continent 1799–1804*, trans. Helen M. Williams, 7 vols (London); facs. repr., 6 vols (New York, Ams Press, 1966).

[37] *The Correspondence of Charles Darwin*, vols 1–14: 1821–36, eds Frederick Burkhardt and Sydney Smith, with David Kohn, et al. (Cambridge: Cambridge University Press, 1985–2004), vol. 4, II, p. 434.

[38] Sir John Saunders Sebright (1767–1846), Whig politician, wrote *The Art of Improving the Breeds of Domestic Animals* (1809) and on hawking (1826), animal instinct (1836) and selective breeding (1838). Darwin's friend, the naturalist and stationer William Yarrell, was a mutual acquaintance.

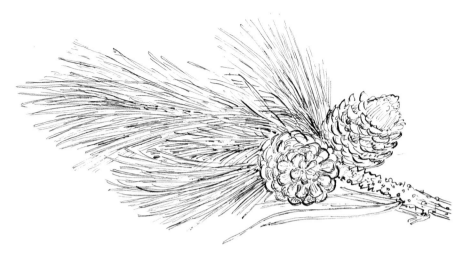

FOUR

*The Ornamental Grounds:
the Bank, the Terrace and
the Flower Garden*

The laying out of the drive, a lawn and a circumnavigating walk; the planting of a screen of shrubs to hide both the slums of Frankwell and the busy road below the garden wall; the making of the terrace and its walk along the top of the steep river bank, with a lower, parallel connecting walk, were, in all probability, Dr Darwin's earliest projects in The Mount's gardens.

There was certainly a flower garden of some sort by 1815. A letter from Bessy, wife of Josiah Wedgwood II, written on a visit to The Mount on 28 June 1815, describes the scene at Shrewsbury when celebrating the earlier surrender of Napoleon Bonaparte: 'the bells are ringing and the guns firing away at a great rate... . We are here in the middle of the hay-harvest, and the flower-garden looks beautiful.'[1] Moreover, as already described in Chapter One, letters from Caroline, Susan and Catherine to their brother Charles, written in the 1820s and 1830s, make several references to their gardening activities.

The Severn, its cliff-like bank – or escarpment – and the Terrace Walk along its top formed the most striking features of this garden. Today the river can hardly be seen from the terrace or the mansion. It, and the walk below, are hidden in a thicket of self-sown trees, bushes and ivy.

THE BANK

There is a conflict of interest here, as the prime reason for building a house on this site was its fine views of the river and beyond; there can be little doubt that when the Darwins lived here the bank's vegetation was, unlike today, well controlled. Its deterioration, once The Mount had ceased to belong to the Darwins, was sadly quite rapid. Henrietta Darwin, Charles and Emma's third child, visited The Mount in 1880, thirteen years after it had passed from the family's hands, and found it already overgrown and neglected: 'All the pretty walks in the bank have been let to grow up so that you don't see the river and are stuffy and dank. The little summerhouse where all the children used to play, is in ruin. Poor old house.'[2]

In 2012 the bank was bought by the Shropshire Wildlife Trust, with the intention of opening it up to the public as a memorial to, or recreation of, Charles Darwin's early days. I made the following account[3] of the bank's vegetation in the Darwins' time in part to advise the Wildlife Trust on the commencement of their project.

Emma Elizabeth Wilmot (1820–98) made a drawing of the Terrace Walk on one of her visits to The Mount in either 1842 or 1843. She was a first cousin to Charles, her father Francis Sacheveral Darwin (1786–1859) being a younger half-brother of Robert Darwin. Her drawing shows the mansion and bank, with the river and its meadows below, low shrubs and trees clothing the western end of the bank, and tall, slender trees trimmed to a fair height, framing the view.[4]

An etching of 1884, from the opposite bank, shows the north front of the house in full view, with only low shrubs and sparse trees covering the bank below.[5] However, a later photograph taken from nearly the same point as

Emma Wilmot's drawing shows that the view is already becoming obscured by trees and bushes.[6] Whatever the bank's original vegetation may have been, it is apparent from the Diary that Robert Darwin started planting it with trees and shrubs as soon as the property was purchased. He also built an ice house halfway down the bank beside the 'Middle', 'Lower' or 'Bank Walk'. The Middle Walk was linked at each end to the Upper or Terrace walk, which in later years became known as 'the Doctor's Walk'.[7]

The Diary frequently mentions the River Severn, which was accessed from the bank by steps situated just below the ice house, and where the Darwins' boat, used for fetching and carrying gravel and other materials, was kept. Usually, in December, January or February, loads of ice – up to twenty-nine cartloads – for the ice house were brought in. Occasionally, the river and the pond in Bank Meadow froze enough to avoid cartage from further afield. The actual river froze enough to fill the ice house in 1841 and 1844.

At other times, the Severn caused serious damage by flooding. Massive floods in 1852 – one of the Severn's highest floods for sixteen years – caused slippages to the Middle Walk, needing six men to work on its repair, driving piles or 'stanks' (supports), boating gravel, cutting drains and so on. Some twelve entries in the Diary for the March of that year relate to the preparing of piles, 10 ft and 13 ft long, for the Bank Walk.

The fence separating the whole of the bank, and the palings and hedge of the Bank Meadow to the west, also needed frequent mending and had to be kept in good repair, as did the public towpath, or 'Barge Path'.

The Diary constantly refers to trees on the bank and terrace, usually in connection with the removal of branches or their felling, with the implication that either judicious thinning was needed (for the sake of the view) or that their roots had become unstable. In this respect, the Diary mentions ash, beech, birch, elm, fir, horse chestnut, lime, oak, quince, walnut and yew, as well as the 'Halston oak' mentioned in Chapter One. Replacements were sometimes planted and the timber of the felled trees was invariably used for fencing, stakes or rails.

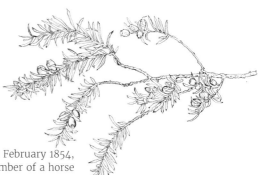

An exception occurs when an ash tree, felled on the bank in February 1854, was sawn up in the December of that year, along with the timber of a horse chestnut felled on the terrace in the same month, to make wheelbarrows. The Spanish chestnut beside 'the Doctor's Walk', in which Charles and his youngest sister Catherine played when they were children (see Chapter One), was apparently still standing in 1892.

Another ash tree by the terrace was one of several trees that the Doctor regularly measured. It might well have been one of the trees he planted when he first came to The Mount, as by 1838 it was fairly mature, being 3 ft 6 ins in girth at 2 ft from the ground. It had increased by 1½ in the following year, and another 2½ in by 1842, but no measurements were recorded for it thereafter. This could have been the 'ash by house' that was cut down in 1851. An ash tree by the ice house was felled in 1857.

The Diary mentions two beeches growing on the bank, one by the towing path, the other by the ice house; they were cut down in 1839 and 1849 respectively. The timber from the tree by the towing path was made into stanks for the Bank Walk, the Severn having caused another serious flood in 1836. A young oak replaced the second beech. Another tree, growing by the ice house and cut down in 1849 for rails, was an elm.

A fir and a walnut on the north side of the house were felled in 1840. They, too, could have been planted when the house was new and, forty years later, would have obstructed the view. However, twelve 'spruce firs' were planted on the bank in 1860. There are a few references in the Diary, in September 1853 and June 1854, to the hemlock spruce (*Tsuga canadensis*). This tree, according to Charles M'Intosh in 1832, was 'almost unknown to the generality of our pleasure-grounds', but it is not clear if the twelve 'spruce firs' were of that variety.[8]

Yews, laurels and hollies are among the trees most frequently mentioned in the Diary, as they were used extensively for clothing the bank, lining walks, screening the garden from the outside world and hedging, both in the garden and in the fields. They were kept trimmed and clipped, especially along the

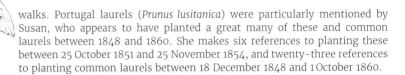

walks. Portugal laurels (*Prunus lusitanica*) were particularly mentioned by Susan, who appears to have planted a great many of these and common laurels between 1848 and 1860. She makes six references to planting these between 25 October 1851 and 25 November 1854, and twenty–three references to planting common laurels between 18 December 1848 and 1 October 1860.

Rhododendrons were also planted on the bank and terrace, but no varieties are specified for this or any other part of the garden, except for six plants that came from Waterer's nursery at Woking, Surrey, along with two *Kalmias* and an *Arbutus* in 1856.[9]

The Upper and Middle Walks traversed the entire width of the bank. They were made of gravel, with mown turf verges and yews, laurels and hollies lining their sides. The walks received regular re-gravelling, cleaning, the removal of moss (scuffling), brushing and mowing, and the hedges were regularly clipped and laid. As mentioned by Henrietta Litchfield (above), this discipline had already disappeared by 1880. There is certainly no sign whatsoever of the Darwins' careful maintenance today.

THE TERRACE WALK

According to the Sale Map of 1867, the Upper – or Terrace – Walk was 600 ft long. In front of the Mansion it was about 10 ft wide, but narrower at either end. There were steep steps linking the Terrace Walk to the Middle Walk at the western end, and shallower steps (both of which can still be seen) halfway along the top terrace, to ease the gradient downwards towards the east, the eastern side of the property being about 25 ft lower than the western side.

A low wall, 140 ft long, ran along part of the walk on the bank side, from a vinery (which once stood to the east of the house) to the end of the stable block on the west.

From Wilmot's drawing and a photograph in Arthur Keith's *Darwin Revalued* (London, 1955) it can be seen that this wall is no more than 1–2 ft high and made of brick with a broad stone coping, triangular in section. The Diary shows that an earlier wall was taken down in 1841 and replaced by a new one, the work beginning on 9 December and finishing on 30 December, with a couple of days off for Christmas. It looks as if this same wall, or parts of it, still exists today.

The walk was re-laid once the new wall was completed, and then, six months later, in the summer of 1842, trees at the eastern end were felled and a wall in the Terrace Walk was removed, in order to join the Terrace Walk to the flower garden (28 June 1842, 'working at new walk to flower garden with the steps', and 1 July 1842, 'Removing Terrace wall to join the walk to flower garden'). The shallower flight of steps was also part of the 'new walk' to the flower garden. The Diary mentions, as well, in 1840 and 1848, a 'wire fence' along part of the terrace walk, planted with roses and honeysuckle.[10]

The terrace was a major feature of the Darwins' garden. It formed a long, high, gently sloping promenade along the length of The Mount's grounds, with the mansion at the higher end and the flower garden at the lower. It would have had grand, extensive views of the Severn and farmland to the north, while The Mount's lawns, shrubberies, kitchen garden and borders hid most of the town of Shrewsbury to the south.

I suspect that a walk along the terrace was part of Robert Darwin's daily routine, as this promenade was still known as 'the Doctor's Walk' in 1902 (see Chapter One). Charles, while staying at The Mount in the early 1840s, sent a charming letter to Emma, describing their little son's behaviour there, on seeing a frog: 'I fear he is a coward – a frog danced near him & [he] danced & screamed with horror at the dangerous monster, & I had a deal of kissing at his open bellowing mouth to comfort him – he threw my stick over terrace wall, looked at it as it went and cried tatta with the greatest sang-froid & walked away.'[11]

Charles also had the habit of walking 'as usual an hour or two on terrace' and going 'for a turn on the terrace several times a day'.[12] The sand walk at Down House in Kent was later to provide him with the same benefit.

FERNS ON THE BANK AND TERRACE WALL

Hart's tongue, curly bracken, rue-leaved spleenwort, *Osmunda regalis*, brake and polypodiums were planted in the terrace wall and on the bank in the decade between August 1852 and April 1862. This is the only period during which the Diary mentions ferns, but it occurred when the 'fern craze' or 'Pteridomania', which began in the early 1840s, was in full swing.

It looks as if fern-collecting was one of the pastimes enjoyed by the Darwin sisters, but there is no indication that Susan and Catherine foraged for ferns themselves. The Diary merely states that they 'planted ferns on bank from Tan-y-bwlch and Festiniog'[13] (villages in the Welsh mountains not far from Snowdon), and 'ferns we brought from the lakes'.[14] A 'rue leaved spleenwort fern planted came fr. Orme's Head by Margaret Haycock', the Haycock family being local family friends, while other ferns (possibly from nurserymen or fellow gardeners) came from nearby Grinshill, Acton Scott and Bicton. The fern craze became even more intense in the 1860s and 1870s and The Mount's Sale Particulars of 1867 include a fernery among the 'conservatories', but the Diary makes no mention of such a feature.

THE TERRACE LAWN

A steeply sloping, north-facing lawn (sometimes called the terrace lawn), some 12-18 ft wide and 100 ft long, lay between the windows of the mansion's drawing room and dining room and the Terrace Walk. The shadow of the three-storey mansion would have covered the whole of it for most of the winter and only a little less in summer.

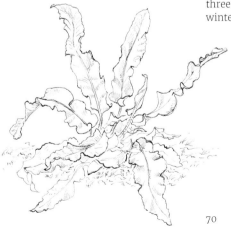

The Sale Plan of 1867 shows that the north sides of the vinery, stove-house and greenhouse (conservatory) on the east of the house and the kitchen, dairy and laundry on its west side were screened by trees and shrubs. This screen, as mentioned by Susan in the Diary for 1850, included mountain ash, laurel, yew, an ilex (presumably *Quercus ilex*), holly, Chinese box, some 'lauristina' bushes by the housekeeper's room, an acacia tree (probably the false acacia or *robinia*) by the kitchen window and, in 1840, planted by the laundry, a 'Paeona tree'.

As mentioned in Chapter One, the laundry was Erasmus's and Charles's boyhood laboratory. It was situated in the stable-yard next to the dairy. Like the dairy, its north wall faced the Terrace Walk, and was covered in ivy, which needed constant clipping.

FLOWERS AND SHRUBS IN THE TERRACE BORDER

Along the side of the Terrace Walk, beyond the shade cast by the mansion, there was a border edged with tiles ('laying Tiles down as edge to Border on Terrace', 20 June 1855). It lay between the vinery, an octagonal summerhouse and the flower garden lawn. The Diary provides the names of the moisture-loving, sun-loving annuals, perennials, bedding, climbing and shrubby plants in the terrace border, but gives no hint of their disposition, except to say that *Acorus gramineus* (Japanese rush) was planted by the Terrace Walk when it was extended in the summer of 1842, which suggests that this area was damp (Diary, 11 August 1842).

As well as *Acorus*, the plants mentioned in the Diary include antirrhinums, *atragene*, berbery/barberry, box trees, calceolaria, cheiranthus, cistus, *Clematis flammula*, silk convolvulus, double gorse, everlasting pea, fuchsias, geraniums, heaths, late honeysuckle, jasmine, jonquils, *Laburnum* 'golden chain' (five shillings' worth), 'little red' pinks, rhododendrons, small roses, 'Brompton' and 'German' stocks, and double yellow wallflowers.

Geraniums were planted out regularly in May, and roses and honeysuckle were grown on the wire fence; probably the atragene, clematis, jasmine and everlasting peas were grown upon it too. Everlasting peas and a barberry tree, originally planted on the terrace, were later moved to below the terrace wall (6 November 1849) and stocks were planted 'to the wall' (17 August 1840).

THE FLOWER GARDEN

The flower garden was a favourite haunt of all the family, as can be seen from the letter on p. 32 from Caroline, written in February 1826 to Charles ('Bobby') when he was a seventeen-year-old medical student in Edinburgh. However, once Marianne, Caroline and Erasmus had left home, many of the activities in the flower garden seem to have been, as her father put it, 'by Miss Catherine's direction' rather than Susan's.

The flower garden appears to have demanded much more attention than the other beds and borders in The Mount's pleasure grounds. Apart from the usual, necessary weeding, mowing of grass walks, cleaning and renewing gravel paths, trimming box edging, pruning and laying the rose hedge, manuring or 'soiling' the beds, and the sowing of annuals, the tender perennials needed planting out in spring and taking up again in autumn. This bedding-out system ensured a constant display of flowering plants for most of the year. It also entailed the taking of cuttings and transferring to pots, and the use of some sort of winter shelter; in this case either the greenhouse (conservatory), the hothouse or the stove-house.

The Sale Map of 1867 and the Shrewsbury Town Map for 1882 show a large, circular flower garden at the eastern end of the Terrace Walk. (This site is now covered by the houses and gardens of nos 2, 3 and 4 Darwin Gardens.) Its shape was rather unusual for its time. The gardens shown on contemporary Shrewsbury town maps and the nearby countryside do not possess geometric flower gardens, let alone any like the circular garden at The Mount. In keeping with a garden created mainly to enhance the natural landscape, it is placed at a considerable distance from the mansion and is relatively simple in design, which is strikingly similar to the children's cottage garden laid out by Humphry Repton for Endsleigh in 1814.

The Mount's flower garden formed a tangent with the north wall of the kitchen garden and was about 65 ft in diameter, with a rectangular summerhouse on its southeastern edge. Three paths formed concentric rings and beds within the perimeter, with a circular bed in the centre. Small radial cross-paths divided the concentric beds into separate compartments. One radial path allowed entry from the Terrace Walk on the east and another, on the same axis, gave access to the flower garden lawn opposite. This lawn extended 100 ft to the west, where there was another, octagonal, summerhouse.

The placing of this geometric flower garden on the north side of a kitchen garden wall that would have robbed it of a good deal of sunlight is puzzling. The only explanation is that it might, originally, have been intended to form a decorative entrance to the kitchen garden, of the kind described by Charles M'Intosh, in *The New and Improved Practical Gardener*.[15] This argument is strengthened by the fact that the central, north–south kitchen garden cross-path lines up exactly with the centre bed of the flower garden. However, this hypothesis also requires a communicating door or gateway in the wall between the flower garden and the kitchen garden, and there is no such opening marked on either the Sale Map or the Ordnance Survey Map of 1882. Nor are there any references in the Diary (which is rich in references to all the other doorways in the garden walls) to any door in this particular wall, which supported, on its north side, a number of fruit trees; two plums (a 'Magnum Bonum' and a 'Winesour'), a pear and some morello cherry trees.

Diary entries made between 1838 and the early 1850s suggest that the flower garden once looked quite different, consisting of isolated or island flower beds in various forms. It might well have been the type described by John Claudius Loudon as 'dug compartments placed on [a] lawn [and] … surrounded by an irregular border of flowers, shrubbery, and trees'.[16] No isolated beds are shown in the Sale Map of 1867, but the Doctor recorded

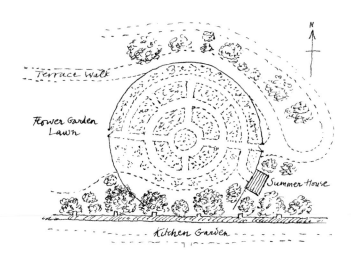

the making of a 'sage bed below flower garden' in September 1838[17] and, in November and December the same year, two round beds: a small one 'by flower garden' and a 'large round bed in flower garden'. Both were for roses. There was also a 'yellow rose planted in the grass in flower garden' (November 1840) and 'Cath's oblong bed in flower garden' (March 1852).

According to Susan's entries in the Diary, flower garden alterations began on 9 October 1854, following the building of 'an octagon bed' earlier that year on 1 April: 'begun to build the octagon bed in f.g.' The reference to its being 'built' suggests that this was a raised dome-shaped bed, possibly acting as the central focal point of what already was, or was about to become, the circular flower garden. It was finished by 5 April and planted with geraniums on 19 April 1854, but there are no other references to it, apart from the following year when it was again planted with geraniums.

'Altering Flower Garden' (10 October 1854) continued into November when tiles were 'put round F. garden' and a new walk was made to it. In July 1857, Susan's *Ageratums* were removed from the flower garden: 'a bed by themselves is best'. Another walk was opened into the flower garden in October 1858.

Two years later, in April 1860, Susan reported that she was again 'making [a] new flower garden', which was bedded out in May, ornamented with 'tubs covered in bark' in June, and, three years later (2 April 1863), '6 little arbae vitae shrubs' were planted in it. This last, late date makes it fairly certain that she is referring to the circular flower garden shown on the Sale Map of 1867, but the earlier references cited above indicate that there might have been beds of a different layout beforehand.

WALKS AND EDGINGS IN THE FLOWER GARDEN

The walks within the flower garden appear to have been of mown grass until February 1850, when Susan first mentions 'gravelling flower garden'. This was repeated in June and November 1854, at the same time as her first alterations in the layout of the flower garden were being made. Scrutiny of the Sale Map of 1867 suggests that there was a wide band of grass round the outer perimeter, with narrow paths (of gravel?) between the beds. Whatever the case, the band of grass in the flower garden continued to be mown until the Diary ends.

The beds were edged with box but, as noted above, tiles were put around the flower garden in 1854 and a reference by the Doctor, in December 1843, to 'pruning the wire fence round Flower Garden' suggests that its several beds, including the *Verbena* beds, were enclosed by a wire fence supporting a hedge of roses. In December 1856, a round bed (the octagon bed?) was adorned with wire 'like [a] basket, and painted with two climbing roses planted over it'.[18]

THE NORTH BORDER OF THE FLOWER GARDEN

As early as 1839 the Doctor mentions 'the North Border in the Flower Garden', 'the Upper Border' or 'Upper Bed'. This bed was planted with three kinds of peony: Moutan, 'Poppy' (*P. papaveracea*, a variety of Moutan) and the hardier 'Siberian' (*Paeonia albiflora*). The Moutans, as mentioned in the Chapter One, were taken into the greenhouse to flower in early spring.

Here too were cypripediums, azaleas, yellow gentians (presumably *G. lutea*, the root of which would have been of pharmaceutical interest to the Doctor), dahlias, golden ribes and the *Ribes sanguineum* that was the Doctor's first entry in the Diary: 'sowed *ribes sanguinea*'. No details are given as to how the cypripediums were grown, or their variety (other than a 'yellow cypripedium from Miss Arden', July 1843), but they were, in the summers of 1841 and 1842, given nitrate of soda in one of the horticultural experiments conducted by Dr Darwin for Charles (see Chapter Three).

This area also contained the 'North Peat Border' or 'Bog Bed' which was used for cuttings of gum cistus, golden ribes and a rose 'from Chirk Castle', as well as plantings of unspecified bulbs and dahlias, and for 'planting' or plunging pots of plants, such as the peonies mentioned above, cistuses and azaleas. These would spend the summer outdoors before being taken into the greenhouse in autumn for the winter. This system, according to M'Intosh, writing in 1847, was relatively new: 'The introduction of tender greenhouse exotics as flower garden plants, is an improvement in floriculture of comparatively recent date, and is, when judiciously carried into effect, capable of raising the smallest garden to the highest possible grade of keeping.'[19]

The gum cistuses (also known as rock roses and considered at that time hardy only in southern England) were planted out in the north border in spring or put out in pots on the terrace in July and taken back to the greenhouse in the autumn. The Doctor mentioned a little yellow *Cistus* put out in the north border in April 1839 and a small *Cistus formosus* (probably the plant now named *Helianthemum lasianthum* sub sp.*formosum*) being brought in from the same border in October of the same year.

Some azaleas were grown outdoors, flowering in late spring, but others, like the tree peonies and cistuses, were grown in pots and plunged outside

in midsummer in the north border, then taken up in autumn, re-potted in heath soil, and forced in beds of tan in the stove-house to flower indoors in the new year. No varieties of azalea were named except one, which was 'white-flowered', and, in 1854, six 'Indian' azaleas, which came with six epacris, 'from London'.[20]

ROSES, FLOWERS AND SHRUBS IN THE FLOWER GARDEN

As already noted, the Doctor referred to two round beds in or 'by' the flower garden. In October 1852, two years before she began building her 'octagon bed', Susan planted four rose trees in the 'Flower Garden round bed'. These appear to have been underplanted with the dwarf shrub Rose de Meaux, the layering of which is a frequent occurrence in the Diary. 'Rose de Meaux' (*Rosa centifolia*) also formed the rose hedge encircling the flower garden, and Susan's basket of wire in her round bed was planted with two climbing roses in December 1856. An entry for the following July reads: 'taking up red roses in round bed & leaving only the Provence'. Other roses were grown by the summerhouses in the west border and against the south front of the mansion (see Part 3:1).

The flower garden had two summerhouses, an upper one at the end of the terrace walk and a lower one facing the flower garden lawn. On the Ordnance Survey maps of 1867 and 1882 the upper summerhouse is shown as rectangular, while the lower one is octagonal. There are few indications as to which of the two houses the Diary entries refer to, but it does tell us that rhododendrons, azaleas and the climbing rose 'Felicité' grew by the upper house; that in December 1838 Susan had an iris bed 'by summer house'; that a cobaea and two other roses ('Mrs Elliott' and 'Giant of Battles') were planted 'by summer house' in October 1850 and that box trees were planted 'behind summer house' in April 1851. (Part 3:1 lists the plants that were specifically given in the Diary as growing in the Flower Garden.)

[1] *Emma Darwin: a Century of Family Letters, 1792–1896,* ed. Henrietta Litchfield (London: John Murray, 1915), vol. 1, p. 67.

[2] Edna Healey, *Emma Darwin* (London: Headline, 2001), p. 271. Unattributed quote.

[3] Susan Campbell, *'Its situation … was exquisite in the extreme: …'* The Journal of the Garden History Society, 40:2 (2012), pp. 6–10.

[4] Private collection.

[5] Frontispiece opp. p. 12, in Edward Woodall, *Transactions of the Shropshire Archæological & Natural History Society,* 8 (1884).

[6] Arthur Keith, *Darwin Revalued* (London: Watts & Co., 1955), fig. 1b, opp. p. 46.

[7] *Charles Darwin: His Life told in an Autobiographical Chapter, and in a Selected Series of his Published Letters.* ed. by his son, Francis Darwin (London: John Murray, 2nd edn, 1902), p. 2.

[8] Charles M'Intosh, *The New and Improved Practical Gardener* (London: Thomas Kelly, 1847), Vol. 2, p. 139.

[9] Garden Diary MS (28 and 29 February 1856). The rhododendrons are also listed on the front page of the Garden Diary (see Part 3:1 E for this list).

[10] A 'wire fence' at this time meant a neat, ornamental and sturdy barricade of railings or trellis made from drawn wire, usually half an inch in diameter, and supported by cast-iron uprights. It was not intended to be seen, and for this reason was often painted green and covered with plants.

[11] CCD vol. 2, p. 296.

[12] *Ibid.,* vol. 2, pp. 314 and 399.

[13] Garden Diary MS, 22 August 1852.

[14] *Ibid.* (20 September 1852).

[15] M'Intosh, op. cit., p. 21.

[16] John Claudius Loudon, *An Encyclopaedia of Gardening* (London, 1830), p. 791, fig. 540.

[17] Garden Diary MS (20 September 1838). The fact that he also noted 'first sage [flower] sent in at breakfast' the following spring (25 May 1839) suggests that the sage was *S. patens,* which was introduced only in 1838.

[18] 'Rose baskets may be … formed merely by fixing wires in the ground; the lower part being covered with roses pegged down, and their branches covered with moss, and the handles to the basket being formed of wire, over which climbing roses have been trained', Jane Loudon.

[19] M'Intosh, *op. cit.,* p. 828.

[20] The Indian azalea is the evergreen greenhouse variety (*Rhododendron simsii*) as opposed to the 'Ghent' or American azalea, which is hardy.

FIVE

Borders, Lawns and 'the Glade'

The west border was nearly 120 ft long. It ran along the outside of the west kitchen garden wall and was separated from the lawn by a grass verge and a wide gravel walk. At the south end there was the main door into the kitchen garden, which meant that the west border formed one side of an elegant, ornamental box-edged approach from there to the mansion.

From the Ordnance Survey Map of 1882, the west border appears to have been filled with small standard trees. The Diary confirms, in 1839 and 1850, that the border stood at the base of a fruit wall supporting an apricot tree, baking pears, cherries, three plums and a greengage, as well as a 'jessamine' and roses. More roses grew in the border, with a few herbaceous plants and annuals. Roses predominated. They included: '7 new roses, mostly moss roses fr Mr H. Wedgwood[1] planted in a row before W. Wall outside K. Garden', in 1838; a 'Gloire de Rosamane ... from Eaton' and a rose 'from

Mr Wakefield's sale' in 1840; a 'small moss rose from Instone' in 1841, and 'white Provence roses from Maer Hall' in 1843. Fifteen unnamed rose trees were planted in November 1852, and in November 1856 six standard roses came from Paul's Cheshunt Nursery in Buckinghamshire.[2] The herbaceous plants included mignonettes, fuchsias, crocuses, ranunculus, sweet peas, chrysanthemums, hepaticas, azaleas, rhododendrons and, on one occasion, in June 1839, 'love apples' (tomatoes).

THE FRONT BORDER

The front of the mansion faced south, with a warm and sunny border below its ground-floor windows. This border, referred to in the Diary as 'in Front of House', ran from the kitchen courtyard gate on the west end, past the windows of the Doctor's study and his consulting room, to the entrance of the front or hall door. The border then continued eastwards, past the windows of the library, the morning room and the greenhouse or conservatory. It was quite wide, edged as usual with a grass verge and fronted by the gravelled carriage sweep.

The walls of the house by the Doctor's windows (he referred to his study window and his closet window) supported a 'Sweetwater' grapevine, and a *Clematis florida* (with another outside the morning room). Below them was a purple Cistus. In August 1851, two climbing roses were planted by the hall door. The following August a *Magnolia grandiflora* was planted by what was once the Doctor's study window and, in the same year, a *Clematis azurea* (syn. of *Clematis patens*) was planted by the hall door. The mansion's walls also supported roses, *Cobea scandens*, a 'Yeulan' magnolia, a pomegranate, myrtle trees (which had to be covered up in winter), a *Clematis flammula*, which had been moved from the terrace border in 1841, and a Wisteria. There were mignonettes in the window boxes, geraniums by the hall door and the rest of the border was planted with verbenas, belladonna lilies, stocks, gorse, small hollies, hibiscus and chrysanthemums.

A grapevine, which the Doctor referred to as 'the tree from Mr Rowland', cropped very late, in October or November. It actually provided the family with 'a large plate of grapes' on Christmas Day in 1839. Even more surprising is a reference to a tree 'in front' from which thirty-one almonds were taken on 12 November 1838.

LAWNS

Lawn-mowing, rolling and raking are recorded throughout the Diary. These procedures usually began in mid-April and continued throughout the summer until early November. It could take three days to mow all the lawns, and mowing was repeated at ten- to fourteen-day intervals. There were four lawns: the small north or terrace lawn, the more extensive lawn at the front of the mansion, a small lawn in front of the vinery, and the flower garden lawn. The flower garden itself, and the grass verges on the terrace walks, also needed mowing.

The Mount's lawns were presumably cut with a scythe until 7 July 1857, when Susan recorded that the flower garden lawn was mown with a mowing machine. This appears to have been sent on trial, as ten days later she wrote: 'mowing machine bought £5. 7. 6'. A new mower costing that amount (about £400 today) at this date would have been the cheapest available – a 14-in hand mower. However, it is possible that hers was a larger, donkey-powered machine bought second-hand as, three years later, on 22 May 1860, she recorded 'mowing lawn with a donkey'. She did not name the mower's manufacturer but a Shanks patent mowing machine was among the garden items in the sale of The Mount's effects in November 1866.[3] A Shanks donkey-powered mower would have had a 25-in cutter and a new one would have cost more like £12 10s (about £880 today). A mowing machine saved a good deal of labour; advertisements of the day claimed that a man with a mowing machine could mow in three hours what would take ten hours for a man with a scythe. However, M'Intosh, writing in 1847, did not think this new invention was 'at all likely to lead to the entire disuse of the more antiquated mode of cutting with the scythe'.[4]

Trees specifically mentioned as growing on the main lawn in front of the house include a Cembra pine (given to the Doctor at some unspecified date by a Mr Wilding, but cut down in 1840) and an *Araucaria imbricata* sown from seed donated in 1844 by Isaac Secker, a lawyer friend of Harry Wedgwood, and planted out on the lawn in 1849. It was a slow grower; by 1858 Susan found that it had grown to a height of only 2 ft 5 in.

A 'white' cedar was blown down in 1839 and a 'red' cedar was cut down in 1849, but another cedar survived; it was being pruned in 1850. There was also a beech (probably the one below which the experimental letter 'D' was made with nitrate of soda; see Chapter Three) with white and yellow crocuses beneath. Here, too, was an Ilex (planted in 1854) and an Arbutus (planted in 1858). A scarlet oak was cut down at the top of the lawn in 1849.

There were fruit trees, too, on the lawn. There was a quince by the greenhouse/conservatory, and some fruit trees (including a Ross Nonpareil apple and a red and a yellow crab apple) appear to have been grown as a little orchard in the lawn by the kitchen garden door. An old Chaumontelle pear grew at the top of the lawn and another at the bottom. Other kinds of trees doubtless grew here too, but there are no specific references. Laurels were planted by Susan from 1848 onwards at the top of the lawn to screen the road and new houses from sight.

THE GLADE

'A glade,' according to *A Glossary of Garden History*, is 'a clearing in a wood',[5] but nothing resembling such a clearing can be seen on any contemporary map. The Diary makes only two references to the glade's position, namely 'near the hot house' and 'behind the hot house'. This is presumably the Doctor's pet hothouse, which lay between the vinery and the greenhouse/conservatory. However, if this was truly the site of the glade, there must have been some Darwinian irony attached to its name. 'A glade' conjures up a sylvan lawn, with sunlight filtering through the leaves and branches of the trees that grow about its edges. If the glade at The Mount was actually

situated beside the north-facing yard behind the vinery and the hothouse (containing the boiler house and potting sheds), it would have provided only, at best, a view of the north lawn at the top of the terrace walk, with glimpses of the Severn in one direction and the front lawn in the other.

The Diary shows that it was planted mainly with evergreens such as hollies, *Rhododendrons*, a barberry and Box trees, their purpose presumably being to hide the boiler house and potting sheds. The only deciduous trees to be planted there were two pink hawthorns (1849). A birch tree 'by the glade' was cut down in 1846 and an ash in 1849 ('cut down for rails'). A gravel walk in the glade was widened in 1843; this would have led from the north side of the mansion to the front lawn and the rest of the pleasure gardens at The Mount.

[1] Henry Wedgwood (1799–1885), brother-in-law of Robert Darwin.
[2] The roses from Paul's Cheshunt Nursery are listed separately in the front of the Diary. See Part 3:1.
[3] Sale Catalogue, Auction of the contents of The Mount, 19 – 24 November 1866 p. 60, lot 25, 'Shanks' patent mowing machine'.
[4] Charles M'Intosh, *The New and Improved Practical Gardener* (London: Thomas Kelly, 1847), Vol. 2, p. 752.
[5] Michael Symes, *A Glossary of Garden History* (Princes Risborough, Shire, 1993), p. 58.

SIX

The Glasshouses

When compared to the size and number of glasshouses in any of the larger and more stately gardens in the country around Shrewsbury, such as Attingham, Longner, Chirk, Walcot, Apley Park, Berwick, Hardwick and Wynnstay, those at the town house garden of The Mount look relatively small and insignificant. However, their productions were impressive, especially during Dr Darwin's time.

Apart from the 'greenhouse' or conservatory attached to the mansion, there were three more glasshouses at The Mount. There was the Doctor's small but favourite hothouse just to the east of the mansion (labelled 'plant stove' on the Sale Map) and a very large vinery beside it. There was also a sizeable glasshouse in the kitchen garden, plus a large brick melon frame.

The Diary uses a variety of names for its four glasshouses: the conservatory attached to the Mansion is always called 'the Greenhouse' or 'G.H.' 'The Stove' refers both to the stove-house beside the mansion and the glasshouse in the kitchen garden; the latter is usually called 'the Stove in the K.G.' The word 'Vinery' never appears in the Diary, but the larger of the two glasshouses to the east of the mansion, with a large border in front, would have been a vinery. However, this structure is always referred to as 'the Hot House'.

THE GREENHOUSE

This was one of the most distinguishing features of The Mount. It was an extension of the morning room, large and south-facing, 25 ft long and 15 ft wide. It is not known when this addition to the mansion was made, but it is mentioned in the Diary throughout. Three steps were made into the garden as late as March 1856, according to Susan's entry in the Diary.

It is labelled 'conservatory' on the sale map of 1867 and because it forms an extension to the house, that is what it would be called today, but the words 'green house', 'greenhouse', 'G. House' and 'G.H.' rather than 'conservatory' are consistently used throughout the Darwin Correspondence and the Diary.[1]

Moreover, there is a difference, because, according to M'Intosh: 'The green-house is distinguished from the conservatory, by having all the plants portable, and generally placed on stages: whereas, in the conservatory, the major part are usually planted out permanently in beds or borders prepared for them.'[2]

This was indeed so; the greenhouse was equipped with stands filled with an ever-changing display in pots, vases and boxes, of flowering shrubs, forced bulbs, hothouse plants and the Doctor's collection of citruses.

The Sale Map shows that the back wall on the north side of the greenhouse supported two sheds, one for a boiler and the other possibly for use as a potting shed. These sheds were hidden by shrubs on the terrace lawn (mountain ash, laurels, yew, an ilex, holly and Chinese box). On the south side of the greenhouse there is a continuation of the border in front of the mansion. The interior of the back wall was stuccoed, but the roof, front and one end wall were of glass, which is referred to, almost monthly, as being cleaned or mended.[3]

The boiler fire was lit in October or November; there is no reference as to when the heating was turned off, but many of the plants, and especially the citruses, were taken outside in summer.

The greenhouse was presumably heated by hot-air flues, rather than hot-water pipes, before February 1832, as in a letter from Susan to Charles she says: 'We have had pipes laid down in the Greenhouse & the regular warmth of the hot water makes the morning room very comfortable as it was apt to get very cold at night.'[4]

Two years later, Caroline writes to Charles: 'We have had workmen without end this summer about the House new slating &c, & latterly pulling down and rebuilding the green house on rather a larger scale than before – the wood was so bad that it was not supposed safe – so that we might have had a grand clash of glass some day.'[5]

The greenhouse was accessible from the morning room by wheelchair and was much enjoyed by the Doctor in his last years, right up to the day before he died, when Catherine wrote to Charles (then living in Downe, Kent): 'He is so excessively faint and exhausted often, and requires air, that he is constantly wheeled into the Green House – and sits there, – it is a great blessing having it for him.'[6]

This place seems to have been a particular source of pleasure, too, for Susan. She recorded the number of Rhododendron buds or flowers on more than one occasion, and twice refers to it looking 'very gay' with its *Camellias*, hyacinths, Epacris and Primulas all in flower.[7]

By skilfully heating this glasshouse and moving plants either outdoors for the summer to rest or bringing them in from the warmer glasshouses as autumn approached to force them into action, an exotic show of flowering plants was obtained, especially throughout the winter months and to a lesser extent during the rest of the year.

Part 3:1 lists the plants grown in the greenhouse on page 209.

THE HOTHOUSE
(also known as THE PLANT STOVE)

A constant display of tender and exotic potted flowering plants in the greenhouse, especially throughout the winter, meant that there was a continuous exchange between it, the flower garden and the three other heated glasshouses. The smallest but very much the warmest house was just a few yards away from the mansion in the garden. It is labelled 'PLANT STOVE' rather than 'hothouse' on the Sale Map, and measures 20 x 12 ft. It, too, has sheds behind it on the north side. There is a pump beside one of these sheds in a small triangular yard, one side being formed by more sheds behind another, much larger structure marked 'VINERIES'.

The plant stove was known at first as 'The Hot House' in the Darwin family, and the building of it in 1831 and its first plantings (which included a banana tree and a pineapple) are described in the letters to Charles from his sisters in Chapter One. It was something of a luxury, a novelty and a hobby for the Doctor's retirement. At this period the description of a hothouse as a 'stove' indicates that its heat was maintained at a tropical level. There were,

in gardens at this time, two sorts of stove-house: a dry stove, suitable for plants such as succulents, and a bark or moist stove, in which pineapples would be grown. The latter would contain a pit filled with fermenting bark or tan. It is not clear which type of stove the plant stove was, but as pineapples were grown there, it was probably a bark stove.[8]

It is first mentioned in the Doctor's account books in 1832, when the sum of £746 3s 9d (£52,800 today, and one-third of his professional income in that year) appears under 'Hot House &c'.[9] This is presumably what it cost to build, sometime between 1831 and 1832. The Doctor had by now reached the age of sixty-six and a year later, with increasingly bad health, he decided that it was time he 'left off business'.[10] According to his accounts for 1833, the hothouse cost almost £42 (about £3,000 today) to run in that one year.[11]

The Doctor's Garden Diary, which commenced four years later in September 1838, makes no mention of a banana, although pineapples continued to be grown in the hothouse until 1840. Pears were put to ripen there on two or three occasions, and when the Doctor received the gift of a blue water lily from Lord Hill in 1840, it was planted 'in glass' in the hothouse. It flowered three years later, to be replanted in a tub in 1844.

Confusingly, by the time the Diary begins there are references to another stove as well as this one. The second stove was in the kitchen garden and, even more confusingly, from 1841 onwards there are references not only to 'the Hothouse and Stove', but also to a 'first' and 'second' hothouse, which could refer to the two halves of the vinery.

There are no records of when the kitchen garden stove was originally built; it may have already existed when the Doctor's new, 'pet' hothouse was created in 1831.

THE VINERIES

It was long and careful analysis of entries in the Diary that indicated that those 'first' and 'second' hothouses must be the double structure marked 'VINERIES' on the Sale Map. This was a large building, 40 ft long and 18 ft wide, with a wide border in front of it and a long shed behind. It stood beside the plant stove or the Doctor's little 'pet' hothouse, facing southeast. It was divided in two, thus leading to references to a first and second hothouse and providing adjoining sections for a succession of early and late fruit, which would allow for the first being two months ahead of the second.

The system for growing grapes at The Mount appears, for some vines at least, to have been that by which young vines are planted with their roots outside the vinery and 'introduced' or 'taken into' the vinery via slots cut in the outer wall when forcing begins. After their leaves have fallen in winter they are pruned or even cut down, and then pulled out of the house, to overwinter outside.

This system could also be applied to vines in pots and there are references to 'vines in pots', but it is not clear from the Diary entries alone which method was used at The Mount. There were clearly some vines planted in beds within the hothouses as well. References to vines being cut down (in order to encourage shoots from the base of the plant) occur in February, May and November.

Forcing began in the first hothouse in February or March for the production of grapes in early June and July. These came from a Sweetwater vine; other early grapes were a 'Dutch Water' and a Hamburg. Forcing began in the second house in mid– to late April, though there are references to the vines being 'put into the second house' as early as 12 March. Hamburg, Tokay and Lombardy grapes were gathered in August. Champion grapes ripened in September and the second house provided Lombardys again ('not quite ripe') in September. In 1845 the Lombardy growing in the second house was

replaced by a Canon Hall. Canon Hall and Muscat were gathered in September and October.

Cuttings were put into pots in November and December; three months later they were 'taken into a Hothouse'. They were then either left in pots or planted in beds inside the hothouses/vineries.

Tying to wires within the houses began as soon as the shoots were big enough, in March and April. Thinning the fruit began in May and continued into July. A certain amount of summer pruning also took place.

The vine border, which extended the full length of the vinery and was 15 ft wide, was manured in mid-winter. Turf was put over it in November and around it in May. The 'Black Hole' in the kitchen garden (see Chapter Eleven) was emptied in April, and part of its contents was put on the vine border. It was planted with both salads and flowers between February and the autumn. Lettuce and celery were sown first, then came sweet peas, mignonette and stocks, vegetable marrows, green curly endive and more lettuce.

There were grapes at The Mount for nearly six months of the year. The earliest recorded picking occurs in 1842, when the first grapes, an unnamed variety from the stove in the kitchen garden, were cut on 30 May. In 1856 the last hothouse grapes (also unnamed) were cut on 5 December. In only one year (1838) were grapes bought; these were from nearby Berwick, '4 pound at 2s 6d a pound'.

Although the vine on the front of the house, the Sweetwater 'from Mr Rowland', was an early cropper, some of its fruit was left on the vine until November. This enabled 'a large plate of grapes from Front of House' to be presented at table on Christmas Day 1839, as mentioned previously in Chapter Five.

The vinery was not only heated by hot-water pipes; each half contained a tan bed, or pit. These beds were used in winter for forcing the Doctor's 'Passion trees', bulbs, roses, mint and rhubarb (which was ready to eat in December).

Strawberries and French beans were also forced here. They would have been grown in pots placed on wide planks running just under the roof of the vinery.

A Diary entry for 5 March 1859 says 'Hothouse & Stove Painted pale blue inside'. There was a popular belief at the time that this colour discouraged insects.

THE STOVE-HOUSE IN THE KITCHEN GARDEN

The stove-house in the kitchen garden also contained vines. This house is simply labelled 'GREENHOSE' on the Sale Map. It measured 35 x 10 ft and faced south; it also contained a tan bed for making hot-beds and forcing. A small shed was built at one end in 1840. Like the vinery, it was divided into two compartments, created in 1851 and provided with brick flooring in 1853. The north-facing back wall was planted with morello cherries. Being situated in the kitchen garden, it was more utilitarian than the greenhouse or hothouse/vinery, and was mostly used as a forcing house, and for seed sowing, cuttings and the potting of plants, mainly culinary but also ornamental. The Doctor had a guava tree there in 1841, which fruited in the July of that year.

It was used constantly for the raising of cucumbers, of which the family must have been very fond, as they were also grown outdoors. In December and January, this glasshouse was used to force rhubarb and new potatoes, which would be ready by the end of March; in February, there was the indoor sowing of cauliflowers, tomato and melon seed and mustard and cress; in March, capsicums would be potted there; in April, the first indoor cucumbers were ready for eating, and continued to be so as late as January.

The kitchen garden stove's usefulness petered out somewhat during the summer months, but by September its tan bed was being revived, with roses, a 'sweet olea' and *Stephanotis* in pots growing there. In October and November geraniums and *Cinerarias* were potted there, the first seakale was put to force

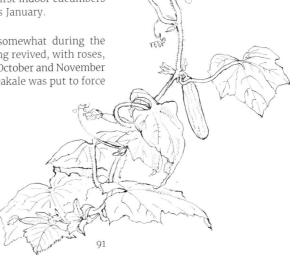

indoors, and the first cucumber seeds would be sown. In December, bulbs and roses were put there to force, while the stove's seakale would be ready for eating on Christmas Day.

THE KITCHEN GARDEN FRAME

Frames were mainly used in kitchen gardens as supplementary structures for the containment and covering of hot-beds, which were heaps or pits containing fermenting horse manure, leaves or tanners' bark. Soil would be heaped on top of this hot, fermenting material, for the growth of the appropriate plants, seeds, seedlings, cuttings or layers. The bed would then be covered with sashes of glass to contain the heat, which needed skilled management. These structures could be temporary or permanent.

They were, at first, largely used in the production of pineapples, but were more especially useful in the cooler months for starting off early salads and vegetables. Vast brick-built 'frame yards' were constructed at large establishments, but The Mount gardens sufficed with one or two frames at most.

According to the Diary, work began on 7 November 1839, in 'pulling down and altering the Frame in the Kitchen Garden'. This work continued into December, when it was filled with four loads of tan, indicating that this frame was fairly large.

Only five years later, on 19 January 1844, the foundations were laid for a new brick 'Melon Frame' or pit in the kitchen garden. It measured some 15 x 3 ft and, again, work on the building of it continued for over a month, every working day, until 23 February. This may or may not be the same frame as the one shown on the Sale Map, as two years later, in February 1854, Susan writes '1,000 bricks carted to K.G. for new Frame'. This is followed on 6 March by 'Phillips began to build Brick Frame in K.G.', this job being finished only a week later.

Since frames could be temporary and moveable, and made of any size, of timber as well as of brick, it does appear that there were several other frames built at The Mount from time to time. The large one built in 1844 was used mainly for growing melons, but cucumbers, celery, cauliflowers, potatoes, lettuce, *Phlox drummondii* and dwarf larkspur are all mentioned in March alone as being grown 'in a frame' over the years. *Cinerarias*, endive, carnation layers and dahlias followed, with the first melons ripening in July, and rhubarb and seakale being forced in November. Some frames were even made specifically for forcing one particular crop, such as potatoes or cucumbers.

[1] The confusion over what is and what is not a greenhouse is increased by the fact that the glasshouse in the kitchen garden is labelled 'GREENHOSE' on the sale map.

[2] Charles M'Intosh, *The New and Improved Practical Gardener* (London: Thomas Kelly, 1847), Vol. 2, p. 886.

[3] Garden Diary ms (4 December 1855), 'repairing stucco on Wall behind Greenhouse'.

[4] CCD vol. 1, p. 207.

[5] *Ibid.*, vol. 1, p. 409.

[6] *Ibid.*, vol. 4, p. 182.

[7] Garden Diary, 5 February 1858 and 23 February 1860.

[8] 'Stove-houses' were originally exactly that; glasshouses heated by small, charcoal-burning stoves.

[9] The Account Books of Robert Waring Darwin, Darwin Manuscript Collection, Cambridge University Library, DAR 227.5.82.

[10] *Ibid.*, DAR 227.5.140.

[11] *Ibid.*

SEVEN

The Kitchen Garden

It would be nice to be able to say that my own kitchen garden is managed in exactly the same way as the one at The Mount. It is, up to a point … but not quite so professionally. Nor is it as large, or quite so prolific.

The kitchen garden occupied the lowest, southeast corner of the property, with high brick walls on all four sides. Its east wall was bounded by Drinkwater Street and the south wall was bounded by a narrow alleyway known as Hermitage Walk. The Mount's pleasure gardens lay outside the north and west walls. Two doorways provided access: one was in the southeast corner at the junction of Drinkwater Street and Hermitage Walk, the other was in the southwest corner, leading into the pleasure garden and towards the mansion.

The Sale Plan of 1867 and the Ordnance Survey of 1882 show that there was a pump in the northeast corner of the garden and a perimeter walk with a wide border beneath each of the kitchen garden walls. There was one central path running north–south. The west half of the garden was further divided by a path running east–west, and the north half of that section was divided again by a path running north–south.

A small, lean-to work and storage shed, which was for a brief time Erasmus and Charles's 'Lab' when they were boys, is also known as 'the Garden House'. It stood inside the south wall (and is still to be seen there today), but, as mentioned in Chapter Six, there was only one glasshouse in the kitchen garden.

A kitchen garden's glasshouse was usually a lean-to against the south face of the north wall, with its work sheds and boiler room hidden on the wall behind it, but in this case such an arrangement would have meant an unseemly intrusion into the flower garden. The Mount's kitchen garden glasshouse was therefore placed in the centre of the northwest quarter. The large melon frame stood in front of this glasshouse. The vinery, stove-house and conservatory, all standing outside the kitchen garden and closer to the mansion, provided ancillary heat and space for the more ornamental plants. It is not shown on any plan, but from various references in the Diary it can be deduced that an orchard occupied a portion of the kitchen garden.

There is no mention in the Diary of any gardeners working at The Mount, other than John Abberley, but he did have additional help from his father ('Old Abberley', also called John). Towards the end of his life the younger John was frequently too ill to work. His absences were possibly covered by a servant named Thomas Harris, who was hired for odd jobs such as pruning from time to time, as was one Benjamin Smith, while jobs such as making fences, gravelling walks, mowing, carting manure and filling the ice house were given to various labourers, an arrangement that seemed to be sufficient for this kitchen garden.

THE FIELD GARDEN

Its one-and-a-half acres were large enough to support the Darwin family and its servants, given that there was also a 'Field Garden' in one of the Doctor's meadows to the west of The Mount.[1] See illustrations on pp.156-7.

Here, coarser root crops such as potatoes, beets, Jerusalem artichokes, mangelwurzels, carrots, turnips and parsnips were grown, as well as occasional cabbages, beans and spinach. In short, Dr Darwin's account books show that vegetables were never bought, though his gardeners' wages and the running of his hothouses amounted to over £200 a year.[2]

'FIRSTS'

Both Dr Darwin and Susan habitually recorded the first appearance of various fruits, flowers and vegetables, whether natural or forced. The 'perpetual' form in which the Diary was kept was therefore very useful for comparing one year's 'firsts' with that of another.

The first fruits included rhubarb, currants and gooseberries, which were invariably made into tarts, being only just ripe, followed by strawberries, raspberries, cherries, melons, apricots, peaches and nectarines; then autumn fruits of apples, figs, medlars, quinces, plums, pears and grapes. Of vegetables there were forced new potatoes, green peas and beans, asparagus, carrots (orange and white), beetroot, turnips, hothouse cucumbers, green salad, tomatoes, and celery, salsify, seakale, endives, Brussels sprouts and cabbage, plus Jerusalem and globe artichokes.

Several 'firsts' were considered to be worthy of the honour of being first served for Sunday dinner, birthdays or dinner parties. These meals featured

nearly all of the above, as well as vegetable marrows and couve tronchuda (Portuguese kale).

The latter two appear as novelties. Exotics such as passion fruit and guavas are mentioned once or twice; a pineapple just once (on a Sunday). These rarities were raised, almost to the end of his life, by the Doctor, but not by his daughter, whose horticultural activities were less ambitious. However, in 1862, when the fifty-nine-year-old Susan's diary-keeping was already fairly spasmodic, her only entry for the whole of March appears on the 25th and is given an exclamation mark: '1st young Potatoes!'

FRUIT TREES AND THE ORCHARD

The inner sides of all four kitchen garden walls were amply covered with trained fruit trees, as were the outer sides of the north and west walls. The borders of the kitchen garden paths were lined with standard fruit trees.

Apples, pears and mulberries were grown in other parts of The Mount's gardens. Plums were trained on the coach house wall, an almond and a pomegranate grew by the mansion's front door, quinces and a walnut tree had been planted by the terrace and figs and morello cherries grew in the kitchen-cum-stable-yard.

The precise position of the orchard is not easy to determine. Neither the Ordnance Survey Map of 1882 nor the Sale Map of 1867 show an orchard within the gardens at The Mount, nor is an orchard, as such, listed in the sale particulars, but 'the Orchard' is mentioned so often in the Diary that there can be no doubt of its existence. Fortunately, there are a few helpful diary entries which indicate where it might have been.

In 1840 a new cottage was built by Dr Darwin for his butler, Edward Evans, on land directly opposite The Mount's front gates. They screened it from view by planting yews and laurels on the lawn (9 November 1840). Another new house was built within sight of the Mansion in 1858 and Susan writes: 'moved large Holly into Orchard to hide the new house' (26 November 1858). An earlier entry reads: 'Large cherry tree in Orchard cut down to open the view of the Castle' (23 August 1844).

These three references show that new houses just beyond the walls disturbed the privacy of the Darwins and the tranquillity of their garden, but on the other hand the sight of a noble, ancient edifice (Shrewsbury Castle) on the skyline was thought to be enhancing. And they prove that the orchard occupied a portion of the kitchen garden, probably the southwest quarter, as a line drawn eastward from the mansion to the castle cuts right across that area. Weight is added to this conclusion with the knowledge that the kitchen garden's west wall, hothouse, garden shed and garden door are all mentioned in close proximity to the orchard, a walk being made in 1855 'in Orchard from Hothouse' (17 October 1855).

The orchard was therefore quite small; it could not have occupied more than a quarter of an acre. However, some thirty varieties of fruit tree grew there – apples, apricots, a cherry, a medlar, pears, plums and quinces – with more fruit on the walls. The orchard trees were manured with liquid manure from the kitchen garden, with bones from Wem and with spent tan from the hothouse. It was mown for hay in June and again in October, to supply grass for the hot-beds. Susan twice mentions putting her young calves (Vashti, Ruby and Fairy) to rear in the orchard, and twice there is a mention of sweet peas growing there, 'round the trees' and 'over manure'.

[1] The size of the household fluctuated over the years. Before the death of Mrs Darwin in 1817, and until the children left home, the family consisted of eight, with probably the same number of living-in servants, if not more. The Census return of 1841 listed a family of five and nine living-in servants. After the Doctor's death in 1848, the household consisted of his daughters Susan and Catherine, again with several living-in servants. After the death of their sister Marianne, in 1858, her two eldest children joined their aunts at The Mount. The Census of 1861 listed three family members and seven servants. Hampers of produce were sent to places wherever members of the family were staying, and baskets of fruit were regularly given to family and friends.

[2] Equivalent to £13,400 today. Robert Darwin's Account Book for 1833; Cambridge University Library DAR 227, 5: 140.

EIGHT

Susan

Susan Elizabeth Darwin (3 August 1803–3 October 1866) was the third child of Dr Robert and Susannah Darwin. She lived at The Mount all her life, having never married. Had she become a wife she might have had her portrait painted but, possibly for this reason, I have been unable to find a portrait of her unless, that is, she is the subject of the pastel drawing by Ellen Sharples, dated 1816, of a serious-looking young girl with a book in her lap, now at Down House in Kent. This portrait is one of four by the same artist, all to be seen at Down House.

The other portraits are of Dr Darwin, Erasmus Alvey Darwin and the well-known double portrait of a seven-year-old Charles with his youngest sister Catherine. The date corresponds to a visit made to Bath by the entire Darwin family. During the stay, one imagines there would have been an opportunity to have portraits made of all of its members by Ellen Sharples, a Bristol artist well-known for her work in pastels.[1] However, maybe there was not enough time to include Mrs Darwin and her other two daughters, Caroline and Marianne; maybe the portraits of them are to be found elsewhere.

If this is Susan (and there are some authorities who say it is, in fact, her older sister, Caroline), she would have been thirteen years old. Her face is long and oval, almost almond-shaped, with a porcelain complexion. She has brown hair arranged in flat curls close to her head. Her mouth is firm and not large. She has her mother's nose (straight, not pudgy like a Darwin's) and brown eyes.

Except for her complexion, this description of Susan's appearance is totally different from the one offered by Irving Stone in his book *The Origin*. Here, after describing Susan, at the age of twenty-eight, as 'tall, high-spirited, the golden beauty of the family, adored by her father, the only child who was', he goes on to tell us that she had the 'long, golden curls, the flashing sea-green eyes, the complexion as creamy white and shell pink as the most delicate of vases Susannah Wedgwood had brought to Dr Robert Darwin as part of her dowry'.[2]

According to her niece, Henrietta Litchfield (Charles Darwin's eldest surviving daughter), Susan 'had been her father's favourite daughter, and was greatly beloved by her brothers and sisters'.[3] She makes her first appearance in family memoirs and letters as a young girl of seventeen. In a letter to her aunt, Fanny Allen, from The Mount, dated 30 November 1820, Elizabeth Wedgwood (Susan's cousin, then aged twenty-seven) describes 'a most prodigious friend' of Susan's. This would be Fanny Owen, 'a very little girl of sixteen', later to become the first love of the young Charles Darwin's life. Charlotte Wedgwood, a younger sister of Elizabeth's, was also staying at The Mount, where a Mr Sor (who 'says such amusing things with such amusing looks that it is impossible not to laugh') was employed in teaching music to this merry group of girls.[4]

Many years later Henrietta described the characters and appearance of Charles's sisters, Caroline and Susan Darwin, in their youth:

> Both had high spirits, abounding life and deep feeling. Caroline was not regularly handsome but her appearance was very effective; she had brilliant eyes and colouring, and black hair growing low on her wide forehead... . Both were tall, and Susan had both beauty and sweetness. Fanny Allen spoke of Susan as pleasing her extremely; she is so handsome, so gay, and so innocent.

She goes on to say that Susan and another Wedgwood cousin, Jessie (daughter of John Wedgwood and the beauty of the family), were both great flirts 'in an innocent way'. They were given the nicknames of 'Kitty and Lydia' in allusion to the Kitty and Lydia in Jane Austen's *Pride and Prejudice*, 'but we were always told that Susan had a settled resolution against marrying'.

Be that as it may, Henrietta adds in a footnote that 'my father told me that anything in coat and trousers from eight years to eighty was fair game to Susan'.[5] And as a young lady she was at the heart of the many 'very flirtish, very noisy, very merry and very foolish' revels that took place in the houses of the Wedgwood and Darwin cousins, along with the Owens from Woodhouse, Susan's reputation as a flirt being 'the only one in the family who has the least talents that way'.[6]

As in the novels of Jane Austen, there was a constant round of balls, parties, games, archery contests, play-acting and excursions on horseback among the families of the Darwins, the Owens and the Wedgwoods until well into the 1830s, with Susan and Catherine enjoying 'wicked times' at Maer for a whole month in October 1827.[7] As for the parties at Woodhouse (the home of the Owen family, which lay halfway between Maer and Shrewsbury), according to Susan, 'we never talked a word of common sense all day'. These occasions were perhaps the most rackety, with 'more than half the gentlemen ... a little too much stimulated'. There were bets as to which table could make the most noise at dinner, and 'quantities of waltzing, dancing and games &c going on till about 1 ... this has gone on for nearly a week'[8] (though Mr Owen, a peppery squire, had a preference for 'instantly dissolving' any revels that continued after midnight).

Another memorable party took place in 1837, at Wynnstay (home of the aforementioned banana-grower, Sir Watkyn Williams-Wynn) when Susan would have been a more mature, but rather sporting, thirty-four-year-old. It was a birthday party with more than 200 people attending 'a magnificent dinner upon plate & a ball & supper afterwards'. However, 'their carriage pole broke on arrival, & Susan came home sitting at the bottom of the carriage' (lent to them by the young Sir Watkyn): 'it was rather a squeeze'.[9] Somewhat surprisingly, by the same account, 'The Dr has been as pleasant as possible, and I never saw [him enjoy] anything so much as Susan's account of all her gaieties.'[10]

EXCURSIONS AND CAMPAIGNS

The Doctor, when his health allowed, was fond of little sightseeing excursions with his butler, Edward Evans, in attendance, plus Harry Wedgwood and one of his daughters for company. During one such trip, to London in November 1832, Susan and Catherine found themselves alone at home. A new carriage had been specially made for this occasion to accommodate the Doctor's enormous frame, which 'most unluckily did not quite answer his expectations as Hunt was careless about the measurement', making it difficult for him to get in and out. 'Catty and I feel very odd with the house, horses, Carriages and servants all at our command without Papa sitting in his Arm chair by the fire.'[11]

In May 1833, Caroline wrote to Charles, then in Patagonia on the third year of his great voyage on the *Beagle*, 'My Father is grown quite larky – he is going next week to see York and I go with him.'[12] The trip lasted ten days and they saw the new-fangled railroad, 'but did not go on it', while Susan and Catherine took the opportunity to stay for three weeks in London with their brother Erasmus, driving about with him in his stylish 'cab'.[13]

Shortly after the trip to York, the Doctor 'is planning another little journey, in the South of England to see the cathedrals of Winchester & Salisbury',[14] with Susan and Harry for company. This 'Architectural Tour' included Gloucester and ended at The Hill in Abergavenny. It took place in late October 1833, again with Evans in attendance. Unfortunately, once arrived at The Hill, the Doctor was 'laid up 17 days with the worst fit of gout he ever had in his life'. Susan and he came home as soon as he was fit to travel again.[15]

The two youngest Darwin sisters rarely left home without the company of their father, but in the summer of 1829 Susan and Catherine made a sightseeing trip to London, escorted by their Wedgwood cousins Joe and Harry, who wrote to his sister Emma:

> Jos [Joe] will carry this to you … I don't think he has seen much, certainly not when compared with the never-enough-to-be-sufficiently-fatigued Darwins… . I had the melancholy task of seeing them out of London, and though Susan had hypocritically dressed herself in black, a merrier parting never took place – the young ladies were all in roars of laughter as they came downstairs and we drove off for Islington in a coroneted Jarvey… .[16] In Oxford Street I saw a chariot with better horses (ours were miserable), so I tumbled them both out into the street with their bags &c in their hands and transhipped them – the Jarvey must have thought it a manoeuvre to puzzle pursuers. At Islington we drank tea in a lively apartment looking down 5 roads[17] and there I washed my hands of them.

The Darwin girls did have other occupations apart from partying. One of them, as already mentioned, was gardening. Two more were support for the newly emerging anti-slavery campaign and, later, fighting child slavery. A third occupation was working at their infant schools.

The Wedgwood and Darwin families' opposition to slavery is well documented. In 1826, in a letter from Catherine to Charles (then studying medicine in Edinburgh), she says: 'Susan is hotter than ever about slavery – John Bull pretending that the Slaves lead a life of <u>Comfort</u> and <u>Happiness</u> really seems as if he was quizzing the subject.'[18] In March 1833, Susan wrote to Charles

(still on the *Beagle*, having reached the Falkland Islands), that she was hoping that 'Slavery will be certainly done this session,'[19] and seven months later she wrote, 'you will rejoice as much as we do over Slavery being abolished'.[20] Later, in 1852, according to Charles:

> Susan has been working in a way, which I think truly heroic about the scandalous violation of the act against children climbing chimneys. We have set up a little Society in Shrewsbury to prosecute those who break the Law. It is all Susan's doing. She has had very nice letters from Ld Shaftesbury & the D of Sutherland, but the brutal Shropshire Squires are as hard as stone to move.[21]

THE INFANT SCHOOL

An infant school in Chapel Street, Frankwell, was established sometime after Mrs Darwin's death in 1817 by her eldest daughters, with financial help from the Doctor. It was one of the first infant schools in Shrewsbury and 'with characteristic readiness to welcome every improvement', it was furnished 'with the appliances which had lately been introduced by Pestalozzi and other educational reformers'.[22] Mrs Jos Wedgwood II described a visit there in 1824:

> and I could scarcely refrain from tears, but not tears of sorrow, at seeing the little creatures, all at the word of command, drop down on their knees and say the Lord's Prayer. They sung two hymns very tolerably and a whole set of them, none more than four years old, seemed to me quite perfect in their multiplication table... . At the same time, the reality is not so picturesque as the description, which a person who wishes to put it into practice must be prepared for. She must not expect to see rosy little cherubs in white frocks & pink sashes, but on the contrary perhaps, for the most part, pale sickly and dirty little children.[23]

There appears to have been a 'new' infant school built some nine years later, apparently on the same site. Until her marriage in 1837 it was chiefly in Caroline's care. In September 1833, she wrote to Charles, then on the *Beagle*, which was surveying the Argentinian coast:

> Susan's present hobby is [needle] work, as it was when you went – she is now doing a magnificent bunch of flowers in an enormous frame. <u>My</u> hobby is a new Infant School, now finished & the children & governors all properly established in it.[24]

An account in 1849, in the local newspaper, of a celebration for the twentieth anniversary of the school puts these dates at odds with Caroline's, but whatever the case, nearly 200 children (clearly not all of them 'infants')

> proceeded from the school to the 'Doctor's Field', where they were treated with a liberal supply of tea and plum cake, at the expense of the Misses Darwin [Susan and Catherine]... . After tea had been well attended to, numerous pastimes were devised for the little ones, who after engaging in them for some time, returned to the schoolroom; they and their attendants, when opposite the residence of the Misses Darwin, giving three hearty cheers.[25]

The Doctor makes no references whatsoever to the infant school in his portion of the Diary, but between 1840 and 1858 it is frequently mentioned by Susan, mainly in connection with the maintenance of its garden, playground, hedges and fences, and its annual Tea Feasts which were held in one of the Darwins' fields in July or August, after the hay was cut. Two years after Susan's death in 1866, the school, with its ninety-six infants, was transferred to the Church of England school of the local parish church, St George's.

GRANNY

Although Charles was now aged twenty-five, Susan (only four and a half years older than him) could still not resist correcting his spelling (his nickname for her was sometimes 'Chucky' but more often 'Granny', which seems particularly ironic at this point). He was sending the family marvellous accounts of his voyage bit by bit, but she wrote: 'there is one part of your Journal as your Granny I shall take in hand namely several little errors in orthography of which I shall send you a list that you may profit

by my lectures tho' the world is between us'. The misspellings are: loose (instead of lose), lanscape, higest, profil, cannabal, peacible and quarrell.[26] I cannot resist adding that although Susan's own spelling was impeccable, she had one foible, which is that in the Diary her spelling of 'rhododendron' is always 'rhododenrhon'.

Susan was 'Aunt Susan' to nine nephews and seven nieces. Warm and funny, concerned with human rights, caring and businesslike, her capabilities with finance and housekeeping were also recognised by the rest of the family, not least by Charles who made frequent requests, while on his voyage, for more funds from his father via letters to Susan. Later still, she was apparently the go-between regarding loans made by the Doctor to Charles when setting up at Down House where, following a visit in November 1843, she supplied a breakfast service and a quantity of furniture. She also came in handy some years earlier when, as newly-weds, Charles and Emma appealed to her for help with buying linen and kitchen paraphernalia.

> I have asked Susan to come if possible, to London for a week in early January to buy
> a few pots & pans &c &c. do try & persuade the good dear old soul to do so, for she
> will save us much trouble, & will do it, I daresay, very well.[27]

The Diary also reveals Susan's love of the Darwins' house cows, with Alderneys and Guernseys being the breeds of the family's choice. Her father, while recording all the occasions when his cows went 'to the bull', calved or were moved from one pasture to another, rarely refers to any by name, preferring to call them (as he did with his horses) by their colour or the place from which they came – unlike Susan, who gave them all names.

She had an extraordinary fondness for guinea fowl as well. These birds were never mentioned by her father and were obviously her own pets (see Chapter Ten).

If any of the Doctor's daughters wished to leave home on a short holiday or visit while he was alive, there was always an obligation for one of them to stay at home as his companion. With his death in 1848, which was felt sorely by Susan, this constriction vanished. She went abroad for six weeks with her sister Catherine in 1850, on a tour which 'answered capitally' as Charles put it,[28] and she frequently went to London to stay with her brother Erasmus, often combining these visits with a trip to Down House to stay with Emma and Charles.

TENBY AND THE ISLE OF WIGHT

According to the Diary, Susan made three visits to Tenby between 1852 and 1861, where she would have stayed with three of her many Allen aunts: the widowed Jessie Sismondi, and the unmarried Emma and Fanny. The first visit, in April 1852, was made a year before Jessie died. The house was called Heywood Lodge, where Jessie described how, in 1840 when she herself was a visitor, she did 'little but look out of the window at the coming and going sea, the bathers, the walkers, the merry dogs, riders and ass riders that cover the shore'.[29] Susan's second visit was from 12 February to 6 March 1858, and the third in May 1861. Tenby had also been a favourite destination for Emma Darwin from an early age;[30] even getting there from Shropshire or London was an adventure, as the last part of the journey involved a voyage by paddle steamer from Bristol.

On 18 August 1858, Susan wrote in the Diary 'Go to the Isle of Wight'. The date is puzzling, as it looks as if she might have been there for only one day. Charles had written to a friend on 4 July: 'I have had death & severe illness & misery amongst my children & am going at once to leave home for some weeks for their health.'[31]

Charles and Emma's daughter, Henrietta (Hetty), aged fifteen, had been struck down with diphtheria in mid-June, with one of the Darwin's nurses suffering from the same illness. Four days later both their youngest child Charles Waring, aged eighteen months, and his nurse caught scarlet fever, from which the little boy died on 28 June. The two nurses recovered, but three of the younger children were still at risk. Anxious for Hetty's recuperation and seeking an escape from a disease which was then often fatal and raging in their home village of Downe, the Isle of Wight became their destination. In mid-July the Darwins decamped, first to Sandown and then to Shanklin.

At the same time Charles had a different but equally urgent matter to deal with – the writing of a detailed abstract of the work which was eventually to become Chapter I of *The Origin of Species*. The need to do this was prompted by the recent and alarming publication of Alfred Wallace's paper *On the Tendency of Varieties to depart indefinitely from the Original Type*. With the publication of his abstract needing his attention, Charles went home on 11 August, to be followed eight days later by Emma and the children. This was just one day after Susan wrote 'Go to the Isle of Wight', presumably to be a help and companion to Emma and her children at an exceedingly difficult time. There is no mention of Susan's arrival in Emma's diary, and no further entries for a whole month in Susan's Garden Diary. However, there had been another sad event in the family that summer, with the death of Charles and Susan's eldest sister Marianne, on 18 July. Susan appears to have dealt with the dispersal of various items from Marianne's garden at Overton during August and would have been almost certainly needed at that time by Marianne's family as much as she would have been by Charles's.

THE PARKERS

Marianne's husband, Dr Parker, had died in 1856. The three eldest Parker children had, by 1858, presumably left home, leaving only the two youngest, Mary (aged twenty-two) and Charles (aged twenty-seven), and so after Marianne's death they were 'adopted' by Susan and went to live with her at The Mount.[32]

Susan was at this time living alone, as Catherine had decided in October 1857 to take a small house in London.

Susan clearly enjoyed the company of her niece and nephew and shared a trip with Charles to Beesby in Lincolnshire in 1861 to look at farms bought by the Doctor as an investment on her behalf many years earlier. She had done the same trip in 1851 with Frank Parker, Marianne's third son, then aged nineteen. On that occasion, according to Emma in a letter to Charles, she arrived home 'in tremendous spirits. The tour had answered most brilliantly. She never saw such trees, such post-horses, such civil waiters & such good dinners. And as for Frank Parker, she is in love with him. It has done her a world of good.'[33]

Mary Parker was to marry Edward Mostyn Owen of Woodhouse at St George's, the church just over the kitchen garden wall, in April 1866, thereby uniting the families of Owen and Darwin after many years of close friendship. A wedding breakfast must surely have taken place at the Mount, but by this date Susan had given up keeping the Diary.

There had been another marriage before this. In 1863, somewhat to the family's surprise, Catherine, then aged fifty-three, married Charles Langton, the widower of Emma Darwin's elder sister, Charlotte. He was then aged sixty-two. According to Henrietta Litchfield, the rest of the family viewed the marriage with misgivings: 'Catherine had neither good health or strong spirits, and both she and Charles Langton had strong wills,' while Charles and Emma Darwin 'were doubtful of their happiness and thought the marriage a somewhat anxious experiment'.[34] The couple lived nearby, in Shrewsbury, but by 1866 Catherine had returned to The Mount to be near Susan who was by then in failing health. Very shortly after this, Catherine herself was to die, to be followed only six months later by Susan.

In 1896, some twenty years after her Aunt Susan's death, Henrietta was to write to her brother George, thanking him for sending the list of what their recently deceased mother (Emma Darwin) had left them. It included 'Aunt Susan's inkstand [which] I think was broken 20 years ago or so. It was the one that the ink dried up in one moment, but I shall like its remains if they exist.'[35]

[1] Ellen Sharples was the mother of the even better-known painter Rolinda Sharples.

[2] Irving Stone, *The Origin* (Doubleday, 1980), pp. 30-31. There is no reference to the source of this description, its date, the artist or the portrait's whereabouts.

[3] *Emma Darwin: a Century of Family Letters, 1792–1896*, ed. Henrietta Litchfield (London: John Murray, 1915), vol. 2, p. 184.

[4] *Ibid.*, vol. 1, p. 139.

[5] *Ibid.*, vol. 1, p. 141. Jessie was to marry Harry, yet another Wedgwood cousin and brother of Emma Wedgwood, who was to marry Charles Darwin in 1830.

[6] *Ibid.*, vol. 1, pp. 162, 163. Letters from Mrs Josiah Wedgwood II (Bessy) to her sister Fanny Allen, 6 October and 15 December 1824.

[7] *Ibid.*, vol. 1, p. 210, Emma Wedgwood's diary.

[8] *Ibid.*, vol. 1, pp. 225-66, letter from Catherine Darwin to Emma Wedgwood.

[9] *Ibid.*, vol. 1, p. 283, letter from Emma Wedgwood to her sister-in-law Mrs Hensleigh Wedgwood.

[10] *Ibid.*, vol. 1, p. 284.

[11] CCD vol. 1, p. 283, letter from Susan to Charles.

[12] CCD vol. 1, p. 310.

[13] *Ibid.*, vol. 1, p. 318. 'Cab' is short for cabriolet, a small carriage.

[14] *Ibid.*, vol. 1, p. 334.

[15] CCD vol. 1, p. 356.

[16] A hackney carriage.

[17] *Emma Darwin: a Century of Family Letters, 1792–1896*, ed. Henrietta Litchfield (London: John Murray, 1915), vol. 1, pp. 217-18, 19 June 1829. This would be the junction now known as The Angel, in Islington, where the modern A1 begins. The stagecoach journey home to Shrewsbury would start from here.

[18] CCD vol. 1, p. 40. *John Bull* was a pro-slavery activist newspaper.

[19] *Ibid.*, vol. 1, p. 299.

[20] *Ibid.*, p. 337. The bill for the Abolition of Slavery was passed on 28 August 1833.

[21] Letter from C.D. to W.D. Fox, 7 March 1852. CCD vol. 5, p. 84. 'The act against children climbing chimneys' was passed in 1840, but rarely adhered to. In 1875 Lord Shaftesbury eventually managed to have a law passed that licensed only chimney sweeps who did not employ children.

[22] Edward Woodall, *Charles Darwin, a paper contributed to the Transactions of the Shropshire Archaeological Society* (London: Trubner & Co., 1888), p. 14.

[23] Litchfield, *op. cit.*, vol. 1, p. 163.

[24] CCD vol. 1, p. 330.

[25] *Eddowes Shrewsbury Journal.* Watton's Cuttings, vol. 6, p. 407.

[26] *Ibid.*, vol. 1, p. 366. Letter sent on 12 February 1834, Charles's twenty-fifth birthday.

[27] Charles to Emma, CCD vol. 2. p. 133.

[28] 10 October 1850, letter C.D. to W.D. Fox (CCD vol. 4, p. 362), but it is noticeable that during this trip entries in the Diary appear only occasionally, with some twenty-six days on which nothing is entered; the writing appears to be Susan's for the days that are accounted for, which implies that there was a notebook kept by Abberley to which she could refer on her return.

[29] Litchfield, *op. cit.*, vol. 2, p. 15.

[30] Though Charles disliked going there owing to the proliferation of Allen cousins.

[31] Charles to W.B. Tegetmeier, CCD vol. 7. p. 127. The three girls had suffered from scarlet fever ten years beforehand.

[32] Litchfield, *op. cit.*, vol. 2, p. 184.

[33] CCD vol. 4, p. 143.

[34] Litchfield, *op. cit.*, vol. 2, p. 180.

[35] Edna Healey, *Emma Darwin* (London: Headline, 2001), p. 343.

NINE

Servants at The Mount

There was no lack of servants at The Mount. Apart from the four 'top' positions of gardener, butler, coachman and cook/housekeeper, there were ladies' maids, housemaids, charwomen, kitchen maids, grooms and odd-job men, all living-in or nearby. When the family included young children, there was a nanny (called Nancy) and nursemaids as well.

GARDENERS

The Doctor's gardeners at The Mount tend to be mentioned only briefly in the biographies of Charles Darwin. There are references in The Correspondence and in the Doctor's accounts of the 1830s to a gardener named Joseph. This would have been Joseph Phipps, whose head was 'turned' by growing a pineapple (see Chapter One).[1] His occupation is given as 'gardener' in the local Parish Records of St Chad's in 1818, so he was possibly employed at The Mount at least from then, if not before.[2] Joseph died in 1835 aged forty-six. He may well have had young John Abberley, the gardener who succeeded him, as an under-gardener. The Garden Diary mentions other men (names of Harris, Smith, Barrett and Rogers) working at various times in the garden, as well as an 'Abberley' and 'old Abberley', who is recorded as mending fences for Dr Darwin in 1838[3] and 1857.[4] This would be the gardener John Abberley's father, a haulier, also called John.

John Abberley the younger (1814–57) is described in the Census of 1841 as born in Shrewsbury, a servant, aged twenty-seven and living at The Mount. By the Census of October of 1851, he is married to Ann Munslow, another servant at The Mount, and his occupation is given as 'gardener'.[5] He, his wife and four of their five sons lived in a small house belonging to the Doctor opposite The Mount's front gates, which had previously been occupied by Edward Evans, the butler. It had its own garden, beehives, stable, coach house and yard. Of the five sons, one appears to have died in infancy, since two were named John.

Our John Abberley, five years younger than his master's son, Charles, suffered poor health from the age of thirty-nine, mainly from what Susan called 'gout'. In June 1856 he had a 'paralytic stroke' and he died aged forty-three in 1857, having been put on board wages for the last six months of his life. He was clearly a much-valued part of the extended family, loved and respected by Susan, who recorded all the occasions on which he was poorly, ill, confined or better, sorrowfully entering, on 31 August 1857: '18th August, 1857. Poor Abberly died this day. Just when I got back fr. London.'

She also more happily mentions that he went to the Chester races in 1850, to the Great Exhibition in London 'for a week' in 1851, and to the railway station at Shrewsbury in 1852, when Queen Victoria passed through on her way from Balmoral to Windsor.[6] He would have watched that event with 20,000 other citizens.

Abberley's position as head gardener, with his own house, horse and carriage, put him on a par, socially and economically, with the other 'top servants' at The Mount – Edward Evans the butler, Mark Briggs the coachman, and Mrs Grice the cook/housekeeper. It is speculation on my part that Abberley learned his trade from Joseph Phipps, the previous gardener at The Mount, but he was clearly highly proficient, running four glasshouses, a large glass frame and hotbeds with productions (and temperatures) ranging from the tropical (for plants such as maracujas, guavas, capsicums and orchids) to the more mundane (for forced flowers, grapes, winter salads and cucumbers).

He was responsible for all the ornamental flower beds, the upkeep of the lawns, drive and walks, the trees, hedges and floriferous shrubberies, as well as, and not least, the productions of a variety of fruit trees on several walls and other sites, as well as the kitchen garden, the orchard and the vegetable garden in the field.

He would have also had to keep a record (with his primitive spelling but beautiful writing) of all the activities in The Mount's garden in notebooks of his own, which could be passed on to the Diarists on a weekly, if not a daily basis, as Diary entries continued even when the Doctor and Susan were away, to be recorded in their own writing on their return.

It was almost a year after Abberley's death before Susan decided to find a replacement; her Garden Diary entry for 17 July 1858 reads: 'settled to look out for a head gardener!' George Wynne, born the same year as Abberley, was engaged on 18 September 'at £60 a yr & house rent free' to start work on 1 October. There is every possibility that Wynne was Marianne Parker's gardener, as according to the census of 1851 he was then living at Overton. Moreover, Susan's decision was made on the very day before Marianne's death, when his employment with the Parkers would have come to an end. He remained at The Mount until 1867, staying on for a year after Susan's death in 1866.

BUTLERS

Edward Evans (1797–1846) was the Doctor's butler certainly from 1831, as he is mentioned at that date in a letter from the Doctor to Josiah Wedgwood II.[7] His duties did not extend to the gardens, so there are very few references to him in the Diary. However, prior to the voyage on the *Beagle*, he was given several tasks and errands by Charles, such as sorting his gun and packing his carpetbag with items such as slippers, a microscope and a book on taxidermy.[8] Edward was also in attendance on the Doctor's three sightseeing trips. He went to London in 1832, to York in June 1833 and to Gloucester, Winchester and Salisbury in October 1833. His wife, Ann, is described by the Doctor as 'servant to my daughters' in his account book, but elsewhere[9] she is described as the cook.

In 1840, the Doctor built the house which is now known as 'Darwin Cottage' opposite the front gate of The Mount for the newly married Edward.[10] The Doctor frequently refers to this house, later Abberley's residence, as 'the new Powell Cottage', as it was built on the site of two smaller cottages, one of which was lived in by one Anne Powell until she died in 1810. In the Diary, on 8 March 1841, he records 'planting box at Powell Cottage'.

Edward Evans died on 10 November 1846, and the Doctor noted in his account book: 'Edward Evans died this day, a faithful friend and servant.'[11]

Thomas Thonger (1809–?), is entered in the Census of 1841 as a servant at The Mount, and in the Census of 1851 as a farmer of 118 acres, living on the south side of The Mount. The Darwin Research Society here describes him as Dr Darwin's last butler. His wife, Jane, is listed as sister of the late Edward Evans. Ann Evans, a widow aged eighty-one, is described as Jane's mother. She should therefore not be confused with the Ann Evans who was Edward Evans's wife.

The Census of 1861 names a Jane Thonger, aged eighteen, as a kitchen maid at the Mount. She does not appear in the previous Census of 1851, but that may be because she was not at home on that particular occasion.

Thonger's post as butler at The Mount lasted only two years, as the Doctor died on 13 November 1848, with Thonger and Mark Briggs, the coachman, 'one on each side of him the whole night'.[12] His career as a farmer appears to have commenced after that event, with only one entry referring to him in the Diary. This was made by Susan, on 3 February 1849: 'Sold calf to Thonger.'

COACHMAN

Mark Briggs (1806–?) was a servant at The Mount certainly by 1826, when Marianne wrote to Charles, then studying medicine in Edinburgh, about his little dog, Spark, who had been left in her care: 'She had been shut up as Mark said he did not think she would bear tying up … and made her escape.'[13] The consequence was sad; the dog became pregnant and died after giving birth.

Mark was then twenty years old, and probably only a groom at that point. It is not clear when he actually became the Doctor's coachman, but by 1827 the Doctor's yellow chaise was a familiar sight in the environs of Shrewsbury, as was his coachman who, because of the Doctor's great bulk, tested the floorboards of old and fragile houses before allowing his master to enter. By 1832 Mark was married, albeit somewhat reluctantly at first, to a laundry maid at The Mount, and by 1833 he had become a father. Their house, known as the Coachman's Cottage, was part of the stables at The Mount.

In 1836 Catherine writes, in a letter to Charles, by then with the *Beagle* in Sydney, Australia: 'Papa is very well, and walks surprisingly about the town again. The Carriage drops him in the town, and then he walks a great deal about it, and the carriage goes to pick him up again.' Mark does, indeed, sound like a very good man; in the same letter Catherine describes how he allowed Marianne's eldest boy, 'Parky', to go 'on the Box of Grand Papa's Carriage … hoping to be trusted with the Reins for a few minutes'.[14]

As mentioned, Mark was at the Doctor's bedside with Thonger the whole night before he died. (He was also to perform the same act of kindness and nursing when John Abberley died, in August 1857.) Although the Census of 1861 lists him as 'coachman', it looks as if that role came to an end after the Doctor's death. Before 1844 the Diary makes no mention of him. Between 1844 and 1857 Susan refers only to his activities as a farmer, rearing cows, killing pigs, making hay, complaining about the weather and, in 1855, suffering from gout. With the Census of 1871 the connections between the Darwin family and Shrewsbury were over and he is listed as a cowkeeper and widower but, as promised by Charles's brother Erasmus, he was living on £20 per annum and his house was rent-free.[15]

COOK / HOUSEKEEPER

In every reference in the Diary, the cook/housekeeper is called either 'Mrs Gryce', 'Mrs Grice' or 'the Housekeeper', which is confusing, for she is clearly the cook. According to the Census return of 1841 'Jane Grice', aged thirty-five, is listed as a servant at The Mount, but with the Censuses of 1851 and 1861, she has become 'Housekeeper'. All the Censuses refers to her as 'unmarried', the 'Mrs' being a courtesy title customarily given to female head cooks. Another Grice, Mary, appears as a kitchen maid in the Census of 1851; presumably she was a young relation of Jane's.

The Diary reveals that Jane lived at The Mount, with her own room on the ground floor.[16] All five references to her in the Diary relate to the business of preserving or drying fruits (greengages, apricots and angelica) or vegetables (artichokes and tomatoes). She would also have had a hand in the preserving and pickling of other fruits and vegetables mentioned in the Diary, such as cucumbers, cayenne pods, red cabbage, 'seeds of kale', radishes and radish pods, dwarf beans, walnuts and green tomatoes.

Her repertoire appears to have included the making of redcurrant jelly; the preserving of quinces, shaddocks, soft fruits and rhubarb; the making of vinegars from gooseberries, crab apples, rhubarb and tarragon, and the production of a regular supply of tarts containing the thinnings of apricots, Lammas plums, cherries, 'green' currants, raspberries and what appears to be one of the Darwins' favourite ingredients – gooseberries.

Emma Darwin's recipe book, dated 16 May 1839, includes instructions for the making of another five dishes 'from Mrs Grice':[17] quince marmalade, the salting of bacon and hams, 'white sauce', 'fish sauce' and soft bread rolls.

[1] CCD vol. 2, p. 256.

[2] Parish Register of St Chad's, Baptisms, entry number 960, p. 120, and Robert Darwin's Accounts 1833–35, Cambridge University Library, DAR 227.5:140 and DAR 227.5:95.

[3] Cambridge University Library, DAR 227.4:46.

[4] Garden Diary MS (6 March 1857).

[5] Parish Register of St George's, Frankwell, Marriages, entry number 120, p. 60.

[6] The first railway line into Shrewsbury ran from Chester in 1848, and from Birmingham in 1849. Shrewsbury's magnificent Gothic-style railway station was built in 1848.

[7] CCD vol. 1, p. 132.

[8] Ibid., pp. 143, 148.

[9] Henri Quinn, *Charles Darwin, Shrewsbury's Man of the Millennium* (Shrewsbury: Redverse Ltd, 1999), p. 23.

[10] Donald F. Harris, *The Story of the Darwin House & other Darwin Property 1796–2008* (privately printed, 2008). The house was also described in successive census lists as 'No. 1 The Mount' and '46 Frankwell'.

[11] DAR 265:9, 'Red Account Book', p. 40.

12 CCD vol. 4, p. 182. Thonger is on all occasions incorrectly referred to as 'Thurger' in the Correspondence.

[13] CCD vol. 1, p. 35.

[14] CCD vol. 1, pp. 486–7.

[15] DAR 105 (ser.2), 57. Letter from Erasmus Alvey Darwin to C.D., 3 March 1867.

[16] Garden Diary, 17.ix.1850, 'Lauristina bushes planted by Mrs Grices's room.'

[17] Darwin-online.org.uk. DAR 214. Emma Darwin's recipe book.

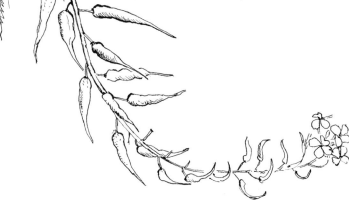

TEN

$Livestock$

Today, whether we live in town or country, we depend on commercial enterprises for our daily supplies of dairy produce, eggs, bacon and ham, but 200 years ago well-to-do country, and even suburban, households kept at least one cow for milk (with the bonus of butter, cream and even cheese). In the same establishments (and at many a cottage) there would be chickens and a pig or two as well. The Darwin household at The Mount was no exception.

COWS

The Darwins appear to have kept between three and four cows (with or without calves) at a time: 'our 3 cows give 13 qts of milk at morning meal'.[1] Three of them were certainly Alderneys at one period: '17 qts milk fr our 3 Alderney Cows'.[2]

An exception was made on 24 April 1855, when Susan bought a Guernsey cow (from Upton) for £16, which gave prodigious amounts of milk until it died of milk fever in 1860. Alderneys and the one Guernsey are the only breeds mentioned. Other breeds may have been included from time to time, as the cows are frequently referred to only by name, colour or size, or even the place or person they came from. The Guernsey cow, for example, was simply called 'Guernsey cow Upton' and a 'Red cow' was always known as 'Red cow Robt. Phipps'.

Ayrshires were considered best 'for a private dairy; but where the main objects are butter and cream the Guernsey or Alderney cows are preferable'.[3] The amounts of milk, butter and cream from her cows were a source of pride for Susan: 26 quarts of milk in the morning and 23 in the evening, in April 1857, 'and Vashti has a first calf to feed!' On New Year's Day 1859, she recorded that there had been 494 lb of butter made in the previous year. Even so, the homemade butter was presumably supplementary to what was bought, as the Doctor's Account Book for 1 July 1832– 30 June 1833 shows that 558 lb of butter were bought that year, at a cost of £28 16s 5d.[4]

Although there was a dairy in the kitchen yard, there is no mention of a dairymaid, a milkmaid or even of a cow keeper; these tasks were presumably undertaken by one or two of the many servants attached to The Mount. Milking took place morning and evening, which would have necessitated someone bringing the cows to the milking place twice a day. I have an account of a late nineteenth-century family in Shrewsbury, living near the Castle. Their house-cow was kept on a pasture on the other side of the Severn, and was brought across the river on a punt twice a day to be milked.[5]

Cows would be taken to the bull three months after calving and dried off four to six weeks before calving. Gestation for a cow is just over nine months; the Darwins' cows therefore calved once a year, these events being well spread out between January and August. Dr Darwin noted the dates on which a cow was taken to the bull, as well as the date on which it calved, but Susan delicately avoids mentioning the date of conception and records only the date of birth. The bulls were owned by various neighbours: Dr Kennedy (Headmaster of Shrewsbury

School), David Davis (one of their field tenants), Mr Gough (who lived at Gravel Hill) and a Mr Bridges.

Occasionally a calf was reared by a cow other than its mother, presumably to eke out the supply of milk to the household. 'Stella' fostered calves from both 'Esther' and 'Gipsey'. Cows past their prime and unwanted bull calves were sent to the butcher, Mr Dawson. Other calves were given or sold to Mark Briggs (the coachman-cum-farmer) or Thomas Thonger (butler), both of whom had their own smallholdings, and 'Mr Woodward'. New cows were bought from sales from Hardwicke Grange, Stretton, Berwick and Upton, and from a 'Jacob Brown at Newport', a 'Mr Davies', 'Mr Bridges' and a 'Mr Birch'.

Grazing for the cows was to be had from the fields closest to The Mount, namely Hill Head Bank or Bank Field, and from the 19 acres of land bought by the Doctor from Jack Mytton in 1820, known as Sparks Field and Bishops Land. These fields adjoined the Copthorne Road. A hovel, or shelter for the cows, stood in the nearer part of Bishops Land. The Darwins made hay for the cows on part of this land, and also cultivated mangelwurzels and kohl-rabi for them in the field and kitchen gardens. Mangelwurzel tops were fed to the cattle before the roots, which were stored for the winter in the hovel. In March 1840, hops were taken to the cows after 'the brewing' was done, though whether this was a home-brew or a local enterprise is not known.

When the grass stopped growing at the end of autumn, winter feed was essential. So too was shelter for the cows; in early November they would be brought in at night (the last entry in the Diary is for 17 October 1865, 'Cows put up at night'). They were not allowed to lie out again until April or mid-May.

In her last years it was the cows and her guinea fowl that seem to concern Susan most; there are more diary entries about them than there are about the garden. With the exception of 'the Guernsey cow Upton', she habitually referred to each cow by name, whereas her father was less concerned to do so, happily calling the Alderneys 'small', 'large', 'old', 'fawn coloured' or 'white', and others as merely 'black', 'red cow (Robt Phipps)' or just 'heifer'.

Lilly, Nancy and Rose are three cows that were named by the Doctor; Susan gives us Sabrina, Esther, Vashti, Fairy, Ruby, Gipsey and Stella. Whereas the last four are quite usual names for a cow, and Sabrina is presumably named after the River Severn (Sabrina being the Roman goddess of the River Severn), Esther and Vashti seem curious choices. I can find no explanation for this.

The Sale Plan of 1867 shows a commodious piggery next to the stables, and entries referring to the keeping of pigs at The Mount are, like those relating to the Darwins' milk-cows, continuous throughout the Diary.

PIGS

Two different fates befell the Darwins' pigs: some were reared for pork and some became bacon. No particular breed is mentioned, but they were bought three at a time for fattening, rather than being bred and reared on the premises. Their weights when killed were recorded in virtually every instance by both the Doctor and Susan, pork pigs weighing at anything between 4 and 8 score – far less than their bacon pigs, which weighed anything between 10 and 17 score (one score equals 20 lb).

The Darwins paid from 18s to 22s apiece for small, unfattened bacon or 'store pigs', while twice as much was paid for unfattened pork pigs. This discrepancy in price is not explained by *Cassell's Household Guide*, which states that bacon pigs were sold fully grown and then fattened, while pork pigs were bought at about eight to ten weeks old, then fattened and killed at about five months.[6]

The buying, fattening and killing of pigs took place between October and March. The fattening process appears to have been quite brief – only a matter of four to five weeks, with the household consuming three or four bacon pigs and one or two pork pigs per year.

Both bacon and pork pigs were killed in winter – in November, December, January and February – but only pork pigs were killed in March. There was

no pig buying or killing in the warmer months, between April and mid-October, when the first pigs were put up to feed. One of Charles Darwin's letters to Susan, dated 26 April 1838, thanks her for the gift to him and his brother Erasmus, both then living in Great Marlborough Street, London, of a very fine ham; other members of the family or friends may have benefitted over the years in a similar way, but there are no such mentions in the Diary.

Apart from a reference (2 November 1857) to the pigs being given mangelwurzel, there is no indication of how they were fed. Frequent notes by Susan, of manure being taken from the pigsty to the kitchen garden between May and August (including six cartloads in December 1852), suggest that this includes manure from the adjacent stables.

On 2 December 1857 Susan records the killing of a pig under chloroform. Discovered as an aid to painless childbirth in 1848, chloroform was not used at every subsequent pig-killing but it was repeated on three more occasions, in 1858, 1859 and 1861. This 'grandest and most blessed of discoveries' was used in Emma Darwin's seventh confinement, in January 1850,[7] and again in her confinements of 1851 and 1856 – Queen Victoria had helped to set the trend in 1853. There is no indication as to why chloroform was used for pig-killing at The Mount but it is possible that it was suggested by Charles Darwin, who was very much in favour of its use in childbirth.

SHEEP

Sheep make a very brief appearance at The Mount. On 26 November 1852 Susan 'bought twelve sheep (Kerry breed) at 21/- per sheep' and promptly had one killed, noting that it weighed 42 lb.

A week later she had 'Troughs [made] for sheep to feed out of chopped hay & peas.' However, the slaughter continued; two weeks later the second sheep was killed, and on New Year's Eve the third met its fate, at 44 lb. There is no accounting for the next four sheep, nor for the eighth, eleventh and twelfth, but

the seventh was despatched on 24 February, the ninth on 18 March and the tenth on 31 March 1853.

Considering that both pork and bacon pigs were being slaughtered at the same time, this makes a massive amount of meat for a modest household, especially as Susan and Catherine were staying with Erasmus in London in late January 1853.[8] No reason is given for the purchase of the twelve sheep, nor is it ever repeated; this enterprise therefore appears to have been something of a whim on someone's part.

POULTRY AND GUINEA FOWL

A large, covered poultry house is shown on the Sale Map of 1867, next to the coalhouse and just by the kitchen door, and there is a reference, in February 1859, to the making of a new chicken pen, but otherwise chickens are referred to very rarely, and then only in relation to the guinea fowl, which, for Susan, were more like pets. The first reference in the Diary to guinea fowl comes from Susan, in April 1850: 'Guinea fowls begin to lay.' Towards the end of her life the Diary is used almost solely to record their activities.

She allowed them to roam, lay and sit freely in the garden, and they were able to make use of the poultry pen, too, as on one occasion in April 1862 a guinea fowl laid eggs in a hen's nest (the hen would then sit on them), and on another occasion just before Susan went to London in May 1856, a hen was put to sit on fifteen guinea fowl eggs, to make sure they hatched. Guinea fowl nests were discovered on and below the terrace, in the backyard, 'under the Mountain Ash' and in the border in front of the house. Laying began in

April and sometimes continued into October, with nests of up to seventeen eggs. Sitting would start about a month after laying the full complement and hatching around a month after that.

However, guinea fowl life at The Mount was not without its disasters. Sittings began too late, the total complement of eggs was rarely hatched; some chicks hatched too early and died of cold while others hatched and were then 'all killed by something'. On one occasion the adults were all struck by disease and killed. All of these problems, and more, are mentioned in *Cassell's Household Guide*: 'no [other] fowl gives such trouble from its wandering habits'; the guinea fowl is 'a very shy bird, and if eggs are taken from her nest with her knowledge, [she] will forsake it altogether, and seek another, which she conceals with the most sedulous care'. They must always have one meal regularly at night, and 'Nothing … will persuade them to sleep in the fowl-house … they usually roost in the lower branches of a tree.'[9]

Susan makes no mention of eating her guinea fowl and, given the trouble she had in rearing them, one can only suppose that she inherited her mother's love of pet birds and liked them for their chatter, their looks and their charming and amusing ways.

HORSES

The correspondence of the Darwin and Wedgwood families is full of references to riding and carriage-driving. Apart from the necessity of getting from place to place, their horses were a source of enjoyment and pride. Riding was a favourite pastime for all the Darwins and their friends when young. Charles was still riding at the age of sixty, and only gave it up after an unfortunate fall; his father was always to be seen in the smartest of carriages, but only one riding horse is mentioned in the Diary. One of Susan's later entries, on 28 May 1859, reads: 'Agnes Salt rode with May – on the new horse bought £70, Berrington.' Agnes Salt would then have been a young lady of twenty-six, the daughter of Thomas Salt, the Darwins' solicitor. I can find no indication of who 'May' might have been; 'Berrington' is a village 4½ miles southeast of The Mount.[10]

All the other Diary references concerning horses are to carting or ploughing, for which a workhorse would be needed. This animal was the frequently mentioned 'Grey horse' which belonged to the gardener, Abberley. It was kept busy; it carted potatoes to the house from the field garden, hay from the field to the stack, and hay from the stack to the stables. It brought loads of ice to the ice house. It carted all the manure from the stables and pigsty to the fields and garden. From the railway it brought gravel for the garden walks and paths and planks to cover a tank, it delivered coal and timber, heath soil from Shawbury, turf and ashes.

This noble creature died on 31 January 1855: 'old Grey horse died a natural Death great age <u>32 yrs old</u>'. There is no mention of a replacement, though the carting continues.

There is, however, mention of a donkey, which was used to pull a mowing machine in 1860 (see Chapter Five).

Hay was needed as autumn and winter fodder for the Darwins' cows and horses. It was made in their own fields and in the orchard, rotating from parts of the Bank Field to Bishops Land, Sparks Field and the field garden, all of which were regularly grazed, manured, weeded of thistles and securely fenced or hedged.

Hay seed for the designated fields would be sown in spring, and haymaking would begin with mowing any time between midsummer and mid-July, depending on the weather. Carrying the hay was followed by making and thatching the haystack, with a tea feast for the infant school.

Crops were measured in tons; they varied between only 2 tons in 1854 and a record 18 tons the following year. A good crop would mean that the hay in a haystack could last for as long as eighteen months. The Diary frequently records the last of an old stack being trussed and carted to the stable loft before the 'new' haystack was cut for the first time.

The Doctor mentions a buzzard, hedgehogs and two ducks. These were all brought into the gardens at various times to act as pest-destroyers (see Chapter Eleven).

[1] *Diary*, 3 February 1857.
[2] *Diary*, 3 August 1857.
[3] J.C. Loudon, *The Villa Gardener* (London: Wm. S. Orr & Co., 1850), p. 260. N.B. Loudon is a Scot.
[4] DAR 227, b5:140.
[5] Letter to the author from Keith Goodway 5.5.2013.
[6] *Cassell's Household Guide* (London: Cassell, Petter, and Galpin, *c.* 1880), vol. II, p. 120.
[7] CCD vol. 4, p. 303, n. 3, in a letter from C.D. to Henslow, 17 January 1850.

[8] CCD vol. 5, p. 113, n. 9. Letter to W.D. Fox from C.D.: 'Catherine and Susan are at present staying with Erasmus in London, & perhaps I shall go up and see them next week.'
[9] *Cassell's Household Guide, op. cit.*, vol. I, p. 218.
[10] Berrington Manor, the home of a branch of the Hill family, was also the source, in 1851, of two store pigs and, in 1861, of a pair of duck-winged bantams.

ELEVEN

=====

Manures, Soil Improvers and Pesticides

The Diary's frequent references to 'manure' may be taken to mean, in general, the droppings, urine and litter of horses, cows, chickens or pigs; other kinds, such as leaf manure and liquid manure, are specified by name. 'Night soil' (the contents of the cesspit) was also used as 'manure'.

Soil improvers are of a different nature; at various times the Darwin garden was treated to bones, tan, turf, ashes, charcoal, lime, nitrate of soda, old mortar and salt.

ANIMAL MANURE

As there were horses, cows, chickens and pigs at The Mount, there would have been plenty of manure from the stables, cowhouse, poultry house, chicken run and pigsty. The Doctor refers to 'the Manuria', by which he presumably meant the dung heap (29 October 1838). The site of this is not clear, but it was possibly in the triangular dairy-yard to the north of the stable-yard. In 1838 a well was made in the same yard 'to receive the night soil'. Another dung heap, of rotted manure, was made in the kitchen garden or orchard, as well as heaps for leaf-mould, bog or peat soil and turf. In March 1852, 'sweet peas were sown in Orchard over Manure', perhaps to form a floral screen around the heap.

Stable manure might well have had a heap to itself, as horse manure is the best kind for forcing frames and hot-beds. It would have been used on the potato frames, the melon beds and the rhubarb and seakale beds. Once spent, it was removed and spread or dug in wherever needed. 'Stable draining', 'saline draining' and 'stable dressing' were put on the asparagus, a crop which seems to have received more manure than any other.

Cow manure would have accumulated only between November and May, when the cows were taken in at night. It was specifically mentioned for the north border by the mansion's 'offices', the rose beds and the strawberry beds, with a mixture of bog soil and bones.

Manure from the pigsty in the stable-yard was plentiful, five cartloads being taken at one time, four for spreading on the fields and one for the kitchen garden. It was known to be rich in nutrients, but it was thought to taint the flavour of fruit and vegetables. Gardeners therefore avoided using it alone. Manure from the dung heap in the dairy-yard was taken by cart to spread on the fields (Bishops Land, Sparks Field and the field garden), winter and summer; both carts and wheelbarrows were used to take it to the kitchen garden.

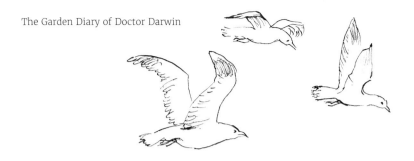

'Marks manure' (from animals owned by Mark Briggs, the Darwins' coachman, who was also a smallholder) is mentioned once (December 1844) and there is one occasion of it being bought at a cost of £5 for spreading on one of the family's meadows, Sparks Field (15 February 1859). Strawberries, asparagus, raspberries, peas, the potato garden in the field, the vinery border, celery trenches and the fruit trees are specifically mentioned as being given manure. In the flower garden the beneficiaries were roses, rhododendrons and the hollyhock bed.

GUANO

Guano – the droppings, other litter and decomposed bodies of seabirds – was put on the asparagus and on the melons. The best deposits are found on rainless, uninhabited islands off Chile, whose farmers, from ancient times, used it as a powerful fertiliser. (Its gathering, which disturbs the seabirds who create it, is now illegal in Chile.) The naturalist and explorer Alexander von Humboldt (1769–1859) first brought it back to Europe in 1804 and analysed its composition, which was found to be similar to, but more concentrated than, that of farmyard manure. It was first introduced to England, via Liverpool, in 1840 by Lord Derby (1775–1851), a keen horticulturalist, in its dried form as a commercial manure. It is first mentioned in the Diary in 1843 and was therefore still a very new horticultural commodity. 'Guano manure' was applied to The Mount's asparagus beds, – advisedly as a dry, sifted powder – in the May of that year and then a year later – as liquid 'guano water' – to the melons.

130

LEAF MANURE

Rotting, fallen leaves were used as well as stable manure to raise the heat in hot-beds and frames. Leaf manure was specifically used to force seakale and rhubarb. Care appears to have been taken to make heaps of different kinds of leaf, as a load of 'Soumach manure' was, on one occasion, given to the raspberries (7 December 1849). Newly fallen leaves would have been used to protect tender plants, such as globe artichokes, from the frost, while well-rotted leaves, 'leaf soil' or leaf-mould was used, again on the raspberry bed and on the laurels.

'BLACK HOLES'

Liquid manure was obtained from 'a hole in the Kitchen Garden' (also referred to as 'the Black Hole') in the Doctor's portion of the Diary, and from 'the Tank by the Hothouse' in Susan's more refined entries. She also refers to 'cleaning and emptying of outdoor places' (23 August 1859). As 'liquid manure' is mentioned in connection with the first three places, and implied in the fourth, it is probable that The Mount was supplied with two, if not more, cesspits, filled with the drainings of the Mansion's privies, water closets, manure heaps, stables, cowhouse and pigsty. Regular emptying of these 'black holes' was a necessity, as a sewerage system in the town of Shrewsbury was not begun until 1848. The smell from these holes would have been obnoxious; between 21 June and 4 July 1855, Susan's tank was covered with planks obtained from the railway then being built at Shrewsbury.

Cassell's Popular Gardening describes liquid manure as 'doubtless the soul of horticulture' and declares that 'money and labour expended in the construction of a liquid-manure tank is well spent, and will yield a more than commensurate return'.[1] The contents of the Doctor's 'Black Hole'

and Susan's tank were therefore deposited on the kitchen garden beds, the vine border and the asparagus, mostly in early spring, although, on 14 July 1843, thirty tubfuls were put on the asparagus beds. 'Manure water' was also put on the roses, on fruit trees grown up walls, on fruit trees in the orchard and on the vine border on lettuces and kale in midsummer. This may be the same as liquid manure, but it could also be water in which a bag of dung has been suspended.

PEAT

Bog soil, also referred to as 'bog earth', 'peat soil' and 'heath soil', was obtained from Shawbury and Rowton, villages some 7 miles to the northeast of Shrewsbury. 'Heath soil' was also obtained from the workings created by the new railway. It was mainly used for the 'peat bed' on the north side of the house, which contained gum cistus and azaleas. In the kitchen garden it was put in the strawberry bed, mixed with bones and cow manure on one occasion, and on the asparagus bed mixed with bones. Asparagus and a purple magnolia were put in a seedling bed of bog soil.

BONES

Bones, in order to be of use for manure, needed to be ground up to form what is today called bonemeal. They were used as manure at The Mount for the fruit trees on the south-facing wall of the kitchen garden, the orchard, and the asparagus, strawberry and raspberry beds. In 1852 Susan notes that 100 lb of unboiled bones costing 7s were put on the corner of Sparks Field. According to Scott's *Orchardist*,[2] unboiled bones were found to be more beneficial than boiled ones, unless the soil was already rich in organic matter, when both boiled and unboiled were equally useful. He recommended using from 12 to 16 bushels per acre.

M'Intosh wrote that 'Bones have of late years been much used for a manure ... and have been strongly recommended for vine borders,' but added that 'The expense of collecting and grinding them is too great to allow of their general adoption.'[3] However, by 1847, the grinding process had obviously become more economical, as he wrote that 'Bones are in general boiled, for the purpose of extracting the oil and gelatine which they contain, previous to their being ground for manure.'[4] The Doctor notes that in 1837 bones were obtained from Wem (a town 12 miles north of Shrewsbury where there was possibly a fat and glue factory), further evidence that he kept a similar Garden Diary before 1838.

TANNERS' BARK

Tan, also known as tanners' bark or tan waste, consists of the bark of oak trees which, being rich in tannin, was used to tan hides. That process involves soaking the raw hides with the bark in large baths. When tanning was finished, the tan waste was discarded and left to ferment. Fermentation caused it to heat up, just as dung heaps do, but tan bark creates a more even, moister heat than horse manure. It is also less messy, cleaner and longer-lasting. It therefore makes a particularly useful hot-bed for pineapples and was preferred for all indoor forcing in places that could afford the expense. Exotic, or particularly favourite conservatory plants, were put into pots and plunged into warm tan beds or pits.

Tan was used at The Mount first for its heating properties and then, when its heat was exhausted, as a manure for the field garden and orchard. Tan 'from the Tan Yard' came in fairly large quantities. The melon frame took four loads of tan to fill it, the tan pit in the first hothouse needed five loads, the second house took three and the kitchen garden stove-house took two.[5] It was used not only to grow pineapples and melons but also for propagating yuccas, growing passionflowers and

forcing potatoes and melons, and for forcing azaleas, rhododendrons, bulbs and roses for the conservatory.

TURF, ASH AND CINDERS

Turf was used for repairs to The Mount's grass paths and lawns and also formed both an edge and a cover to the vinery border. When well-rotted it became 'turf soil' and was added to the compost for the hothouses as well as the cucumber and potato frames. Turf was cut from the Doctor's fields and, in 1856, was taken, as yet another by-product of the work, from the railway being made between Shrewsbury and Crewe.

Ash and cinders were provided by both coal and timber. Coal ashes or cinders would have come from the hothouse boilers, the washhouse and the mansion's fireplaces. Their application usually followed the cleaning out of the backyard and the hothouse stokeholes. They were used to mend walks and paths, the cowhouse floor and boggy patches in the lane, rather than as manure or soil improvers, and were 'put under' the west walk, the Bank Walk and the kitchen garden walks, which were gravelled. This term suggests that the surface was removed, then replaced; the ashes would have presumably improved the drainage of the paths.

Finely sifted coal ashes were made into ash beds, usually for alpines. There are two instances (in July 1855) of plants being potted in 'ash beds below the Hothouse' at The Mount. The plants were not alpines, but cinerarias, 'archiminus' (achimenes?) and primroses. Where wood ashes (presumably from bonfires) are specifically mentioned, they are used as a dressing for the raspberries.

CHARCOAL

Charcoal was recognised as 'a valuable auxiliary to manures and indeed, when applied to the soil without the admixture of manuring substances, it has great fertilising properties.'[6] It was applied mainly to the Doctor's orange trees, and as described in Chapter Three in what looks like an experiment for Charles on the manurial values of charcoal and bones, to four different rows of raspberry canes. The Diary also specifically mentions 'animal charcoal' in the summer of 1841. It was applied first in May, to '2 of the orange trees' (when Charles Darwin was again at The Mount) and next in August, 'to one of the orange trees'. It is not clear if 'animal charcoal' is the same as the plain 'charcoal' that was 'put to' orange trees in pots in February 1841, August 1842 (put at the bottom of the pot) and March 1844 (when Charles was again visiting The Mount).

'Bone-black or animal charcoal' is listed under 'Manures rich in phosphoric acid (seed-formers)' in Cassell's *Popular Gardening*,[7] and 'animalised carbon' is described in 1842 by John Claudius Loudon: 'Animalised carbon consists of nightsoil of great age; it is sent to different parts of Europe from Copenhagen, where it has accumulated during ages in immense pits and heaps, which some years ago were purchased from the city by an Englishman. It is an exceedingly rich manure.'[8] It is not clear if this product is the same as animal charcoal.

LIME AND NITRATE OF SODA

Lime and its effect as an improver of rich garden soil was well known by the 1830s and of all the mineral or inorganic manures it was the one most generally used. It was applied either as quicklime, in order to hasten the breakdown of inert vegetable matter in the soil, thereby freeing nutritious elements for plants to be grown later on, or as slaked or mild lime in order to increase the proportion of 'calcareous matter' and thereby improve the sweetness and texture of the soil. There is no indication in the Diary of the form of lime used in The Mount's garden, but 'lime water' (made presumably from an infusion of slaked lime) was used for the first time with a sowing of tobacco seed in May 1839. Lime was also spread on the kitchen garden in May 1850, on the turf by the front door in January 1855 and on the 'peas &c' in April 1857. These dressings would presumably be of slaked lime, in powder form. It was also put on the field garden and on Bishops Land in the winters of 1842, 1843 and 1855, possibly as quicklime.

'The use of mineral manures is', as M'Intosh observed, 'comparatively modern, and their effects uncertain.'[9] Nevertheless, on eleven occasions beforehand (between July 1840 and June 1842) Dr Darwin recorded the application of nitrate of soda, both in his kitchen and flower gardens, on his orchids and on his fields. Charles had visited The Mount only days previously, so there is little doubt that this was yet another of the Doctor's horticultural experiments on his son's behalf.

DEALING WITH PESTS AND PLANT DISEASES

No description of any pests is recorded other than a 'great blight on Wall fruit' in the April of 1856 and other than smoke, sulphur and tobacco, no pesticides are mentioned either. The smoke could have been provided by burning tobacco or sulphur. The wall fruit trees were 'smoked' in May 1839.

Powdered sulphur was dusted on the orange trees in August 1841 and on unspecified 'trees' in August 1852. Tobacco was applied to cinerarias in December 1854, either as smoke or powder, probably to combat aphids. Soap suds are mentioned once, 'given to Quince tree', but this implies a dressing rather than a pesticide.

However, in autumn 1839 a buzzard 'from Jones pig man' was put in the garden; in December 1840 a hedgehog was acquired from Sundorne, and another two or three years later. In October 1841 two ducks were put in the kitchen garden. The buzzard was presumably meant to kill pigeons, crows and blackbirds; the hedgehog and ducks were probably intended to deal with slugs and snails. The Sale Catalogue of 1866 also lists fumigating bellows and mole traps.

[1] John J. Willis in Fish, *Cassell's Popular Gardening*, vol. 4 (London: Cassell & Co., 1885), p. 171.
[2] Scott, *Scott's Orchardist*, 2nd edn (London: H.M. Pollett, 1872), p. 590.
[3] Charles M'Intosh, *The Practical Gardener* (London, 1828), p. 47.
[4] Charles M'Intosh, *The New and Improved Practical Gardener* (London, 1847), p. 63.

[5] There was a tan yard nearby, in Frankwell.
[6] Scott, *op. cit.*, p. 598.
[7] Fish, *op. cit.*, vol. 3, p. 348.
[8] J.C. Loudon, *The Suburban Horticulturalist* (London, 1842), p. 59.
[9] M'Intosh, *The New and Improved Practical Gardener*, *op. cit.*, p. 67.

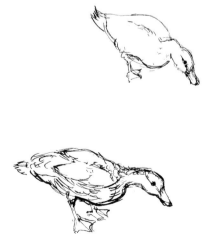

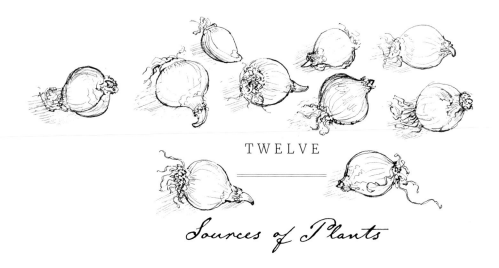

TWELVE

Sources of Plants

The nurserymen of London and its outskirts were the prime providers of plants and seeds for English gardens but, even before Robert Darwin's time, there was no lack of nurseries, flower-growers and seedsmen in the environs of Shrewsbury, many of whom had shops in the town itself. An examination of the local directories of the years covered by the Doctor's Garden Diary reveals that there were at least fourteen such businesses in and around Shrewsbury. This was no doubt because of its importance as a market town and county capital. Many of these businesses depended on supplies from London; one Shrewsbury merchant advertised, with pride, the fact that he could supply a great assortment of the newest garden and flower seeds from there.[1]

SHREWSBURY NURSERIES

Two of the foremost Shrewsbury nurserymen of this era were John Dovaston and Henry John Olroyd.

The Dovastons were based at West Felton, a village some 15 miles from Shrewsbury. John Dovaston senior (1740–1808) was a keen botanist and the originator of the Dovaston, or Weeping, Yew, said to have been planted in 1777 and still surviving.[2] He built up a successful tree nursery based on his original plan to plant a sample there of every tree species in the world (which may explain his nickname of 'Crazy Jack').

His son, also John (1782–1854), qualified as a barrister, but retired to plant more trees on the West Felton estate and to write poetry. He was also an amateur geologist and an ornithologist. The only Diary entry mentioning the Dovastons by name occurs in March 1840: '3 sorts of celery from Mr Dovaston sowed', which implies a friendly exchange of garden plants, rather than a commercial one. However, the weeping yew planted by Susan Darwin in 1849 (possibly as a memorial to her recently deceased father) was surely obtained from John Dovaston's tree nursery.

Susan mentions Olroyd twice, in 1856, when she bought a rose tree from him, and in 1859, when he supplied her with sixteen hyacinth bulbs. He had a shop in the High Street and a nursery (the Portland Nursery) at Beckbury House in Abbey Foregate. He sold a huge variety of plants, including 'flower roots', Dutch bulbs and 'novelties in vegetables and flowers'. As proof that he had dealings, too, with the great plant breeder Henry Eckford (then working at Coleshill, in Berkshire), he sold verbenas named after George and Isa Eckford (most probably his children).[3]

Other nurserymen named in the Diary included Henry Instone, Robert Phipps and 'Mr Woodward'.

Instone had a nursery in Sutton Lane and premises at Abbey Place in 1828 and at Wyle Cop in 1851. He supplied the Doctor with a purple passionflower (1840), potatoes (1840) and a small moss rose (1841).

Robert Phipps (1818–66) was the son of the Darwins' previous gardener, Joseph Phipps, who had died in 1835. He had nurseries on two sites very close to The Mount; one was on the north side of the Copthorne to Montgomery Road, the other was closer to Frankwell, on the south side between New Street and the Copthorne Road, where he also had a house. This site is still a nursery and now belongs to Shrewsbury Council. Phipps also kept cows, one of which ('red cow') went to The Mount in 1839. He supplied a yellow rose tree to the Doctor in 1842 and a 'Lily Rubra' to Susan in 1851.

'Mr Woodward' poses a problem. Susan's Diary entries show that a 'Mr Woodward' was given a calf from one of her cows in 1842 and peaches and nectarines in 1852, which suggests that he was a friend rather than a nurseryman. In this case, he might be Thomas Woodward (born 1791), a neighbouring magistrate. This Mr Woodward had a house and garden adjoining Millington's Hospital and fields bordering the Darwins' pastures further along the Copthorne Road, but he died in 1855 and Susan gave 'Mr Woodward' some orange trees in 1856. As items obtained 'from Mr Woodward' include quicks (hawthorn saplings for hedging) in 1852 and hollyhocks in 1853, it looks as if he was more likely to be John Woodward, a seed merchant in Bridge Street.[4]

PLANTS FROM FRIENDS AND FAMILY

'Bicton' crops up as another source of plants. This is presumably Bicton House, some 4 miles west of Shrewsbury, which had been a nursery since the early eighteenth century. By 1866 it was being run by a Mr Harding. Double violets and ferns were bought from there by Susan in 1852 and 1862, respectively.

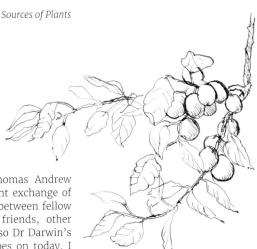

In addition to the connection between Dr Darwin and Thomas Andrew Knight, a pioneering plant-breeder, there was also a constant exchange of plants, seeds, fruit trees and all sorts of greenhouse exotics between fellow gardeners, be they local aristocracy, neighbours, family, friends, other people's gardeners or even servants, many of whom were also Dr Darwin's patients, his debtors, or both. Much the same thing still goes on today. I am constantly reminded of old friends and distant places by the plants in my own garden that originated as seeds or cuttings following visits to their homes.

Knight, who was also a close friend of John Wedgwood, was an early supplier of fruit trees for The Mount. Chapter One already refers to his contributions to The Mount's garden. Members of the Wedgwood family were frequent recipients of baskets of fruit and, as also previously mentioned, in 1840 John gave the Doctor the then rare seeds of a vegetable marrow and, in the same year, a Scarlet Giant Goliath rhubarb plant. He also provided a poppy peony for the greenhouse. However, although John was a renowned horticulturalist and fellow garden diarist, his nephew, the barrister Harry Wedgwood (1799–1885), provided The Mount with many more plants between 1840 and 1854: moss rose trees, fuchsia cuttings, apricot trees, wine-sour and yellow plum trees. Moreover, a barrister friend of Harry, a Mr Isaac Onslow Secker, was the source of twelve *Araucaria imbricata* seeds sown by the Doctor in 1844.

The Owens of Woodhouse, in West Felton, near Oswestry, were also close friends of the Darwins, and it was here, in the 1820s, that the girls joined the young Owens in a giddy social life. Charles went shooting and courted Fanny Owen, his first girlfriend, there. Seeds sown at The Mount 'from Mr Owen, Woodhouse' in the 1840s included lettuce, Dutch aster, a hardy melon and celery. In 1851 Susan recorded 'Charles Owen's Cape lily coming into flower.' Charles Owen was one of Fanny's brothers.

Plants and seeds were also exchanged with neighbours in Shrewsbury. One of the most generous providers of plants (and Alderney cows) was Shrewsbury's

great military hero, General Lord Rowland Hill (1722–1842), who lived nearby, at Hardwicke Grange. A keen gardener and almost certainly a patient of the Doctor's, between the years of 1838 and 1841 he was to send to The Mount 'a new kind of mint', geranium cuttings, potatoes, Myott's Pine strawberry plants, and the seeds of sweet basil and marjoram. Even after his death a white everlasting pea and some British Queen strawberries made their way to the garden at The Mount.

He also sent the Doctor, in 1840, a blue water lily (*Nymphaea caerulea*) from Hawkstone, the old family seat, which was grown in a tub in the hothouse. This was much treasured by the Doctor, who diligently recorded the appearances of its buds and flowers.

Other exchanges took place, as well. Edward Haycock (1791–1870), the County Surveyor and Shrewsbury's leading architect, gave the Darwins tomato and cucumber seed; in exchange Susan sent him quinces by the dozen. Their next-door neighbour was the local vicar, the Rev. John Harding, who provided anemone seeds and received peaches and a budded rose tree by way of thanks. The Darwins' solicitor, Thomas Salt, was given a passionflower and, 'as an experiment' for him, Susan planted gentianellas in a bed with paving stones under them. The Corbets of nearby Sundorne Castle provided potatoes, thyme, roses, geraniums, onions, Emperor cucumber seed, Elton Pine strawberries, a Nepal juniper and a hedgehog, while Dr Darwin gave them three shaddock fruits and a 4 lb 12 oz '*maricuja*' (the Doctor had trouble with the spelling of 'maracuja', also known as a granadilla). The Smythe Owens of Condover Hall sent 'a large scarlet geranium' and kohl-rabi plants, and in return were given shaddock trees, a guava and a 5 lb 1 oz maracuja.

With the completion of the railways connecting Shrewsbury to the rest of Great Britain in 1858, Susan began ordering plants and seeds from nurserymen further afield. From Carter's of High Holborn in London (founded in 1804) she ordered gloxinias and German stocks. Paul & Son, of Cheshunt, from whom, in 1856, she bought roses in great quantities, as well as heaths and hollyhocks, was founded in 1806. Waterer of Woking, Surrey (founded in 1828), provided numerous rhododendrons, kalmias and an arbutus in 1856, and Sutton & Co. of Reading, Berkshire (also founded in 1806), provided twelve hyacinth bulbs for 10s 6d in 1857. All four of these companies are still trading today.

In 1854 and 1859, 'Henderson', who was possibly the owner of a nursery specialising in forced flowers and shrubs on the Edgware Road, London, sent Susan £5–worth of plants and bulbs (about £350 today), including alstroemerias and ixias.

A Mr Guise, listed at the front of the Diary as the supplier of eight standard roses in 1851, is untraceable.

[1] William Powell's advertisement in *The Shrewsbury Chronicle* (9 February 1810), p. 23.
[2] Paul Stamper, *Historic Parks and Gardens of Shropshire* (Shrewsbury: Shropshire Books, 1996) p. 50, ref. 11.
[3] Advertisement, *Eddowe's Shrewsbury Journal* (4 July 1866), p. 4.
[4] Bagshaw's *Gazetteer of Shropshire*, 1851.

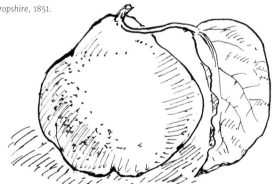

After the Darwins[1]

Susan's last entry in the Diary was made on 17 October 1865 ('Cows put up at night'). Her health had been failing for some months. Catherine Darwin returned to The Mount in the November of that year in order to look after her sister, but she too was far from well. Catherine died on 2 February 1866. The Darwins' connections with The Mount were about to end. As Fanny Allen wrote, on hearing the news of Catherine's death: 'Sad, sad Shrewsbury! Which used to look so bright and sunny.'[2]

By the August of 1866 Susan was, according to her brother, Charles, in 'a terrible suffering state'.[3] In September he was to write to his friend Joseph Hooker: 'She wishes poor thing earnestly for death, & really death is nothing compared with much suffering. It will soon be over.'[4] She died a week later, on the morning of 3 October. She was sixty-three. The cause of her death, according to her death certificate, was 'Exhaustion by long continued Uterine Disease' with Jane Grice, her cook and housekeeper for many years, 'Present at the Death'. For Charles it was 'the end of a most sweet & loving character'.[5]

Her obituary in the *Shrewsbury Chronicle* referred to her generosity to 'the poor in the district where she lived', the 'establishment and maintenance of an Infant School in Frankwell' and munificent contributions 'to various charitable foundations of the town'.[6]

The deaths of Catherine and Susan left Caroline, Erasmus and Charles, the remaining offspring of Robert and Susannah, with the question of what was to become of The Mount. All of them were settled in their own homes. None of them wished to live in their old birthplace. It fell to Erasmus to sort out the papers and legacies and, with the consent of Charles and Caroline, to 'settle something about the house'.[7]

It was agreed that it, and its contents, with the rest of the land owned by the Darwins, should be put up for two separate sales by auction.

THE FIRST SALE AT THE MOUNT

The first sale began on Monday 19 November 1866 and lasted six days. Erasmus and Charles, as executors, had taken care of all the personal papers (which, perhaps, included the Garden Diary), family heirlooms and things left as bequests by Susan. Caroline, meanwhile, as the wife of Josiah Wedgwood III, had quietly bought, before the sale, a number of pieces from Robert Darwin's collection of Wedgwood items, including certain medallions, much to the disappointment of Charles's great friend Joseph Hooker, who had gone to the sale specifically to add them to his collection.[8] This still left seven Wedgwood china breakfast, dinner and tea services, a vast amount of furniture, carpets, linen and draperies, beds, tableware, silver, glass, more china, books and a pianoforte to be disposed of. In addition, there were the accoutrements of the larder, the brewhouse, the cellar, the dairy, the boot room, the laundry, the yard, poultry house and stable, as well as four carriages with harness, a 9-ton rick of hay, a cock and four hens, three pigs and, somewhat poignantly, a 'Black cross-bred Retriever and Newfoundland dog'. Equally poignant were twelve lots of plants and pots from the greenhouse, including orange trees, azaleas, camellias, ferns, etc., and, from the garden, some fifty-three lots of tools, garden furniture, vases on pedestals, forcing frames and a Shanks mowing machine, possibly the one bought by Susan in 1857.[9]

THE SECOND SALE

The second sale included the now empty mansion and the rest of the estate, with the fields bought by the Doctor from John Mytton in 1820. Although these were advertised as 'rich old pasture land of the best quality', there is a hint here as to the future of the entire neighbourhood: they were also described as being 'building sites of unusual excellence'.[10] Sure enough, by 1913 all three fields were occupied by the War Department, as Copthorne Barracks.

This auction took place a week after the first, on 30 November 1866, but only the fields known as Bishops Land, Far Bishops Land, Sparks Field and a piece of land bought by Susan across the river were sold. The reserve price that was put on the mansion, its gardens, the gardener's cottage, outbuildings and Hill Head Bank Meadow (the 'Doctor's field' nearest to the mansion) proved to be too high.

Susan's gardener, George Wynne, remained in his house across the road and kept the garden in order; the mansion was temporarily let and, eventually, a complicated plan for a third sale was devised, in which the site was divided into lots. The sale was held in August 1867 and, as it turned out, the division into lots was unnecessary. The entire property, including Hill Head Bank, was bought for £3,450 by Edward Henry Lowe, a local wharfinger and barge owner, who had recently given up that business and become a builders' merchant.

NEW OWNERS, 1867–1919

Edward Lowe already owned the 2 acres of land lying between Hill Head Bank and The Mount's stables. It was occupied by two villas (one of which, Mount

Cottage, was the home of a recently widowed lady, the wife of the Rev. John Harding, the incumbent of the local church, St George's). Lowe also owned various other properties in Shrewsbury. He chose to let The Mount, rather than live in it.

Two years later Charles Darwin, by now a world-renowned figure, revisited Shrewsbury with Henrietta, his eldest daughter. He was shown round the house by its then tenant, who clung to the party during the entire visit. His love for both his father and his old home was revealed by his remark on leaving: 'If I could have been left alone in that green-house for five minutes, I know I should have been able to see my father in his wheel-chair as vividly as if he had been there before me.'[11]

As related in Chapter Four, Henrietta was to visit 'Shrewsbury' once more, in 1880, and found the gardens much neglected. The house had been lived in by no fewer than four different tenants since 1867.

Lowe died in 1874 and his widow died in 1883, which caused the house (but not Hill Head Bank) to be put up for sale once more. It was bought for £3,000 by John Spencer Phillips, a local banker and a wealthy man. The gardens were probably somewhat restored under his ownership but following his death in 1909 and that of his widow in 1919, The Mount was sold again, this time to Thomas Balfour, for £4,500.

THE MOUNT IN THE TWENTIETH CENTURY

Balfour was a land agent and, as later became apparent, a speculator. He raised a mortgage on the property and then, two years later, divided The Mount and its gardens in half, thus setting in train the destruction of the Darwins' famous and beautiful garden. The mansion, the stables and the small stove-house nearest the mansion with all the grounds between it and the road to the south formed one portion; the entire length of the terrace, the bank and all the grounds to the east of that dividing line, including the vinery, the flower garden and the kitchen garden, formed the second portion.

The part containing the mansion was sold for £5,000 to the Postmaster General. A condition of the deal was that the purchaser must erect a wire fence along the terrace to form a northern boundary to the bank, and a wooden fence along the eastern boundary.

Two years later Balfour sold the second portion to James Kent Morris, a Shrewsbury oil entrepreneur, Justice of the Peace and housing developer, for £1,200, thus making a tidy profit on his initial outlay of £4,500 for the original site.

The mansion was used as offices for various governmental institutions during the twentieth century, including the District Valuation Office for the Inland Revenue. At one point the staff had a nine-hole golf course in the garden to the south of the house.

Morris built a house for himself on the vinery site, incorporating timbers from Hardwick Grange, which he had previously demolished. This property (no. 9 Darwin Gardens) includes the part of the Terrace Walk running along the north side of the mansion, and part of the bank below it. He appears to have had no intentions to develop the rest of his portion of The Mount's gardens, other than to provide a recreation centre for his employees.

The area occupied by the kitchen garden, combined with the garden to the south of the vinery, would have certainly provided enough space for the two tennis courts, the football pitch and the hockey pitch said to have been created there. However, after ten years Morris decided instead to develop the site for housing.

He then cut a road running from east to west along a line formed by the north wall of the kitchen garden (now known as Darwin Gardens) and, in 1933, built eight semi-detached houses along its north side, which were followed by ten more on the south side. Both the kitchen garden and the flower garden are now buried under bricks and mortar, although the southern wall of the kitchen garden and the little garden house that was once the laboratory of Charles and Erasmus are still standing.

Very little else remains of the original garden. There are sets of steps in the terrace and elsewhere in the garden of no. 9. The ice house can still be seen on the bank, now owned by the Shropshire Wildlife Trust. It is even more overgrown than when Henrietta last saw it, and as crumbling as ever. The front gates and the driveway to the house remain the same. There are still crocuses on the lawn in spring.

THE MOUNT IN THE TWENTY-FIRST CENTURY

By 1971 ownership of the mansion had passed to the Secretary of State for the Environment and in 2001 a leaseback was arranged with Mapeley, an international property investment business. In May 2019 came the announcement that an American multi-millionaire had bought the mansion, with the intention of turning it not into a museum but a 'poly university … we aim to make it an important place for digital visitors and that will make it a global destination'.[12] However, a year later that has come to nothing and, as I write this, the future of The Mount as a long-overdue memorial to the birthplace of Charles Darwin is yet to be realised.

POSTSCRIPT

April 2021. News has just come *via* my moles in Shrewsbury that 'Mount House has been bought for nearly £1 million by [a local] businessman, Glyn Jones, who has ambitious ideas to bring it back to life and celebrate Shrewsbury's most famous son. He's expected to spend another £500,000 in breathing new life into the place.'[13]

Mr Jones tells me[14] that he is keen to fully restore the house, which is in 'a very tired state indeed', with the intention of turning it back 'to a place that is lived in'. It will also contain office space for environmental entrepreneurs, a tearoom and a small museum.

I am keeping my fingers crossed, and if he wants to do anything with what is left of The Mount's once beautiful gardens, perhaps he will find this book useful.

[1] Much of the information in this chapter relating to the sale of The Mount is taken from a booklet, *The Story of the Darwin House & Other Property in Shrewsbury 1796–2008* by Donald F. Harris, published in 2008.

[2] *Emma Darwin: a Century of Family Letters, 1792–1896*, ed. Henrietta Litchfield (London: John Murray, 1915), vol. 2, p. 184.

[3] Letter from C.D. to W. Fox, CCD vol. 14, p. 301.

[4] Letter from C.D. to Hooker, CCD vol. 14, p. 337.

[5] Letter from C.D. to Hooker, CCD vol. 14, p. 337.

[6] *Shrewsbury Chronicle*, 5 October 1866, p. 4, col. 6.

[7] Letter from Erasmus to C.D., CCD vol. 14, p. 340.

[8] Letters from Hooker to C.D., CCD vol. 14, 22 November 1866, p. 395 nn. 5, 6 and 7; 12 December 1866, p. 421, n. 7. Hooker constantly teased Darwin for failing to appreciate his inheritance of Wedgwood ware.

[9] Sale Particulars of The Mount, Shrewsbury Archives SC/1/81.

[10] *Shropshire Chronicle*, 16 November 1866.

[11] *Charles Darwin: His Life told in an Autobiographical Chapter, and in a Selected Series of his Published Letters*. ed. by his son, Francis Darwin (London: John Murray, 2nd edn, 1902), p. 3.

[12] *The Shropshire Star*, 1 May 2019.

[13] *The Shropshire Star*, 9 April, 2021.

[14] Personal email, 13 April 2021.

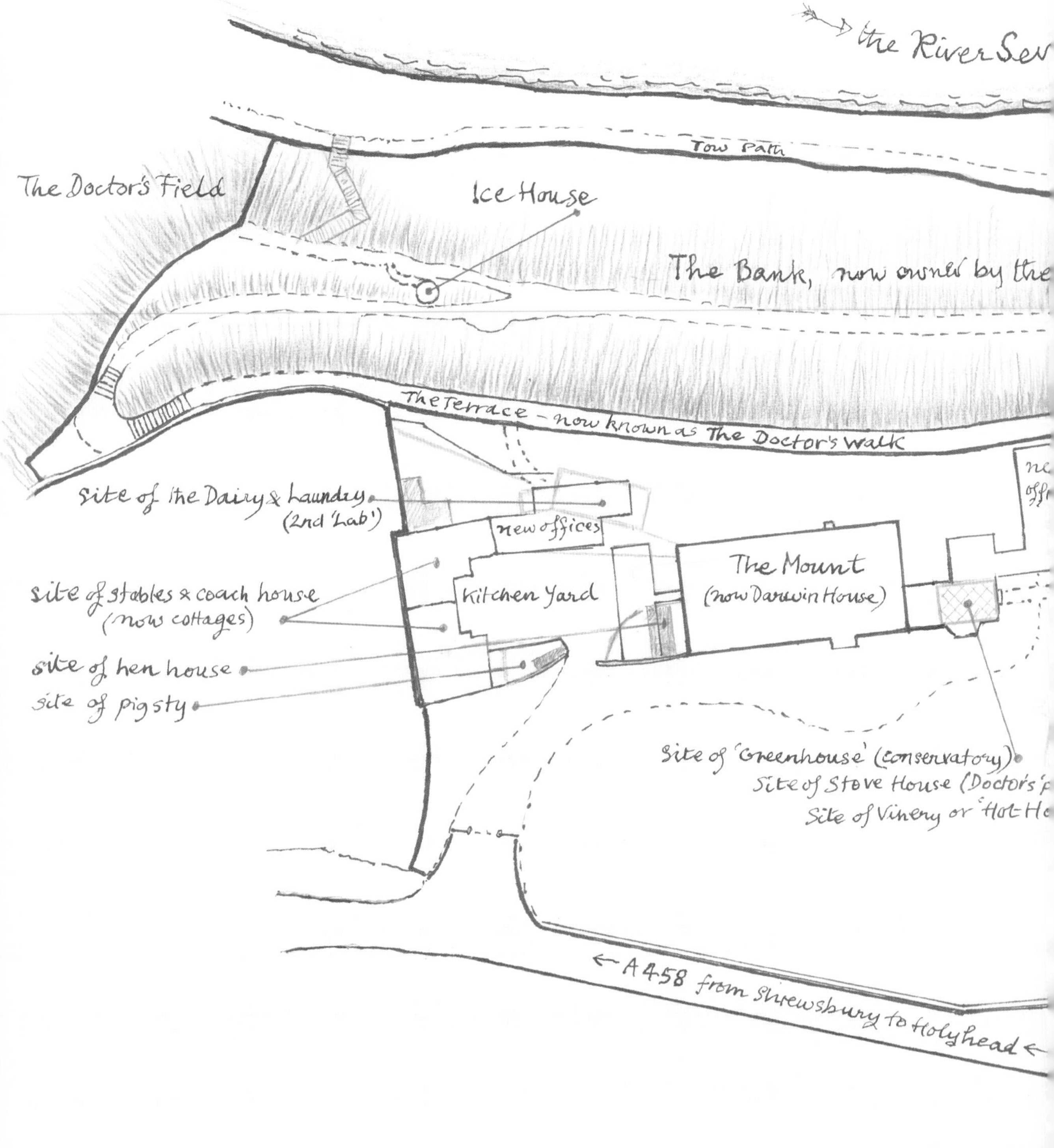

the River Sev

Tow Path

The Doctor's Field

Ice House

The Bank, now owned by the

The Terrace – now known as The Doctor's walk

Site of the Dairy & Laundry (2nd 'Lab')

ne
off

new offices

Site of stables & coach house (now cottages)

Kitchen Yard

The Mount (now Darwin House)

site of hen house
site of pigsty

Site of 'Greenhouse' (conservatory)
Site of Stove House (Doctor's p
Site of Vinery or 'Hot He

← A458 from Shrewsbury to Holyhead ←

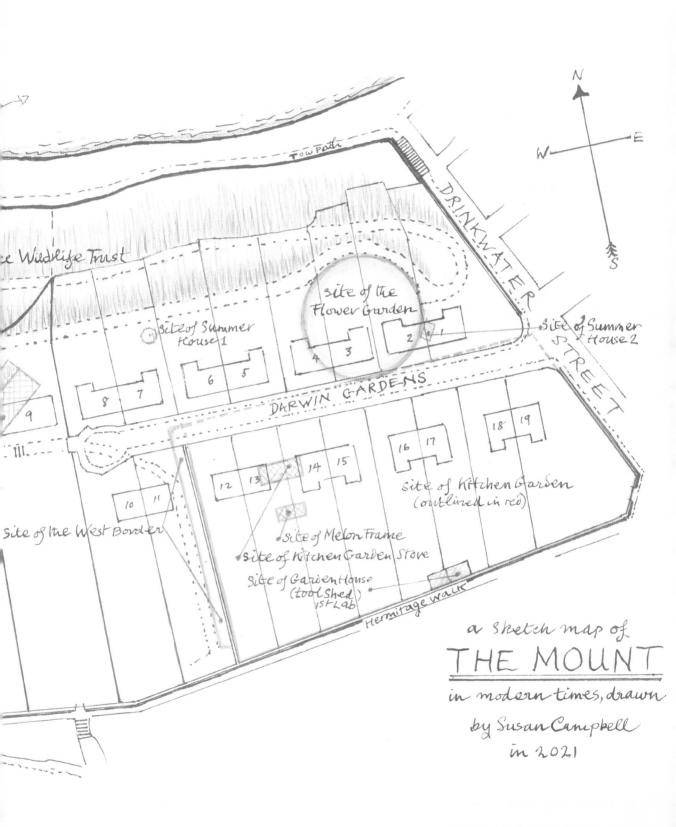

Tow Path

Wildlife Trust

DRINKWATER STREET

N
W — E
S

Site of the
Flower Garden

Site of Summer
House 1

Site of Summer
House 2

3   2   1
4   3
6   5
8   7

DARWIN GARDENS

9

18   19

16   17

12   13   14   15

Site of Kitchen Garden
(outlined in red)

10   11

Site of the West Border

Site of Melon Frame

Site of Kitchen Garden Store

Site of Garden House
(tool shed)
1st Lab

Hermitage Walk

a sketch map of
THE MOUNT
in modern times, drawn
by Susan Campbell
in 2021

Pastel drawings by Ellen Sharples, possibly made in Bath in 1818 and now hanging in Down House, Kent. Reproductions courtesy of Historic England and Down House.

Dr Robert Darwin

Erasmus Alvey Darwin

Possibly Susan Darwin

Charles and Emily Catherine Darwin

The Mount in 1884, seen from the opposite bank of the Severn

The Mount, seen from the same bank in 2014

Illustration of the Terrace Walk shown in a drawing by Emma Wilmot (1842)

View from the garden of the Terrace and the Severn, from Sir Arthur Keith 'Darwin Revalued' (1954)

PART TWO

An Almanac of Work done
in the Garden

An Almanac

'An almanac of work to be done' is often to be found in old gardening books. Here I have compiled a monthly account of the 'work that is done' at The Mount's garden during the years of 1838–66, with the inclusion of outside events where they have been noticed in the Diary.

I have started with November, because for gardeners the year seems to end in October with the harvests of autumn; the days become shorter and the weather gets cooler. We start putting things away, spending less time outdoors. We are not exactly dormant, or hibernating; it is a time for planning the next year's crops and mending tools, paths and fences.

November

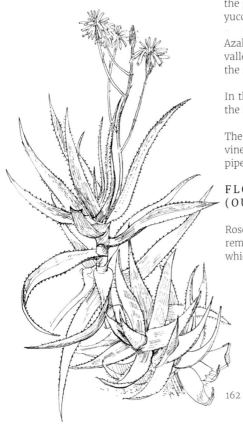

WORK UNDER GLASS (INDOORS)

Work for the gardeners indoors, in their work sheds and glasshouses, includes making cuttings of vines, roses, geraniums, calceolarias, gooseberries and currants. Geraniums, roses and cinerarias are potted.

The endless shuffling of plants from stove to hothouse to greenhouse begins, in order to have decorative plants showing at their best within the mansion, during the winter months.

Tender plants and the roots of ornamentals such as tigridias, gladioli, marvel of Peru, dahlias, verbenas, aloes and the smaller yuccas are taken up from the garden and brought into the shelter of sheds or glasshouses. (The larger yuccas are left in place and tied up to protect them from snow.)

Azaleas, hyacinths, cistus, clianthus, peonies, magnolias and lilies of the valley are brought in to flower in the greenhouse (the conservatory within the mansion), where the first fires of the winter are lit.

In the warmer stove-houses, the first cucumbers are sown and planted and the forcing of more camellias, roses, hyacinths and azaleas begins.

The vine rods are pulled out of the vinery to stand the winter outside. The vinery is whitewashed and cleaned and, in 1850, it has boilers and hot-water pipes put in.

FLOWER BEDS, TREES AND SHRUBBERIES (OUTDOORS)

Roses, hollyhocks, spring bulbs and peonies are planted, dead plants are removed and beds are 'cleaned' (the word 'cleaned' is preferred to 'weeded', which occurs only four times in the Diary).

Yews and laurels are moved. The myrtle tree is covered to protect it from frost. Box hedging is renewed in the flower and kitchen gardens. The ivy on the laundry is trimmed. Roses are pruned.

FRUIT

The last of the apples, pears, quinces, plums and medlars are gathered; their storage places (in a storeroom over the coach house and cellar under the hothouse) are checked.

The Sweetwater vine 'from Mr Rowland' produces its late crop of grapes. In the vinery the last of the grapes are cut.

Old fruit trees and other trees are cut down and new fruit trees are planted against walls in the orchard and in the kitchen garden.

Pruning begins of the vines, raspberries, gooseberries and currants and also of pears and apples.

WALKS AND LAWNS

The gravel walks throughout the gardens are 'cleaned', renewed and, where necessary, repaired. Gravel in the early years comes from a hole by the laundry, but later it is fetched from the new railway.

The lawns are mown for the last time.

FIELDS

Hedges of 'quicks' (hawthorn) are planted on the field and river boundaries, and old hedges 'pleached' (cut and laid).

The haystack is cut for the first time (1842, 1844, 1852).

MAINTENANCE

Fences of posts and rails are mended in the fields, with timber sawn from The Mount's own trees. Garden frames are painted, drains are made in the garden, a door to the cowhouse is made, a shed is thatched and the hovel repaired.

Garden benches are put under cover.

In 1852 the wall below the neighbour's garden (the Rev. Harding) is mended, 'wet and earthquake' having 'thrown it down'.

KITCHEN GARDEN

The seakale bed is manured and forcing is begun by putting some of the roots in pots indoors, some in a frame and covering them with leaves, and covering some outdoors. Rhubarb is given similar treatment.

Beans are gathered for seed, onions and root vegetables dug up and stored. Asparagus and globe artichokes are cut down, then covered with leaves and, in 1839, with cedar boughs. These undoubtedly came from the cedar tree blown down the previous winter (see January).

The asparagus beds are manured and dressed with salt. Onions, hardy lettuces and cabbages are planted, endive tied up to blanch, celery earthed up for the last time and the roots of runner beans dug up 'to keep for next year'.

FIELD GARDEN

Mangels, parsnips, Jerusalem artichokes, beets and turnips are 'got up'.

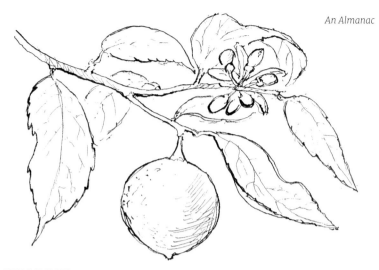

WEATHER

This is hardly ever remarked upon by the Doctor, but Susan records it throughout the year, usually on a Sunday. This month it is wet, frosty, foggy and mild by turns, with easterly and north-easterly winds. The thermometer falls to 18° F (−8° C).

The earthquake that destroyed Mr Harding's garden wall in 1852 occurs at 4.00am, after seven days of rain, causing the Severn's first of two floods that month.

SPECIAL EVENTS

On Thursday 15 November 1849, there is a Thanksgiving Day 'for Cholera being stopped'. This is to mark the end of the second outbreak of the pandemic which, like Covid-19, has caused much concern in the medical world and fear among the people. Shrewsbury, with a population of 23,095, has 116 deaths from cholera in 1849. This figure, compared with the 53,293 deaths in the country as a whole, is modest, but its causes are the same: poor sanitation, crowded, unclean houses and polluted water. The Thanksgiving Day is decreed by Queen Victoria. It is marked by the shops being closed and services being held in all the churches.

December

WORK UNDER GLASS (INDOORS)

More cucumber seeds are sown and cuttings of vines, camellias, clematis and roses are taken. Feverfew, hyacinths, primulas and bulbs are potted, and put into tan beds to force in the stove-house.

In the greenhouse, camellias, primulas and roses are flowering. Roses, lilac, mint and rhubarb are being forced in the hothouse.

Shaddocks are gathered in the hothouse, sent to friends and preserved. Orange and shaddock trees are in flower.

FLOWER BEDS, TREES AND SHRUBBERIES (OUTOORS)

Wisteria, roses and honeysuckle are pruned. Box hedging is renewed. Old trees are felled. Flower roots are taken up, replanted or divided. Yuccas are tied up or taken into the hothouse. Magnolias, peonies and sollia are taken into the greenhouse.

New roses are planted.

FRUIT

New fruit trees are planted.

The pruning of gooseberries, currants, raspberries, vines, pear, apple, peach, pomegranate and apricot trees continues, with the additional tasks of root-pruning and the nailing of wall fruit trees.

The last grapes are gathered from the vinery, and a large plate of the Sweetwater grapes from the front of the mansion (possibly stored from when they were gathered, see November) is served on Christmas Day 1839.

Baskets of pears are brought into the cellar under the hothouse to ripen.

Strawberry plants are potted for forcing.

WALKS AND LAWNS

The gravelling of garden walks continues. Fresh turf is laid on the grass verges. The drive is covered with gravel and stones. Leaves are cleared from the lawn.

FIELDS

The pleaching of hedges in the fields continues. A little hay is taken from the stack for the cows (1836).

MAINTENANCE

Repairs to fences and palings are made. An ash tree is sawn up to make wheelbarrows. A beech tree by the towing path is cut up to make 'stanks' (wooden supports) for the bank's middle walk.

The pond in the field is cleaned out.

There are bonfires. Ice is put into the ice house.

KITCHEN GARDEN

The warmth of the kitchen garden stove provides the first seakale. In 1856, the first cut is sent to the recently widowed Marianne (Susan Darwin's eldest sister).

Potatoes are put to force and cucumber is sown in the kitchen garden stove and in the large brick frame.

Outside, the first couve tronchuda is cut, and the first Brussels sprouts are ready. The remaining carrots, beets and parsnips are dug up, endive stacked. The first peas, radishes, carrots and broad beans are sown and lettuce, onions and asparagus planted. Cabbages, early peas and beans are planted out.

Trenching and manuring is done. Celery is earthed up one last time. There are bonfires.

FIELD GARDEN

There is more trenching, 'turning of soil', ploughing and manuring.

WEATHER

It is wet, mild and then frosty, with the first snow. The thermometer veers from 16°–52° F (-9°–1° C).

It is cold enough in 1841, 1844 and 1855 to fill the ice house with ice from the river, but so mild in 1851 that this cannot be done.

SPECIAL EVENTS

Christmas Days are celebrated but recorded without much comment in the Diary. It is only a one-day holiday for the servants, so if it falls on a Sunday, Monday is regarded as Christmas Day instead. The first seakale of the season is saved for Christmas Day 1858, and there are twenty-three to dinner. Whether this is a similar dinner to that of the Christmas dinners of 1854 and 1855, when all the servants' wives dine there, is not clear.

January

WORK UNDER GLASS (INDOORS)

Peonies, cinerarias, hyacinths, camellias and lilac are flowering in the greenhouse.

Roses, a peony tree, a rhododendron, hyacinths, lily of the valley and lilac are taken into the hothouse to force; here, as in the greenhouse, there is some 'cleaning', 'altering', 'tidying', white-washing and painting.

More plants are potted: alstroemerias, oxalis, geraniums, roses, strawberry plants for forcing, cinerarias, geraniums, narcissi, calceolarias and 'a scarlet rhododendron'.

In 1839 and 1840 there are pineapples in the hothouse. More shaddocks are gathered, the orange trees are washed and cuttings of the Bergamot lime are made in the plant stove-house, as well as cuttings of verbena, roses and geraniums.

FLOWER BEDS, TREES AND SHRUBBERIES (OUTDOORS)

The first camellias, snowdrops, primroses and crocuses are flowering, tulips are planted. The clipping of ivy continues.

FRUIT

More fruit trees are planted. Pruning of orchard and free-standing trees continues, as does the nailing of the trained peach, pear and morello cherry trees on the walls. (This is an arduous job, entailing the undoing and pruning of the year's previous work, and re-nailing the branches in their correct positions.)

Gooseberries and currants are pruned. Pomegranate seeds are sown (1839).

WALKS AND LAWNS

The gravelling and rolling of walks continues; this work takes place throughout the year.

FIELDS

Hedging and the mending of fences continue. And the ice house is loaded with ice every winter, except for 1851 when the weather is so mild it cannot be done.

Hay is brought from the stack.

MAINTENANCE

The felling of trees, particularly on the bank, occurs over several years. Sycamores, oak, acacia, birch, beech, holly, ash and horse chestnut all meet their fates, and are made into posts and rails or, as in the January of 1855, a continuation of the job begun in the previous month, of making wheelbarrows.

KITCHEN GARDEN

More rhubarb and seakale are covered to force and potatoes are put to force in the hothouse and frame. The first seakale is cut from the stove-house, in 1839, 1854 and 1856.

Sowing continues (some of it in boxes indoors), with peas and beans, mustard and cress, celery, carrots, lettuces, radishes, cauliflowers and spinach. Early onions, peas and beans are planted out.

Pigsty manure is spread on the kitchen garden. Horseradish is dug up; there are mushrooms for dinner.

FIELD GARDEN

Manure is spread and trenching continues.

WEATHER

It brings snow, sharp frosts, thaws, floods, rain and the occasional 'beautiful day'.

Most winters are marked as very mild, or 'open', but the winter of 1854 is recorded as '<u>very severe</u>'. It kills a myrtle and a rhododendron, and the temperature drops to 5° F (−15° C). There are severe floods in 1849, 1856 and 1859, and severe frosts in 1854 and 1855.

A gale on the night of 6 January 1839 necessitates the replacement of lead on the roof of the mansion and blows down a white cedar tree.

SPECIAL EVENTS

No particular reason is given for putting glass 'on the wall by the Coal House' in 1849, and 'on the top of wall by the K.G.' in 1856, but presumably there had been unwelcome intruders at those times.

A new cart is bought in 1849 for £6 10s.

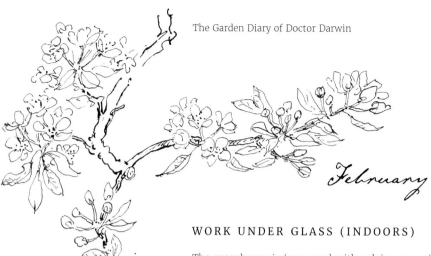

February

WORK UNDER GLASS (INDOORS)

The greenhouse is 'very gay' with salvias, geraniums, camellias, hyacinths, epacris, primulas and azaleas all in flower.

The hothouse contains strawberries already in flower, vines in pots, mint and French beans for forcing, as well as melon and cucumber seedlings, roses, lilac, a passionflower, tree cucumbers, and an erythrina tree.

More cuttings are made of roses, verbenas, clematis, petunias, fuchsias, heliotrope and chrysanthemums. Some are ready for potting, to be joined by salvias, achimenes and *Clianthus puniceus*.

Bergamot limes are gathered.

FLOWER BEDS, TREES AND SHRUBBERIES (OUTDOORS)

The first snowdrops and crocuses are accompanied by dog-tooth violets and a white camellia.

Ranunculus, rhododendrons, kalmias and arbutus are planted out. Roses are laid in the flower garden and rose cuttings planted at the infant school.

Manure is put on the garden borders.

FRUIT

Straw bands and boards are put up to protect fruit blossom from frost.

The nailing of fruit trees on the walls continues throughout this month.

Cherry, peach and apricot trees are pruned (a practice that has since been dropped at this time of year, after it was discovered that it encouraged the blight known as peach-leaf curl).

The vines that were taken to the outside of the vinery in November are returned to the inside and forcing begins.

The first flowers of apricots, a pear and nectarines are open.

WALKS AND LAWNS

The lawn is sometimes mown for the first time of the year in this month. The kitchen garden walks are gravelled.

FIELDS

There is still more planting and pleaching of the hedges to be done in the fields, and palings and fences to mend.

Hay is cut and brought home and hayseed sown by the pool in Bank field.

Manure is put on the fields. The ice house is filled.

MAINTENANCE

Repairs and maintenance this month include the making of ladders, a new chicken pen, re-glazing the hothouse, making more drains, repairing steps on the terrace, making and mending fences and mending the entrance gate piers.

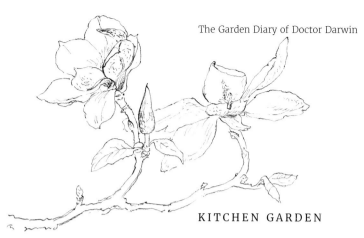

KITCHEN GARDEN

A new brick melon frame is made here, a job that takes almost the whole of February 1844 to complete.

Mint, angelica and thyme are planted.

The early seakale from forcing indoors is now ready to eat. More potatoes and rhubarb are being forced in the frame and the stove-house, where capsicums, mustard and cress and tomatoes are sown.

Outside sowings include parsley, lettuces, radishes, cauliflowers, turnips and more peas, beans, carrots and celery.

The asparagus and strawberry beds are manured.

New box hedging is planted.

FIELD GARDEN

Preparing the ground for carrots.

WEATHER

Bitter east winds, frost, snow, rain, thaws and more floods. In 1852 they have the highest flood on the Severn for sixteen years. (February 2020 will long be remembered for the floods there, the worst ever in England.) In 1855 there is frost for five weeks at Shrewsbury; the Severn freezes over and the pumps become short of water. The temperatures that year sink to 5° F (–15° C) and rise to no more than 28° F (–2° C). Bonfires in the kitchen garden provide respite for the gardeners.

SPECIAL EVENTS

On 10 February 1840, a 'Holy day rejoicing for the Marriage of the Queen' is declared. Since holidays, apart from Christmas and Easter, are rarely recorded in the Diary, this must have been a welcome event for the gardeners and servants.

March

WORK UNDER GLASS (INDOORS)

The days are noticeably becoming longer, spring is on the way and although the indoor work of potting and making cuttings still has to be done, there is less excitement in the greenhouse, with only rhododendron and peony flowers remarked upon.

There is an unusually early crop of French beans from the hothouse in 1839. These are sent to Susan's sister, Caroline (married to Josiah Wedgwood III and living at Fenton), a few months after she has lost her first baby.

There is not much of note in the plant stove-house, except for a near miss with the stephanotis in 1857, due to 'neglect of a fire at night'.

FLOWER BEDS, TREES AND SHRUBBERIES (OUTDOORS)

Work, especially in the flower garden, west border and terrace border, is on the increase. Dahlias are sown from seed, along with sweet peas, American groundsel, mignonettes, *Phlox drummondii* and dwarf larkspur.

Cuttings are made of geraniums, clematis, salvias, verbena, chrysanthemums, the coral tree and willows.

Calceolarias, cinerarias, gladioli, achimenes, verbenas, petunias and dahlias are potted.

Seedlings and young plants of ranunculus, carnations and pinks, stocks, hollyhocks, fraxinella, cobeas, tuberoses and *Arundo donax* are planted; roses are planted and laid and yuccas untied.

The Yeulan magnolias are in flower.

Hedging still has to be done, this time with the additional clipping of holly, yew and laurel hedges as well as the box edging in the flower garden and the kitchen garden and 'berberis by the gate'.

FRUIT

Among the fruit trees the first blossoms appear on the peaches, apricots, nectarines, plums and greengages. As in the month before, boards and cedar boughs are used to protect the blossom from frost; in 1852 pea-rods do the job, and in 1856 and 1857, 'Shaw's tiffany' (a light cotton fabric) is used. A beehive is moved into the garden.

The work of pruning and nailing the wall fruit trees is even more relentless than before. As the kitchen garden walls alone provided over 1,000 ft for wall fruit (both sides of the north and west walls being taken into consideration), and as on average wall fruit trees are planted at 15-ft intervals, there would have been about sixty-five trees to be nailed on those walls, without including the wall fruit trees on the coach house, in the yard, on Abberley's house and the mansion itself.

Raspberries are manured and tied.

WALKS AND LAWNS

The lawns are sometimes mown for the first time in this month. Gravel for the walks is brought by boat.

Winter floods cause slippages on the bank, so that its walks need constant repairs.

FIELDS

Fences, palings and posts and rails in the fields are 'put up' or mended. The fields are bush-harrowed, manured and rolled; ruts filled with turfs. Field and road hedges of holly, laurel and yew are cut.

MAINTENANCE

Repairing slippages on the bank walk with piles engages an extra workforce of six men in 1852, with four loads of gravel brought by boat for the path.

Ladders and a summerhouse are repaired.

KITCHEN GARDEN

The first forced rhubarb is gathered for a tart. Other 'firsts' include seakale, spinach and a green salad. The first spears of asparagus are coming through.

Melon seeds are sown in the big brick frame.

Vegetable seed sowing continues; strawberries, shallots, cabbage, beans, fennel and potatoes are planted, plus red and white beets, Brussels sprouts, broccoli, endive, parsnips, asparagus, kale, basil, marjoram, and kohl-rabi for the cows.

Peas are rodded, with pea rods 'from Berwick' just up the river.

FIELD GARDEN

Trenched and manured. Dutch clover is sown, mangels and potatoes are planted there.

WEATHER

This can still bring frosts, snowstorms and bitter, dry, cold east winds. The thermometer's coldest readings, though, are better than the previous month's; only 19 or 20° F (–6 or –7° C). The days are either dismal and wet or bright and sunny.

SPECIAL EVENTS

Easter falls late in March in several years. In 1857 there is a thunderstorm, 'Uncommon in March'.

An even more uncommon event is an eclipse of the sun, which happens between midday and 1.00pm on 15 March 1858. This is described by the Astronomer Royal as 'the most remarkable eclipse of the Sun that will be visible in this country during the present century'. The nearest place to Shrewsbury where it is to be seen at its best is Blisworth, just south of Northampton. Elsewhere, cloudy skies disappoint potential viewers.

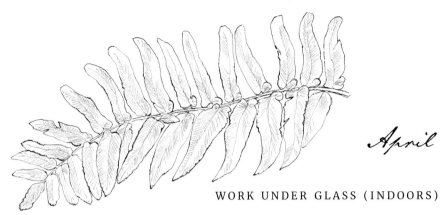

April

WORK UNDER GLASS (INDOORS)

The warmer weather allows for the total removal of plants from the greenhouse to the hothouse or frame and vice versa, so that, in turn, those glasshouses can be cleaned and, where necessary, painted. The mansion is also painted inside and out.

The aloes are taken out of their shed behind the hothouse and the outdoor yuccas are untied.

FLOWER BEDS, TREES AND SHRUBBERIES (OUTDOORS)

On the ornamental borders and in the Flower Garden there is an intensification of seed-sowing, potting, the dividing of clumps, the moving of shrubs and planting-out of the previous month's cuttings and young plants, accompanied by raking and 'cleaning' (weeding).

Hollyhocks are ordered from Paul & Son in Cheshunt, in 1854, and gloxinias from Carters in London, in 1858. Wynne the gardener goes to Acton Scott for plants in 1859. Ferns are planted on the terrace wall.

The laurel and holly hedges in the garden receive their annual pruning and clipping, as do the yews and box edging.

FRUIT

The previous month's apricot, almond, peach, cherry, quince, crab apple, plum and pear trees are flowering, but frosts in 1856 and 1859 damage the blossoms and fruitlets on peach and apricot trees, and also in 1856 a 'great blight' affects the wall fruit.

Grafting is carried out on pear and apple trees, and disbudding on peach trees.

The nailing of fruit trees is almost finished, the fig trees being the last to be done. The later vines are brought in to the 'second house' and tied up.

Strawberries are in flower.

WALKS AND LAWNS

The lawns are now mown on a weekly basis. The gravelling of walks in kitchen garden continues and box edging is clipped.

Walks on the bank need repairs.

FIELDS

More pruning and clipping is done to the hedges in the fields. The pastures continue to be bush-harrowed and rolled.

MAINTENANCE

Ice is taken from the ice house for the first time. The mansion is painted inside and out and ivy on it is cut.

A hovel is thatched.

The fence and hedge are mended at the infant school.

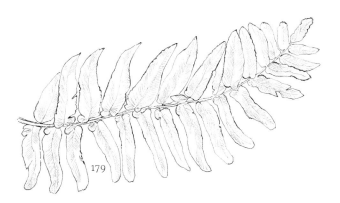

KITCHEN GARDEN

The first new, forced potatoes and cucumbers are served at dinner parties, as are the first rhubarb (in tarts) and asparagus. On 11 April 1851, the first asparagus is cut for Susan, as she is ill with influenza. At a dinner party on 22 April 1856, seventy heads of asparagus are served, as well as new potatoes. Seakale is in regular supply.

The seeds of more vegetables are sown (couve tronchuda, mangelwurzel, dwarf beans, scarlet beans, salsify, more cabbages, peas and beans) and seedlings planted out.

The asparagus beds are given an application of salt.

Peas are rodded, melons potted. Peas and beans are in flower.

Manure from the 'Black Hole' is put on the kitchen garden beds.

FIELD GARDEN

More potatoes, mangels, carrots and parsnips are planted.

WEATHER

As so often in April, it is tricky; mostly mild and showery, or very cold, with snow, frost and wet, but there are also breaks of very dry, beautiful weather.

The potatoes are cut by a hard frost in 1848, when the thermometer hits 28° F (–2° C) and yet on Easter Sunday 1862, the temperature is 64° F (16° C), and on 7 April 1859 it reaches 74° F (25° C).

SPECIAL EVENTS

The 'Fast Day for the War' noted by Susan on 26 April 1854 is the only reference in the Diary to the Crimean War, into which Britain and France have just entered. The war, begun in October 1853, ends in February 1856.

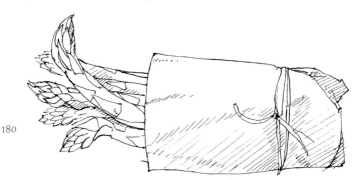

May

WORK UNDER GLASS (INDOORS)

Where the cleaning and painting of the greenhouse and hothouse needs doing, that is repeated, with special attention to cleaning the windows.

Many of the larger plants are now taken outside, including orange trees, peonies, magnolia and tree rhododendrons.

Of the plants left in the greenhouse, the calceolarias, Cape lily, tender rhododendron and andromeda are in flower.

A purple edulis passionflower is planted in the hothouse tan bed.

FLOWER BEDS, TREES AND SHRUBBERIES (OUTDOORS)

The first roses are flowering, as well as rhododendrons, cheiranthus, azaleas and a clematis by the front door.

The gardeners are busy bedding out the flower borders, with dahlias, *Cobea scandens*, penstemons, salvias, verbenas, carnations, gladioli, stocks, geraniums, mignonettes, cheiranthus and petunias.

Sweet peas and nemophila are sown.

The winter covers are removed from the myrtle tree.

Lime is put on the cypripedium in the flower garden.

FRUIT

The wall fruit trees are smoked to rid them of bugs, and the infant fruits disbudded (thinned) on the peach, apricot and nectarine trees, green apricots being particularly favoured for tarts. In 1856, some green apricots are sent to Susan's sister, Marianne Parker, who has recently been widowed. The medlar is flowering.

The thinning of grapes begins in the vinery. This is an even more finicky job than tree-nailing; a number of infant grapes are snipped with scissors from the newly forming bunch in order to allow the remaining fruit to become larger and the bunch to form an elegant shape. The first crop of grapes comes not from the vinery but from the stove-house in the kitchen garden.

The gooseberries are thinned and the first pickings are made into tarts.

The strawberries are flowering. There is a first swarm of bees.

WALKS AND LAWNS

Walks on the bank still need repairs. Gravel is taken out of the river.

Mowing of all lawns is now a weekly occurrence.

FIELDS

Hayseed is sown. Last year's hay is trussed and taken to the stable loft.

Thorns and stones are removed from the Bank Field.

MAINTENANCE

The infant school palings are painted with coal tar.

Fences in the fields are repaired.

KITCHEN GARDEN

A hot-bed is made in the frame for melons and cucumbers.

Lime is put on the beds. Guano water is given to the melons and asparagus, and a solution of nitrate of soda is put on the carrot and asparagus beds.

In 1853 asparagus is sent to London (i.e. to Susan's brother, Erasmus) three times, and from May 1854 a hamper of vegetables is sent to town every week.

The sowing of vegetable seeds continues (vegetable marrow, more peas, beans, carrots, spinach, cabbage), potatoes are earthed up, tomatoes are planted out, the first flowers are showing on the peas, with more rods coming down the river, again from Berwick.

Cauliflowers, celery, dwarf beans, artichokes, tomatoes, lettuces, scarlet beans and broccoli are transplanted.

The first rhubarb is ready.

Lavender seeds are sown in a bed for Susan, angelica is gathered, mint, tarragon, thyme and horehound beds are made, onions are watered.

FIELD GARDEN

More potatoes are planted, as well as dwarf beans, turnips, mangels and Jerusalem artichokes.

WEATHER

May brings the expected, though occasional 'very fine hot weather'; it brings strong east winds and rain too, with snow, frost and hail ruining the scarlet beans in 1850.

SPECIAL EVENTS

Over the years, Susan's visits to London and Down House become more frequent this month and, although she does not appear to have visited it herself, she notes, on 1 May 1862, 'Exhibition opens'. This is the Great London Exposition, a follow-up of the Great Exhibition of 1851. It is held not in the Crystal Palace, which had been dismantled and removed in 1852, but on the site of the present Natural History and Science Museums.

June

WORK UNDER GLASS (INDOORS)

There are still references to cleaning the greenhouse and hothouse, which happens at various times and frequencies during a year. In June and October 1843 the water-pipes in the hothouse are altered.

This month the hothouse is largely used for potting plants. Some of the more tender plants are moved to the stoves, but the Diary's entries are now much more concentrated on outdoor work.

FLOWER BEDS, TREES AND SHRUBBERIES (OUTDOORS)

The planting out of dahlias, verbenas, fuchsias, lobelias and geraniums, etc., continues in the flower garden; carnations and hollyhocks are tied up, withies 'like a balloon' are put round heaths and penstemon and, in 1860, ornamental tubs covered with bark are set out in the flower garden.

Pinks are in flower and gloxinias are 'in beautiful bloom'.

Bees swarm.

FRUIT

The mulberry tree is in leaf, a sure sign of summer. Citrus trees are repotted and put out of doors. The disbudding of peach trees continues.

The first cherries, strawberries and raspberries are gathered. Green currants are made into tarts and gooseberries bottled. There is a glut of strawberries in 1858, when 71 quarts of strawberries are sold 'at 4d pr qt.'

The nailing of fig and peach trees is still practised; this time the intention is to prune superfluous spring growth and to tie in new shoots. In the vinery/hothouse grape thinning continues, with a vegetable marrow, lettuces, celery and stocks planted on the border outside.

WALKS AND LAWNS

The gravel walks are rolled. Mowing is constant.

FIELDS

Haymaking begins towards the end of the month, with much of the workforce doing it.

MAINTENANCE

In 1842 a new walk is made to the flower garden, with steps.

In 1844 the kitchen garden pump is taken up and presumably renewed.

A well and a drain are made by the ice house in 1849.

Benches are put up at the infant school in 1855.

KITCHEN GARDEN

Activities switch between the harvesting of early summer crops such as peas, globe artichokes, green currants for tarts and gooseberries for tarts and bottling, and the sowing and planting-out of autumn and winter crops such as celery, turnips and cabbage.

Herbs (sage, thyme, a new kind of mint and basil) are planted in the herb garden.

The first peas, new potatoes, globe artichokes, rhubarb and 'garden beans' are served 'for the family' with, in 1840, the first 'cabbage for the kitchen'.

The last of the asparagus is cut. (The total number of asparagus spears cut in 1850 is 3,145.)

There are more sowings of peas and lettuces.

FIELD GARDEN

The first potatoes for the family are dug from the field garden. Others are earthed up.

WEATHER

It has its share of thunderstorms, wet days (some of them very wet), and cool and windy days, but there many references to its being very hot, or sultry, even 'deadly hot', with the temperature reaching 86°F (30° C) in the shade on 26 June 1856.

SPECIAL EVENTS

Susan's occasional visits to London continue, but she notes very little that is unrelated to her garden, her fields and her livestock, other than being 'bit by Snap' (a well-named dog) on 16 June 1861.

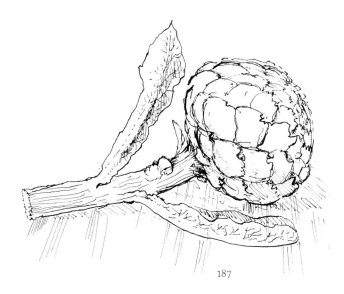

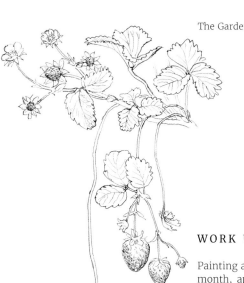

July

WORK UNDER GLASS (INDOORS)

Painting and glazing the greenhouse is the only indoor activity recorded this month, apart from two entries: one, in 1852, reads 'Lily rubra in flower'; the other, in 1855, notes 'Stephanotus in flower beautifully'. The stoves are barely mentioned, apart from an entry in 1841, when the first guava is picked.

FLOWER BEDS, TREES AND SHRUBBERIES (OUTDOORS)

In the borders and flower garden more flowers are planted out. The yuccas, roses and cistus are flowering, and the first sweet peas appear.

Pipings (cuttings) are made of pinks, salvia, gaillardia and geraniums.

Cacti and strelitzia are divided, roses are laid (layered) and budded (a form of grafting).

FRUIT

Budding is also carried out on some fruit trees, citrus trees continue to be put out of doors, the morello, Black Eagle and Florence cherries are ripe, as are summer pears, apricots, greengages and 'Lammas plums' (an early plum, Lammas day being 1 August).

The first *Passiflora edulis* fruit is gathered in the hothouse which, in its guise as a vinery, is busy, with early varieties of grapes to be gathered in the first house, and the thinning of later varieties to be done in the second house.

The first cherries are served.

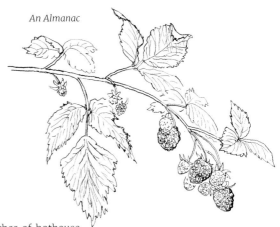

The vine on the front of the mansion is pruned. First bunches of hothouse grapes are served for dinner.

600 green walnuts are gathered for pickling in two days from one tree, in 1841.

Blackcurrants, gooseberries, raspberries, strawberries and rhubarb are preserved. 20 quarts of strawberries are sold in 1858.

Summer pruning is completed.

WALKS AND LAWNS

Walks are still being gravelled.

Lawn-mowing continues with scythes until 17 July 1857, when Susan buys a mowing machine.

FIELDS

It is the height of hay-making time, and the annual infant school tea party takes place as soon as the hay has been carried in. Haystacks are made and thatched.

Manure is spread after mowing.

MAINTENANCE

Wood from the railway is sawn to cover a tank.

The 'wheelbarrow place' is cleaned out and dead laurels cut down.

KITCHEN GARDEN

Kale seeds are pickled. Artichokes and herbs are gathered for drying. Tarragon is added to vinegar.

Two of Abberley's beehives are put in the kitchen garden; bees still swarm.

In the frame the first melons and cucumbers are cut. Dwarf beans are preserved. Cabbages are sold. Celery trenches are planted.

Tomatoes, Brussels sprouts, potatoes, cabbages and cauliflowers are planted out; lettuces, peas, radishes, spinach, turnips, parsley, endive, salsify and broccoli are sown.

The first French beans, peas, young potatoes, artichokes, turnips and carrots are served at dinner. The last asparagus is cut.

FIELD GARDEN

The first new potatoes are served for the family. Turnips and spinach are sown. Broccoli and mangels are planted.

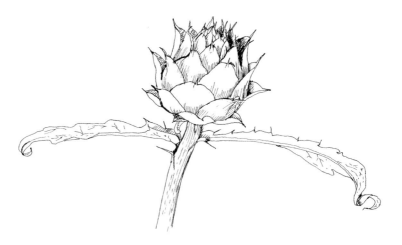

WEATHER

This month it reaches its full summer heat, with temperatures frequently recorded between 70 and 80° F (21 to 26° C). On 12 July 1859, Susan is in London, where the thermometer reads 90° F (32° C).

On St Swithun's Day (15 July), if it rains, tradition has it that it will continue to do so for forty days. Susan notes that date only once, in order to say that it is dry. It does rain quite frequently, however, on other days.

SPECIAL EVENTS

There are none of any note this month, apart from the purchase of a mowing machine in 1857 and the creation of the letter 'D' on the lawn with nitrate of soda during a visit from Charles in 1840 (see Chapter Three).

August

WORK UNDER GLASS (INDOORS)

This is another month for cleaning and painting the greenhouse, hothouse and stoves.

Camellias are brought into the greenhouse, and roses into the hothouse, in order to flower in the winter months. Some lilies are flowering in the greenhouse now, and the waterlily is flowering in the hothouse.

Plants such as verbenas, chrysanthemums, salvias, violets, cinerarias and primulas are potted for the greenhouse.

FLOWER BEDS, TREES AND SHRUBBERIES (OUTDOORS)

In the shrubberies, flower garden and borders, new shrubs such as laurels, yews, jasmines, magnolias, peonies, clematis, yuccas, rhododendrons and roses are planted and transplanted, and old ones moved.

This is also a time for laying and making more cuttings, particularly of carnations, pinks, fuchsias and geraniums, as well as saving seed from geraniums, giant rhubarb and blue salvias.

Plants in flower which are particularly noted are *Hibiscus syriacus*, lilies, cerastium and 'a beautiful Achimenus on the Table at Dinner'.

Yews, rhododendrons and ferns are planted on the bank.

FRUIT

The nailing of peach trees and summer pruning continue.

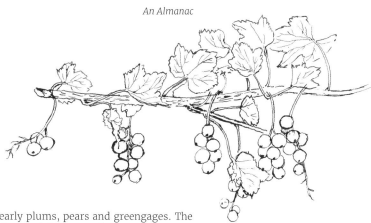

Morello cherries are ripe, as well as early plums, pears and greengages. The first apples, apricots, peaches, nectarines and figs are picked.

The raspberry canes are cut down but more currants, gooseberries and walnuts are gathered.

Orange trees are put into new tubs, the large orange tree yielding nearly ninety oranges in 1842.

There are good crops of Hamburg, Lombardy and Champion grapes.

The last strawberries are gathered and their runners cut for planting.

WALKS AND LAWNS

In 1851 the terrace walk is widened by 7 in.

Grass walks are mown and cleaned, or 'scuffled'.

FIELDS

Apart from a second mowing of hay in 1854, haymaking being finished, the stacks are made, thatched and fenced.

Thistles are cut. The pond in Bank Field is cleaned.

MAINTENANCE

The infant school is painted and whitewashed.

Field fences are mended and gates painted.

The stove in the kitchen garden is 'reduced', cleaned and given shelves.

Timber is sawn for boxes in the greenhouse.

KITCHEN GARDEN

The summer harvest is in full swing. Artichokes and mint are dried; rhubarb is gathered for vinegar; radishes, tomatoes, cabbages and beans are pickled; onions are taken up. The first melons and tomatoes are ripe and the first celery, scarlet beans, salsify and marrows eaten.

200 (powdered) bones are strewn on the asparagus beds, and more pigsty manure.

The sowing and planting out of winter vegetables continues. There are sowings of winter broccoli, cabbage (all sorts), turnips, cauliflower, lettuces, onions, spinach, early peas, purple kale, curly endive, greens, radishes; lettuces, Brussels sprouts, kale, cabbage, cauliflower, parsley, thyme and sage are planted out.

FIELD GARDEN

Cabbages are sown and planted, spinach and turnips are sown. Beet and lettuce are planted.

WEATHER

It being harvest time, the weather stays fine for most of the Augusts in the Diary, but there are windy days when apples are blown off the trees, and there are thunderstorms which 'cool the weather'.

SPECIAL EVENTS

On 3 August 1856, Susan writes 'Sunday. Intensely hot (ther. 88 in shade at Doncaster)'. This is her birthday, but I can find no reference to her having been in Doncaster, so this must have been an item in the newspaper.

In 1848 she has a ripe apricot to celebrate her birthday, but the day goes unremarked in other years, except for 1841, when she is 'ill with ague'.

In 1851, Abberley goes to London for a week in August to see the Great Exhibition, open from 1 May until 15 October. Susan is in London in July, so she has presumably seen it then.

It is on her return from another visit to London six years later, on 18 August 1857, that she finds that 'poor Abberly died this day'.

September

WORK UNDER GLASS (INDOORS)

As a hint that autumn is approaching, the citrus trees and 'greenhouse plants' are put in the greenhouse and rhododendrons are taken into the hothouse, where tomatoes and plums have been gathered and put to ripen.

Sweet olea (olive) and stephanotis go into the plant stove-house and tan beds are made in both the hothouse and the stoves for pots containing 'passion trees'.

FLOWER BEDS, TREES AND SHRUBBERIES (OUTDOORS)

This is the time of year for dividing, potting, taking up and transplanting plants, renewing beds and borders, gathering seed and ordering bulbs for spring flowering. George Wynne, the new gardener, is sent to London in September 1859 to buy plants.

The *Magnolia grandiflora* is flowering against the house. Other plants flowering in the beds and borders are the *Clematis flammula*, strelitzias and neriums (oleanders).

Hollyhocks, cinerarias, wallflowers and ferns are planted and yet more cuttings made of geraniums, fuchsias, verbenas, honeysuckle and calceolaria.

FRUIT

Entries in the Diary referring to the fruit harvest exceed all others. Every variety of plum is ripe; apricots, peaches, nectarines, grapes and figs are gathered, as well as apples, pears and quinces.

Unripe fruit is made into tarts or vinegar or put indoors to ripen.

In 1842 48 baking pears weighing a total of 21 lbs break the branch of the tree they are growing on.

Limes, nuts, berberries (three pints) and a maracuja are gathered. Numerous baskets of fruit are given away by Susan to family, neighbours and friends.

Grapes are to be had 'every day for dessert'.

The trees continue to be pruned.

Old strawberry plants are removed and new ones planted.

WALKS AND LAWNS

Moss is removed from the walks. The usual cleaning and occasional alterations continue.

FIELDS

The first cuts are made into this year's haystacks.

Field hedges are 'brushed' and repaired.

MAINTENANCE

Steps are made by the ice house in 1846, and drains are dug at various places in the garden in 1852 and 1855.

KITCHEN GARDEN

Winter brassicas are planted out, celery earthed up, asparagus cut down and winter salads sown. Green tomatoes, red cabbage and cayenne pods are gathered for pickles and syrup.

Herbs are dried, onions are strung up and potatoes are put under cover in the apple room. Carrots, the first Jerusalem artichokes, parsnips and the last peas are harvested. Dwarf beans are gathered for seed.

197

Spring vegetables such as cauliflower, spinach and lettuces are sown. Kohl-rabi, onions, winter cabbage, broccoli, hardy green lettuces and endive are planted out.

Celery, couve tronchuda and salsify are served at dinner for the first time and beetroot 'for boiled salad'.

FIELD GARDEN

Turnips, potatoes and carrots (including a white variety) are dug up.

WEATHER

This month brings mostly 'very fine autumnal weather', but it is becoming cooler, with occasional 'rather frosty nights'. It also rains quite often, with stormy winds blowing apples down 'in quantities' in 1853.

SPECIAL EVENTS

A new boat is bought for £4 in 1846 and, following a year with no head gardener after the death of Abberley, George Wynne is engaged in September 1858, 'at £60 a yr & house rent free', to start work on 1 October.

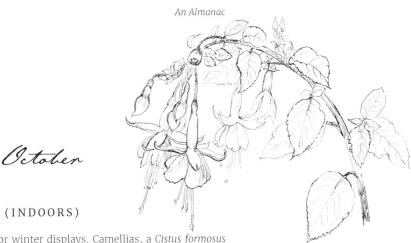

October

WORK UNDER GLASS (INDOORS)

The greenhouse is prepared for winter displays. Camellias, a *Cistus formosus* (*Helianthemum formosum*), tree rhododendrons, chrysanthemums, a sollia, the shaddocks and various flowering plants are brought in after the house has been cleaned.

Cacti, azaleas, eparis, *Chelone barbata*, *Dylitris spectabilis* and cuttings of anagallis, passionflowers and tender plants are put here to force.

Cinerarias, geraniums, hyacinths and other plants are potted in the stove-house.

FLOWER BEDS, TREES AND SHRUBBERIES (OUTDOORS)

On the terrace, in the flower borders and flower garden, geraniums, dahlias, verbenas, azaleas and marvels of Peru are lifted along with gladiolus roots, to be kept in sand. Aloes and blue salvias are taken into the shed behind the hothouse for winter protection.

Fuchsias are cut down. Sweet pea seeds are gathered.

Fraxinellas, syringas, Brompton stocks, ferns, pansies, Rose de Meaux and pinks are planted.

The flower garden is cleaned and cleared; its roses pruned.

FRUIT

This is the penultimate month for the harvesting of fruit, which is still in full swing – mainly apples, pears and quinces, but there are still late plums

(Coe's golden drops), walnuts and the first medlars.

The first Cannon Hall and muscat grapes are gathered.

Countless baskets of fruit are again sent out to friends, family and neighbours. In 1856 one small basket of Astontown pears goes 'to the Rugby boys', namely two schoolboys, William Darwin (Charles's eldest son), aged twelve, and his cousin Ernest Hensleigh Wedgwood, aged thirteen.

WALKS AND LAWNS

The lawns are mown for the last time.

A new walk is made into the flower garden in 1858.

FIELDS

The haystack is first cut (1841).

Hedges cut.

MAINTENANCE

The hothouse has its pipes altered in 1843. It then has a new boiler in 1850, is cleaned and tidied in 1852 and, in 1857, is painted, one half at a time.

A shed is made in the kitchen garden for carrots and mangelwurzel (1855) and a drain is dug by the front door of the mansion.

Timber is sawn for a fence. 'Mud for manure' is taken from the pond in Bank Field.

In 1851 the infant school playground is 'put right' and a drain, a fence and steps are made there.

KITCHEN GARDEN

Some tomatoes are ripe, but the green ones are sent, with red cabbage, to the kitchen for pickles.

A mushroom bed is made in 1838 and 1839, but not thereafter.

Vegetables such as broccoli, cauliflower, cabbage, endive and hardy lettuce are planted for winter.

Asparagus ferns are cut down, celery earthed up; carrots (red and white), parsnips, red beetroot are harvested, and onions 'strung up'.

The first couve tronchuda, salsify, celery and beet in salad are served at dinner.

Dwarf beans are gathered for seed; carrots are stacked; there is more planting of lettuces, cauliflowers, onions, strawberries and endive.

FIELD GARDEN

Potatoes (100 bushels in 1839), carrots, red beet and parsnips are harvested.

WEATHER

It is turning cooler, with rain, winds and the first frosty nights.

SPECIAL EVENTS

Three small dramas are recorded in the Diary for October. The first, from the Doctor, on 1 October 1843, reads: 'Last night somebody robbed the garden.' However, no further references to this are made.

The second, for 14 October 1852, is from Susan: 'The Queen passed thru' Shrewsbury! Abberly at Railway.' The Queen and Prince Albert were on their way by train to Windsor from Balmoral. Although the royal visit lasted no more than a few minutes, bands played and the Queen attended a loyal address in a specially decorated refreshment room. 1,200–1,300 tickets had to be obtained for admission to galleried seats at the station. The numbers thronging the platforms and lines beyond were estimated at 20,000.

The third drama is a sighting, by Susan, on 6 October 1858, of 'the Comet & Arcturus in it quite red!' This was Donati's Comet, one of the brightest comets of the nineteenth century, with an enormous tail. The star Arcturus appeared beside the comet's nucleus on that precise date.

PART THREE

———

A Catalogue of Plants
named in the Diary

Flowers and Shrubs named in the Garden Diary

Incorporating named species and varieties where they are given
(and as spelled by the diarists), times of gathering and positions where
known.

A: ROSES

B: FLOWERS AND SHRUBS IN THE FLOWER GARDEN

C: PLANTS DISPLAYED IN THE GREENHOUSE
(CONSERVATORY)

D: PLANTS GROWN IN THE HOTHOUSE, STOVE-
HOUSES AND VINERY

E: SUPPLEMENTARY LISTS OF FLOWERS AND
SHRUBS FOUND ELSEWHERE IN THE DIARY

A: ROSES

At least forty-four roses are mentioned by name in the Darwins' Garden Diary. A list of fourteen roses on a page dated 1 August 1851 appears on the first page and precedes the Diary proper. The first eight are from 'Mr Guise', an unidentified grower. The next six are from Paul & Son, well-known growers in Cheshunt, originally established in 1806. They are laid out as follows:

'List of Roses Standard
8 fr. Mr Guise
The King – William Jesse – Dr Mark – Charles Duval – Marquise de
Beauvelle – La Sylphide – Minerva (Light) – Louis Buonaparte
King of Battles – Baron Prevôt
Felicité – Mrs Elliott – Persian Yellow – Bourbon Queen – Souvenir de
Malmaison, Triomphe de Tyre –
1856 6 Roses fr. Paul. 1 William Griffith. 2 Augusta Mee. 3 Paul Ricaut. 4
Josephine Robert. 5 Coupe de Hebe. 6 Jules Margottin'

The Diary shows that the '6 roses from Paul' were planted on 25 November and 11 December 1856; Paul also provides fifteen roses (unspecified) in 1853 and twenty-two dwarf standards in 1857. An earlier Diary entry, for 7 October 1849, reads '5 new roses planted. Persian Yellow – Triomphe De Tyre – Giant of Battles – Baron Prevôt – Bourbon Queen – Souvenir de Malmaison.'

Another entry, For 23 November 1855, reads 'Planted 6 roses fr Hinston – Mde Laffay. Crested Moss. Armosa. Boursault Amadis' (the sixth rose is not named). 'Hinston' is possibly a misspelling of 'Hinton', which is a village five miles southwest of Shrewsbury.

The list below is arranged and described according to the classifications in Adam Paul & Sons' *Rose Catalogue* for 1856–7, with occasional remarks from William Paul's *The Rose Garden* (1848). As both the Doctor's and Susan's versions of their roses' names are sometimes erratic, the descriptions begin with the botanical names; alternative names or spellings are in brackets, followed by entries from the Diary, then further information from both Paul sources.

GALLICA ROSES

(Rosa gallica) (Hybrid Bourbons and China Bourbons)

R. Armosa (R. Hermosa): one of the '6 roses from Hinston' planted 23 November 1855. Fl. Cup-shaped, deep pink, abundant bloomer, grey-green leaves. Bourbon.

R. indica: France 1840. Good for massing, front of border; also grown as a standard or in a pot.

R. 'Bourbon Queen': listed as standard, front of Diary, 1851, and one of '5 new roses planted', 7 October 1849. (Also known as Queen of the Bourbons, Reine des Îles and Souvenir de la Princesse de Lamballe.) Listed in Paul's Catalogue for 1841 as 'Queen of Reine des Isles Bourbon', but not included after that date. Fl. Described by Peter Beales as 'semi-double, rose pink, large and cupped. Highly scented'.[1]

R. 'Charles Duval': listed as one of eight standards from Mr Guise, front of Diary, 1 August 1851. Fl. Deep pink, large and full-cupped. Good for growing as pot or pillar, also a handsome tree. Raised at Montmorency.

R. 'Coupe d'Hebe' (Coupe Hébé): listed as one of six standards from Paul, 1856, front of Diary, planted 11 December 1856. Fl. Large and very double, rich deep pink, exquisite in colour, a first-rate show rose. Bourbon hybrid, Laffay, France, 1840. Suitable for growing in pots or as pillar.

R. *fulgens*: 'planted 3 climbing roses fulgens &c', 1 December 1857. Fl. Brilliant crimson, glowing, splendid medium size, full-cupped, fine pillar or standard. Hybrid Chinese.

R. 'Gloire de Rosamane' (Gloire de Rosomène): 'rose tree fr. Eaton, Gloire de Rosamane, planted in West Border', 20 May 1840. Fl. Crimson scarlet, velvety, sometimes shaded with purple and striped white, large double cup. Fine pole rose.

R. 'La Sylphide': listed as one of eight standards from Mr Guise, front of Diary, 1 August 1851. Fl. Rosy blush, fine form, full, cupped. A neat and pretty rose. William Paul also lists this rose under tea-scented.

R. 'Souvenir de (la) Malmaison': listed as standard, front of Diary, 1851. Fl. Flesh-colour, margin almost white, very large and full, compact. A magnificent rose, introduced 1834 by M. Beluze of Lyons. Standard or pots.

HYBRID PERPETUALS

R. 'Augusta Mee' (Auguste Mee/mie): listed as one of six standards from Paul, front of Diary, 1856, planted 11 December 1856. Fl. Light pink, large and full. Very good for forcing and growing in pots.

R. 'Baron Prevôt' (Baronne Prévost): listed as standard, front of Diary, 1851, one of '5 new roses planted', 7 November 1849. Fl. Clear pale rose, glossy, very large and full, compact. A superb kind and one of the largest. Bred in France by Desprez of Yèbles, 1842.

R. 'Dr. Mark' (Docteur Marx): listed as one of eight standards from Mr Guise, front of Diary, 1 August 1851. Fl. Carmine, brilliant, superb, glowing very large and full cup. Introduced by Laffay, 1842.

R. 'Giant of Battles' (also known as Géant des Batailles): 'rose tree (Giant of Battles) planted by summer house', 2 October 1850. Fl. Deep brilliant crimson, shaded with purple velvet, large, very double. Suitable for forcing and growing in pots. Paul classed this rose as *R. indica* and links it with the Rosomènes.

R. 'Josephine Robert': listed as one of six standards from Paul, front of Diary, 1856, 'planted on West Border', 25 October 1856. Fl. Pink, large and full.

R. 'Jules Margottin': listed as one of six standards from Paul, front of Diary, 1856, 'planted on West Border', 25 October 1856. Fl. Bright cherry red, large and full, a superb rose.

R. 'Louis Buonaparte': listed as one of eight standards from Mr Guise, front of Diary, 1 August 1851. Fl. Deep rich vermilion, glowing, very large and full, cupped, very sweet (scented). Suitable for pots, pillars or poles.

R. 'Mde Laffay' (Madame Laffay): one of '6 roses from Hinston', planted 23 November 1855. Fl. Rich purplish rose, very sweet (scented). Too well known to need recommending. Suitable for growing in pots.

R. 'Minerva' (light): listed as one of eight standards from Mr Guise, 1 August 1851. Fl. Rosy pink margin, a lilac tint, large and full, compact, fine foliage and habit and very sweet (scent). William Paul described this rose as a Damask Perpetual.

R. 'Mrs Elliott' (Mrs Elliot): listed as standard, front of Diary, 1851. 'Rose (Mrs Elliott) planted by summer house', 12 September 1850. Fl. Purplish rose, very double, cupped. Laffay, 1840.

R. 'Paul Ricaut': 'planted on West Border', 25 October 1856. Listed as one of six standards from Paul, front of Diary, 1856. Fl. Bright rosy crimson, large and very full. Portemer, France, 1845.

R. 'William Griffith' (William Griffiths): listed as one of six standards from Paul, front of Diary, 1856, 'planted' 11 December 1856. Fl. Pale satin-like rose, large and full. France, 1850. For pots and forcing. (Named after the naturalist.)

R. 'William Jesse': listed as one of eight standards from Mr Guise, front of Diary, 1 August 1851. Fl. Crimson tinged with lilac, superb, very large and double. Laffay, France, 1838. Suitable as a climber, for forcing and for growing in pots.

ROSA INDICA

(original species)

R. 'Bengal': 'first flower open of Alpine rose', 19 June 1840.

BOURSAULTS:

R. Alpine

R. 'Boursault Amadis' (also known as Crimson Boursault): one of '6 roses from Hinston', planted 23 November 1855. Fl. Deep purplish crimson, large and semi-double, climbing, Laffay, France, 1829.

ALBAS: R. alba

R. 'Celestial': 'Pruning roses on west border – planted Celestial rose tree there', 13 August 1838. Fl. Exquisite blush, large and double.

ROSA CENTIFOLIA

(moss, Provence and/or cabbage)

R. 'Crested Moss': 'Double crested Moss rose tree planted in West Border', 12 December 1840, and listed as one of '6 roses from Hinston', planted 23 November 1855. (Also known as Cristata or 'Chapeau de Napoléon' because of the winged cockade of green moss, shaped like Napoleon's hat, around its calyx.) Fl. Bright rose, pale edges, often assuming a lilac tinge, full, globular. Flower buds beautifully crested, the crest sometimes extending to the leaves. First noticed growing on the walls of a convent near Berne.

R. 'Luxemburgh': 'Luxemburgh rose in front of G. House', 24 May 1845. Fl. Deep pink, cup large and full.

R. Rose de Meaux: 'Rose de meaux fr Overton for Caroline', 6 August 1858. (A favourite at The Mount, there are frequent references to this rose: making cuttings, layering and pegging down, potting for forcing and extensively used as edgings to the flower garden and kitchen garden beds.) Fl. Light rose, very small and full, a miniature Provence or Pompon rose.

R. White Provence (also known as Unique): 'White Provence roses from Maer Hall planted in West Border', 19 December 1843. Fl. Paper white, large and full, deeply cupped.

SCENTED TEA ROSES

R. 'Smith(s) yellow': 'Smith yellow rose tree potted. Came from Robert Phipps', 24 November 1842. Fl. Pale straw colour, large and full, globular. A fine forcing rose, seldom opens well outdoors. Noisette.

EVERGREENS

(R. sempervirens)

R. 'Félicité': 'planted climbing white rose (Felicité) by upper summer house', 17 December 1849. Listed as standard, front of Diary, 1851. Fl. Creamy white, beautiful, small and full, in graceful trusses drooping with their own weight. Climber.

AUSTRIAN BRIAR

(Rosa lutea)

R. 'Persian yellow': listed as standard, front of Diary, 1851. Fl. Large and full, globular, of the deepest yellow. Suitable for growing in pots. Introduced in 1837 by Sir Henry Willock.

UNIDENTIFIABLE

R. 'The King': listed as one of eight standards from Mr Guise, front of Diary, 1 August 1851. (This could be King of Roses, also known as Saudeur, described by William Paul as a *Rosa gallica* Chinese hybrid, 'fl. Blush, striped with lake centre, sometimes rosy, large and full, globular. Beautiful in dry seasons, at other times uncertain.').

R. 'King of Battles': listed as standard, front of Diary. 1851. 'Rose budding fr Mr Harding's King of Battles', 7 August 1850. Possibly mistakenly so-called, instead of 'Giant of Battles' (*q.v.*).

R. 'Marquise de Beauvelle': listed as one of eight standards from Mr Guise, front of Diary, 1 August 1851.

R. 'Paul Breant': 'manure on roses – Paul Breant', 2 July 1858. The nearest rose with this name is 'Madame Eugenie Bréon'. Nicholas Bréon was director of the Botanic Garden on the Île Bourbon and is credited with sending the seeds of the first Bourbon roses to France, but I can find no rose named 'Paul Bréon'.

R. 'Triomphe de Tyre': listed as a standard, front of Diary. 1851.

B: FLOWERS AND SHRUBS IN THE FLOWER GARDEN

The following list includes all species, varieties or descriptions (e.g. colour and size) of plants mentioned in the Diary as growing, planted or sown in the flower garden during the period that the Diary was kept. Plant names in bold and in single quotes are as given in the Diary. Details on their position or cultivation are based on Diary entries. The 'north bed' or 'north border' was also known as the upper, peony, bog or peat bed.

In the lists below, sp. and spp. refer to species and subspecies, respectively.

Ageratum: presumably the one used for bedding (*A. mexicanum*) as 'grown in a bed by themselves' after 1857.
Arbor vitae (*Thuya* sp.): (dwarf kind) six put in flower garden in 1863.
Azalea: species and varieties not given, but presumably the hardy 'Ghent' species, as grown outdoors. North bed.
Bocconia cordata (*Macleaya cordata*): the Tree Celandine or Plume Poppy, a

tall decorative subtropical plant grown 'at top of flower garden'.

Box (*Buxus sempervirens*): used as edging.

Calceolaria: species and varieties not given for flower garden. Grown from cuttings, planted out in summer.

Carnation (*Dianthus caryophyllus*): grown in a round wired bed; the only varieties named are 'scarlet' and 'clove'.

Chelone barbata (*Penstemon barbatus*): tall, tender, scarlet-flowered plant, taken in for winter. Also referred to as *penstemon*, see below.

Cineraria: not mentioned by Dr Darwin, but a great favourite with Susan. Planted out in spring and also used as a winter flowering display in the greenhouse.

Cistus: species and varieties mentioned are *C. formosus*, 'purple' and 'little yellow'. Gum cistus in north bed.

Crocus: planted round the rose bed, 1838.

Cypripedium: or Lady's Slipper. Species and varieties not given but hardy, as planted in the flower garden. North bed.

Dahlia: species and varieties not given. Raised from seeds and cuttings and taken up each autumn; planting of entire tubers not mentioned as the fashion then was to train only a single stem.[2] North bed.

'Escholtzia': grown from seed.

Everlasting Pea (*Lathyrus latifolius*): white.

Fraxinella: from Susan's sister, Marianne, at Overton.

'Fuschia' (*F. fulgens,* 'Queen of Hanover' and 'Prince of Wales'): grown from cuttings and planted out in the round bed.

Geraniums (*Pelargonium* spp.): unnamed varieties grown in the flower garden and plunged in the round (? octagon) bed with petunias (1855), as well as 'Frogmore Scarlet' and 'Tom Thumb'. One species mentioned is *P. compactum*; varieties mentioned and probably grown here as well as in other borders and the Conservatory are 'Nosegay Pink'; scarlet (large and dwarf); 'unique'; variegated.

Gentian, yellow: North bed.

Gladiolus (*G. cardinalis* x *gandavensis, gentian, psittacinus* (*G. dalenii*) and *floribunda* (*Chasmanthe floribunda*)): grown in large numbers, presumably in the flower garden, as no other position is mentioned other than 'by greenhouse'. Potted up in winter and early spring, planted out in April/May, taken up in autumn and kept in sand.

Hollyhock (*Alcea rosea*): not mentioned by the Doctor but grown in the flower garden every year by Susan between 1853 and 1859.

Iris ochroleuca: grown 'in Miss Darwin's iris bed' by the summer house in 1838 and in the flower garden in 1843.

Jonquils (*Narcissus* spp.): in flower garden and on terrace.

Linum: flax flower, species and variety mentioned are *L. monogynum* and 'yellow' (probably the same, as the flower of *L. monogynum* is yellow).

Lobelia: used as edging to flower beds.

Marvel of Peru (*Mirabilis jalapa*): treated as an annual, planted out in spring. Mentioned by Dr Darwin 1838–45, but not by Susan.

Nemophila: seeds sown in spring in the flower garden for summer display.

Oenothera: species and variety not named.

Paeony/peony: herbaceous 'poppy paeonies' (*Paeonia papaveraeflora*, a variety of *P. moutan*, the tree peony) and 'Siberian paeonies' (either *P. tenuifolia, P. albiflora* or *P. anomala*) were planted in the flower garden, north bed and north border by the laundry.

Pansy: *Viola tricolor* hybrids. Grown from cuttings.

Penstemon: 'withys put round Heath like a balloon and Penstemon'.

Petunia/'pertunia': grown from cuttings, planted in the round bed in flower garden.

Pinks (*Dianthus plumarius*): 'Mule', little red, pink, white, and 'Anne Boleyn' from Susan's sister Caroline at Leith Hill, Surrey.

Rhododendron: 'matted up' in the flower garden but killed by cold in the severe winter of 1853. Species and variety not named, but see list at end of section E.

Ribes: golden (*Ribes aureum*) and *R. sanguineum*. Grown from seed and offsets, north bed of flower garden.

Rocket: white (*Hesperis matronalis*).

Roses: red, yellow, *Rosa de Meaux* and 'Provence' (see section A). Cuttings in north bed.

Salvia: red, blue, *S. patens* and *S. gesneriiflora* propagated by seed and cuttings, planted out for summer flowering and taken into greenhouse for spring flowering.

Stock: Brompton, German (*Matthiola incana*) and Virginia (*Malcolmia maritima*) sown from seed.

Verbena: grown annually from cuttings. Scarlet and 'Victory' in their own beds fenced with wire.

Violet (*Viola odorata*): 'double' planted round wire bed in the flower garden.

Yucca (*Y. gloriosa*): tied up every winter to keep out the snow. Flowered in July and August. Mentioned continually in the diary from 1838–58, could therefore have become some 6-ft tall. *Y. aloifolia* also grown in the flower garden and tied up in winter.

C: PLANTS DISPLAYED IN THE GREENHOUSE (CONSERVATORY)

Achimenes: used as a table decoration by Susan, no varieties named.
Andromeda: hardy, but one 'with flowers like Lilies of the Valley' grown in greenhouse, 1862.
Azalea: six 'Indian' azaleas bought in 1854, for greenhouse, flowering early February. No varieties named but one described as 'white'.
Bignonia: white, pink: climbers, planted against the back wall. *B. 'jessaminoides'* flowered September.
Cactus: only mentioned by the Doctor, grown from seed, no species or varieties named, but the large *C. sulcatus* moved from greenhouse to hothouse.
Calceolaria: 'Prince of Orange': flowered May, June. Grown from cuttings.
Camellia 'Bourbon': no other varieties named apart from 'pink', 'red' and 'white'.

Chrysanthemum: no species or varieties named, flowered in greenhouse October, also planted outdoors

Cineraria: mentioned only by Susan. Flowered January and March, no species or varieties named except *C. maritima.* 275 plants transplanted in 1853.

Cistus: planted outdoors in spring but taken into the greenhouse in autumn. No species or varieties named apart from 'red', 'purple' and 'yellow', also a 'small Cistus formosus' later known as *Helianthemum formosum.*

Cobaea scandens (Cups and saucers): grown in greenhouse and outdoors.

Convolvulus bryony-leaved (*C. bryonifolius,* syn. *C. italicus*): half-hardy.

Coral tree (*ErythInia* sp.): flowered in August.

Cork trees (*Quercus suber*): put into greenhouse 1838, planted outside by kitchen garden door, 1841.

Epacris: grown only by Susan. No species or varieties named, flowered in February.

Geraniums (*Pelargonium* spp.): grown in pots and boxes in the greenhouse, and also outdoors. Varieties include Tom Thumb, 'Unique', 'Nosegay', Frogmore, 'scarlet', 'white' and 'variegated'.

Guavas: placed in greenhouse only when flowering, otherwise grown in hothouse and stove.

Hyacinth: forced for flowering in January and February.

Lilac 'Persian' (*Syringa dubia* syn. S. *chinensis*): trees forced in hothouse then brought into greenhouse in January to flower.

Lily: no varieties named other than 'rubra', 'alba', 'Cape lily' (*Crinum capense*) and 'Bella Donna' (*Amaryllis belladonna*). The 'Cape lily' flowered in May. The 'rubra' lily flowered in July and August, the 'alba' in August and the 'Bella Donna' in October.

Lime tree Bergamot (*Citrus x latifolia* syns. *C. limetta* and *C. bergamia*): grown from cuttings. Fruits in September.

Lobelia: grown in vases in the greenhouse, 1856.

Magnolia: 'purple' (probably *M. purpurea* syn. *M. obovata*), the only variety mentioned for the greenhouse. It is hardy, and put there in December, presumably to force its flowering.

Mandarin orange (*Citrus nobilis*): part of the Doctor's citrus collection in the greenhouse.

Orange trees (*Citrus aurantium*): raised in tubs in the greenhouse and hothouse. Put outdoors in summer, brought inside September, October. For varieties see Part 3:2 Citrus.

Peony: species mentioned are Moutan, Poppy, and Siberian (see section B). Both the Poppy and the Moutan are grown in pots and put in the greenhouse in the winter, to flower there in March. John Wedgwood gave the Doctor a 'Poppy peony tree' for the greenhouse.

Primula: 'white', 'lilac' and *P. sinensis are* grown in pots, to flower in February.

Rhododendron: *R. arboreum* [sic], scarlet (flowered late March). Also referred to as 'the tree rhododendron'.

Salvia gesneriflora [sic]: taken from the flower garden and potted for the greenhouse, 1856. Introduced 1840.

Shaddock (*Citrus maxima*): part of the Doctor's citrus collection. See Part 3:2.

'Sollea' (sollya): Australian bluebell creeper. Taken into the greenhouse for the winter of 1838.

Yucca aloifolia: Spanish Bayonet, the greenhouse species, also grown in the flower garden.

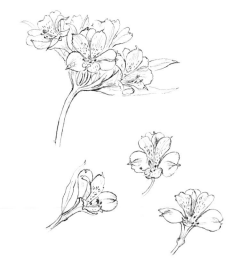

D: PLANTS GROWN IN THE HOTHOUSE, STOVE-HOUSES AND VINERY

Alstroemeria: no species or varieties named, potted in stove-house.
Anagallis: cuttings in hothouse.
Azalea: see above, put in hothouse to force.
Bergamot lime (*Citrus bergamia*): see Part 3:2, cuttings made in stove-house.
Brunsvigia: large brunsvigia put in stove.
Bulbs: various, forced in stove-house only.
Cactus: 'large' *Cactus sulcatus* put into stove and hothouse with others.
Calceolaria: cuttings in hothouse.
Camellia: for varieties see section C. Overwintered in stove-house and hothouse after flowering in greenhouse.

Cape 'jassmine' (*Gardenia florida*) (*G. jasminoides*): cut down in hothouse, January 1839.

Capsicum: grown from seed, stove.

Cauliflower: grown from seed, February, kitchen garden stove, and potted for later planting out.

Celery: grown from seed, January, hothouse and later planted out.

Chrysanthemum: put in hothouse, October, to force into flower.

Cineraria: potted in stove for forcing, October, November. Flowering in stoves, January.

Cucumbers: 'Manchester' cucumbers planted in kitchen garden stove, September, first cut in November. More seed sown and potted throughout winter. 'Four sorts' and 'Sion House' sowed January, 'Walkers improved' sown February, 'Long Spine', 'Southgate' and 'Manchester' in March. First of stove-grown cucumbers cut in April. Thereafter grown outdoors.

Cyrtanthus: flowered in hothouse, October.

'Dylitris' spectabilis: misspelling of Dilatris or possibly Dieleytra (dicentra). Put to force in October.

Erythrina (coral tree): put into hothouse, February, March, moved to greenhouse in June to flower in August.

French beans: grown in pots in hothouse, February, cropped in March and April.

Geranium (*Pelargonium* spp.): taken in from garden in October and potted in stove and hothouse. Put out again in May.

Guava (*Psidium guajava*): purple and white, grown in kitchen garden stove. First fruits ripe July, August. Flowers in April. when moved to the greenhouse.

Kidney beans: planted in pots in hothouse, January.

Lachenalia pendula: flowered in hothouse, October.

Lilacs: put in hothouse to force, December, January, February. Moved to greenhouse in flower, late January to March.

Lilly in valley: potted to force in stove, November, January.

Lime tree (*Citrus x latifolia*): cuttings in stove, January, potted March.

Marvel of Peru (*Mirabilis jalapa*): taken into hothouse from garden in October, planted outdoors in May.

Melons: seed sowed in stove, February and March, planted in stove, April. Thereafter grown in melon frame.

Mimosa sensitiva: seed sown in hothouse for Charles Darwin, December 1838, possibly referring to the more sensitive *Mimosa pudica*, see Chapter Three.

Mustard and cress: sowed January to March in stove.

'Mule' rhubarb: forced in pots, in stove and hothouse, December.

Nymphaea caerulea: blue water lily, in tub in stove, March 1840. Moved to hothouse, December, flowers in hothouse, August, July.

Olea, 'sweet': olive, taken to stove, September. *O. fragrans* in pot, October.

Olea fragrans (*Osmanthus fragrans*): 'we used to have in hothouse', 1860.

Orange trees (*Citrus sinensis or aurantium*): brought indoors, September, taken from hothouse to greenhouse November, January, March and returned to hothouse April, May. Put outdoors, June.

Passion flowers (*Passiflora*), scarlet and purple edulis (*P. edulis*): grown as climbers in stove and hothouse. Fruit gathered September.

Peony (*Paeonia* sp.): 'peony tree' brought in and put in hothouse, November, December.

Pineapples: grown in pots and plunged in tan bed of hothouse, 1839, 1840. Fruit cut in January. Planted in hot-bed in March.

Potatoes: forced in pots in hothouse, stove and planted in frame, January, February. First new potatoes in March.

Rhododendrhon [sic], *R. arboretum*, scarlet and tree: flowered in greenhouse,

March, May. Put outdoors, May. Taken into hothouse, September, October.

Rhubarb (*Rheum x hybridum*): forced in stove, December.

Rose trees (to force): 'china' and Rose de Meaux forced in hothouse, November, December, January and February.

Seakale: forced from November in stove, to be ready for eating in January.

Sensitive plant: sowed in stove, December 1838, for experiment for C.D. See Chapter Three and *Mimosa*, above.

Shaddock tree (*Citrus maxima*): grown in hothouse and greenhouse

'Stephanotus' (stephanotis*) (*S. floribunda*): grown in stove, flowered June, July.

Tomatoes: seed sown in stove, but plants raised outdoors. Unripe tomatoes brought into hothouse to ripen, September.

Tree cucumber (*Magnolia acuminata*): seed sowed in hothouse, February, 1840.

Verbena: cuttings potted in hothouse, March, and stove, April.

Vines: See Part 3:4 for varieties. The hothouse was used as a vinery, divided in two for early and late crops.

Water lily: see *Nymphaea caerulea*, above.

Yew: 'seeds sent by Charles put into a pot in Hot house', November 1840.

Yucca aloifolia and *Y. gloriosa*: taken over winter into hothouse, if small enough. Planted outdoors, May. Flowered July.

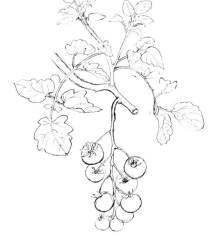

E: SUPPLEMENTARY LISTS OF FLOWERS AND
SHRUBS FOUND ELSEWHERE IN THE DIARY

1: FLOWERS AND SHRUBS IN THE TERRACE BORDER
2: FLOWERS AND SHRUBS IN THE WEST BORDER
3: FLOWERS, TREES AND SHRUBS IN THE
MANSION'S FRONT BORDERS

PLUS THE SUPPLEMENTARY LISTS FOUND AT THE
BEGINNING AND END OF THE DIARY

1: FLOWERS AND SHRUBS IN THE TERRACE BORDER

Acorus gramineus: planted August 1842.

Antirrhinum: planted August, 1855.

Atragene: planted May 1839.

Berbery/barberry: 'Holy [sic] leaved berbery seeds from Eaton sowed in pot', August 1841. Planted on terrace, 1845, moved to below terrace 1849. '*B darwinii in my bed*' (Susan, 1854,) but no indication where this bed is.

Box trees: planted on terrace, and elsewhere in the garden 1850, 1851.

Calceolaria: grown on terrace, 1856.

Cheiranthus: (and see wallflower) 'yellow flower' on terrace. Flowered in May 1861.

Cistus: planted on terrace, 1840.

Clematis flammula: moved from terrace to front of house, 1841.

Convolvulus, silk: planted on terrace, 1839.

Double gorse (*Ulex europaeus flore-pleno*): planted on terrace, August 1849.

Everlasting pea: moved from terrace to below the terrace wall 1849.

'Fuschsia': cut down on terrace, October 1853.

Geraniums: planted on terrace, May 1849, 1850, 1852, 1853, 1854 and 1857.

Heaths: planted August 1855.

Honeysuckle, late: planted August 1840 on wire fence, pruned on terrace, December 1848.

Holly: six hollies planted on terrace, February 1854.

Jasmine: planted August 1849.

Jonquils: planted March 1856.

Laburnum 'Golden Chain': 5 s-worth planted, June 1859.

Pinks, 'little red': planted May 1843.

Rhododendron: two rhododendrons planted below terrace wall, November 1838, and moved from flower garden to terrace August 1845. Moved from terrace to west border, June 1852, moved to terrace, February 1854.

Roses, small: planted December 1843.

Stocks 'Brompton' and 'German': planted August 1840, March 1851, October 1852, 1856.

Wallflower, double yellow: planted September 1849.

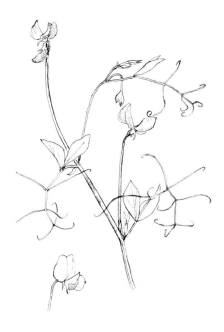

2: FLOWERS AND SHRUBS IN THE WEST BORDER

Apricot: on wall, planted April 1840; root pruned December 1841; nailed December 1840, March 1853.
Azalea: moved to west border, April 1863.
Cherry: on wall, first flower April 1842.
Chrysanthemum: planted March 1856.
Crocus: 'first crocus <u>quite</u> open on west border', 29 January 1843.
Fuchsia: planted May 1840.
Green gage: on wall, flower open May 1841, planted November 1851, pruned March 1853.
Hepatica: plants from Abberley's garden put in west border, April 1855.

'**Jessamine**': pruned on wall, March 1853.

Love apples (tomatoes): planted in west border, June 1839.

Mignonettes: sowed on west border, April 1853.

Pears, baking: tree on wall by kitchen garden door.

Plums, 'red' and Golden Drop: first plums gathered from west wall 'outside the garden' 6 August 1839, 27 July 1840, 22 July 1842, 29 July 1845.

Ranunculus: planted March 1841.

Rhododendron: moved to west border, April 1863.

Roses: white rose planted February 1839 and November 1840. Seven new roses (mostly moss roses) planted in a row before wall, December 1838. Double crested moss rose planted December 1840. 'Small moss rose' planted November 1841, 'white Provence roses from Maer' planted December 1843 'Gloire de Rosamane' from Eaton planted May 1840. Celestial rose tree planted December 1848. Fifteen 'tree roses' planted along west border November 1852 and six standard roses November 1856. Roses in west border regularly pruned in border and on wall. And see Part 3:1 section A, above.

Sweet peas: sowed in west border, April 1856, May 1850.

3. FLOWERS, TREES AND SHRUBS IN THE MANSION'S FRONT BORDERS

Almond: tree in front of greenhouse.
Anenome: in round beds by greenhouse.
Chrysanthemum: planted for autumn flowering.
Bulbs: unnamed, below greenhouse.
Cistus: purple, below the Doctor's windows.
Clematis florida: by study and morning room windows.
Clematis azurea: by hall door.
Clematis flammula: taken from terrace to front of house, 1841.
Cobaea scandens: planted against house.
Geraniums: by hall door, by greenhouse.
Gladiolus: planted by greenhouse.
Gorse: ten gorse plants and chrysanthemums planted front of house.
September 1855.

Grape vine 'Sweetwater' (see Part 3:4). The only vine grown outdoors, by the Doctor's closet window. First grapes October.

Holly: fifteen small hollies planted in front of house, July 1858.

Hibiscus syriacus: flowered late August, front of house.

Lilies, Bella Donna: in flower by house windows, October 1852

Magnolia 'Yeulan': grown front of house, flowered March, April. *M. grandiflora* planted by study window, August 1852.

Marvel of Peru: in front of greenhouse.

Mignonette: planted in window boxes and borders in front of house.

Myrtle, narrow leaved: planted in front of house, May 1849. Covers put on in December, taken off in May. Killed in January 1854.

Pomegranate: sown from seed, January 1839, growing on front of house and pruned, December 1848.

'Portulacca': grown in front of greenhouse.

Roses: climbing, by hall door and *'Luxemburgh'*: in front of greenhouse.

Stocks: planted front of house.

Verbena: planted front of house.

Violet: dog tooth, by greenhouse.

Wisteria: grown on front of house.

E: SUPPLEMENTARY LISTS OF FLOWERS AND
SHRUBS FOUND ELSEWHWERE IN THE DIARY

Below the list of roses from Mr Guise (see Part 3:1, section A), there is a list
of six **rhododendrons** from Waterers, dated 3 March 1856. This appears on
the first page below the list of roses from Mr Guise. All the entries are given
here with the original spellings and capital letters.

Catawbiensis splendens rose   *Rhodo* – Eminent
Gloriosum blush   *Illuminator* scarlet
Cyancum   Guttatum white with spots

The next list below was written on the very last page of the Diary. It names some plants that are not mentioned elsewhere in the Diary.

Climbers in Stove–House 1859 April
N.1 *Passiflora Princeps* (Scarlet Passionflower)
2 *Allamanda obletii [Aubletii]* (Yellow very sweet)
3 *Ipomoea horsfallia* (crimson purple)
4 *Ipomea learii* (Purple convolvulus)
5 *Clerodendron splendens* (Crimson scarlet)

Euphorbia Jacquieniflora back of Stove
Dipladenia Crassinoda Rose colour convolvulus

Ixora coccinea
Croton variegatum
Achimenes meteor
– verschaffelt
daccina [dracena] terminalis
Kennedyea [Kennedia] jacquiflora (Greenhouse Glycine purple)

Cheiranthus yellow flower on Terrace (in pencil)

Another list on a small, loose, pencilled sheet of paper watermarked 1858, 4½ x 7 in, was found at the back of the Diary.

Climbers in Stove
5 *Clerodendron Splendens* – Stove crimson scarlet
Combretum Purpureum – Stove crimson
2nd Allamanda aubletii – Stove yellow very sweet
Dipladenia crassinoda – Stove rose
1st *Passiflora Princeps* – Stove scarlet
Rhyncospermum Jasminoides – Greenhouse white very sweet
3rd *Ipomoea Horsfallia* – Stove crimson purple
Euphorbea Jaquiniflora – back
Ixora Coccinea
Croton Longifolium Variegatum
Dracena Seminalis
Achimenes Meter [meteor]
Achimenes Verschaffelt
4th *Ipomea Learii*

[1] Peter Beales, *Classic Roses*, 2nd edn (London: Harvill, 1997), p. 364.
[2] E.S. Dealmer, *The Kitchen and Flower Garden* (London, *c.* 1855), p. 59.

PART 3:2

Citrus Trees

Some of the Doctor's citrus trees bore enough fruit for the crops to be recorded in the Diary: three limes in 1841, 'near 90 oranges' from one large tree in 1842, and shaddocks in threes and fours, with three sent as a gift to Sundorne in 1840. Unripe shaddocks were gathered while still green and made into a preserve, but there is no mention of the oranges, limes or lemons being used for this purpose.

Family and friends gave or received trees, too. A sweet orange tree, noted as 'Miss C. Wedgwood's', was cut down on 9 March 1839. This would refer to Charlotte, the Doctor's niece. As she had been married since 1832, this entry suggests that the tree had been in the Doctor's possession for some time before that and was now in need of a reduction in size. Other trees came from Lord Liverpool. This would have been Charles Jenkinson, the 3rd Earl, who lived nearby at Pitchford. In 1855 Susan 'gave 2 orange trees to Mr Woodward', a neighbouring seed merchant, and in 1852 she gave a shaddock tree to Frank Wedgwood.

ORANGE TREES

Seven kinds of orange tree are mentioned in the Diary: 'blood red', 'box-leaved', 'horned', 'Mandarin', 'Tangerine', 'sweet' and 'wild'. The horned and wild oranges, being of particular interest to Charles, are described in Chapter Three. A myrtle-leaved orange is also mentioned by Charles as growing at The Mount (see Chapter Three) but is not referred to in the Diary.

The 'blood red' orange may be taken to be the 'Maltese', or red-fleshed blood-orange, botanically known as *Citrus sinensis*. This variety was highly recommended for its delicious aroma, abundant juice and prolific fruiting,[1] but it was mentioned only once, when it was cut down in November 1838.

'Box-leaved' orange trees are also mentioned only once, in September 1938 when they were 'taken in'. They are described by J.C. Loudon as being 'cultivated more as curious varieties than for their fruit'.[2]

'Mandarin' and 'Tangerine' oranges, botanically known as *Citrus reticulata*, need no description today. There is very little difference between these two varieties, except that the former could be said to be larger and flatter than the tangerine and has yellower fruit than the latter, which is a deep orange. References in the Diary are mostly to do with their repotting.

The 'sweet' orange is also known as the China orange (*Citrus sinensis*). It is used in desserts and is distinct from the bitter or Seville orange. There are numerous varieties, but none are specifically named in the Diary.

LEMON TREES

There is only one mention in the Diary of a lemon, on 22 June 1840, when a lemon tree was repotted.

LIME TREES

Referred to on all occasions as the Bergamot Lime, which suggests that this is actually yet another variety of orange, namely the Bergamot Orange (*Citrus limetta*). If so, this is the fragrant, pale yellow, pear-shaped orange from Calabria, famous for the oil from its skin, which is used in perfume and Earl Grey tea. Cuttings were frequently made of it by the Doctor, and three fruits were gathered in November 1841, but its cultivation was not continued after his death.

SHADDOCK TREES

A native of China and Japan, the shaddock is said to have been brought to the West Indies *c.* 1650 by a Captain Shaddock.[3] Originally known as the pummelo, pamplemousse or pomelo (and in modern taxonomy as *C. maxima* syn. *C. grandis*), when crossed with a sweet orange it became the ancestor of the grapefruit. It is a very large greenish-yellow fruit, the size of a child's head, and, according to one authority, often weighing 10-14 lbs.[4] The Doctor's shaddock trees provided a few fruits every year. There was a record of nine in 1840, but they had a tendency to drop off before they were ripe, and they were small, weighing no more than 15–30 oz. They were used unripe in preserves and their flowers were gathered with those of the orange on Boxing Day 1843. Susan also had them made into a preserve, sent a shaddock tree and a guava tree to Condover, and in December 1852 gave a shaddock fruit to her cousin Frank Wedgwood.

[1] The Illustrated Dictionary of Gardening, ed. George Nicholson, vol. II (London: Upcott Gill, n.d.), p. 507.
[2] J.C. Loudon, *An Encyclopaedia of Gardening* (London: Longman, Rees, Orme, Brown and Green, 1825), p. 767.
[3] Or Chaddock, according to O. Wijnands in *Journal of Gardening History*, 1988, vol. 8, pp. 61–86, nn. 2 and 3.
[4] Loudon, *op. cit.*, p. 769.

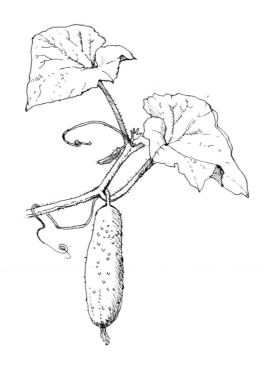

PART 3:3

Vegetables, Salads and Herbs

Incorporating lists of named varieties, times of gathering and positions where known

A: FORCED VEGETABLES

B: OUTDOOR VEGETABLES

C: HERBS

D: PRESERVING METHODS, AND PLANTS TO WHICH THEY APPLY

A: FORCED VEGETABLES

Hot-beds, stoves and the melon frame provided heat for a variety of forced vegetables in winter and early spring, including potatoes, rhubarb, seakale, cucumbers, melons and lettuce.

Capsicums

Capsicum makes a brief appearance between 1843 and 1846. It was possibly grown as a curiosity. Contemporary gardening books class the capsicum with the cayenne (or chilli pepper); the only Diary entry for cayenne occurs in September 1843, when the 'pods' were pickled. These are therefore likely to be the fruits of capsicums sown and potted earlier that year. The Doctor mentions the source of his capsicum seeds as 'Hopton Court, near Cleobury Mortimer, belonging to the Botfield family'.[1]

Cucumbers

Like new potatoes, these made their first appearance from hot-beds in the stove-house in early April, although they may well have been cropped there earlier than that, as on one occasion (13 January 1855) Susan writes 'last cucumber cut'. The stove was prepared for their seed in September, and their cultivation continued throughout the winter.

> *Cucumbers*
> '3 seeds from George at Mr Haycock's' (outdoor; George Jones was the Haycock's gardener)
> Emperor: possibly Roman Emperor, sown May
> Grangers: from neighbours at Sundorne, planted September
> Hothouse or Sion/Sion House: for winter cropping
> Long spine: for ridges, outdoor
> Manchester: for hothouse
> Mills New: sown April
> Southgate: sown May
> Walker long: sown May
> Walker's improved: potted March
> White cucumber: outdoor

Beans, kidney and French

Both these kinds, when planted in pots in the hothouses in January, could be eaten as early as March. The pots would be placed on long planks which acted as shelves running the length of a greenhouse, just under the roof. Strawberries in pots were also forced in this way.

Lettuces

Lettuces were sown and planted out at The Mount virtually all the year round. This activity began by sowing hardy, overwintering types such as 'Hardy Green Cos', 'Brown Dutch' and 'Tennis Ball' from late summer and autumn onwards. The seedlings were grown on in the melon frame, making the first salads available by late March. Late spring and summer types such as 'Golden Cos' and the 'Malta' lettuce were sown in early spring and summer and planted out on the warm south-facing borders of the kitchen garden and vinery.

Mustard and cress

The mustard of mustard and cress is the white mustard (*Sinapis alba*) and the cress is garden cress (*Lepidium sativum*). Both are eaten in their seedling stage and together they form a sharp, peppery salad. M'Intosh states that they should be grown in little boxes measuring 4- or 5-in deep and 1-ft broad, filled with light mould and placed over the flues of a hothouse.[2] This is how it would have been grown at The Mount in January, February and March, in a frame and in the stove-house. It could have been grown outdoors in the summer, but it does not appear to have been, possibly because other sorts of salad, including American cress, were plentiful. Susan does not mention mustard and cress, but the Doctor gives it eight entries.

Potatoes

The first early potatoes were forced, in some years, as soon as the end of December, though the process usually began in the first three months of the year. To be successful it required a mean temperature of around 57°F (14° C)and was carried out in frames, hot-beds, pots, or tan beds in the stove-house. A dish usually appeared on the family's dinner table in April or May, and sometimes in March.

Rhubarb

For winter forcing the mature, dormant roots were taken into a warm, dark place indoors, in succession, to provide a refreshing fruit dessert from mid- to late winter. At The Mount, roots lifted in November and put in pots in the hothouse had stems ready for eating within a month. Plants forced and blanched outdoors were ready to follow on for eating in early spring.

Seakale

This was forced in a similar way to rhubarb. For a welcome mid-winter crop, forcing would begin in November or December. The roots or 'thongs' would be dug up and placed in pots, which were then kept in a warm, dark place. The delicate white shoots, which are in fact leaf-stalks, were ready for cutting for the Darwins in three or four weeks. Warmth and darkness are essential, as I have discovered for myself, by having to wait until the end of February for forced seakale from my own garden shed, which is dark, but also very chilly.

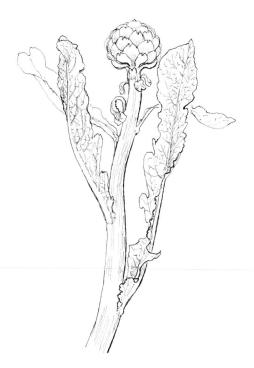

B: OUTDOOR VEGETABLES

Artichokes (globe)

Both green and purple artichokes were grown here. The Diary mentions eating them fresh from early June until August, when they are then gathered in order to be preserved or dried. The drying process entails boiling them until the inedible 'chokes' can be removed, then baking them 'until they be dry as Wood'.[3] They are reconstituted by soaking for two days in warm water and boiling again. They can also be preserved 'moist' by boiling in plain water, then covering them with brine and a thick layer of fat. The purpose of these procedures, as with all preserving, is 'to give Variety at Seasons when they are not to be had otherwise'.[4]

Artichokes (Jerusalem)

These useful autumnal roots were grown in the field garden rather than in the kitchen garden.

Asparagus

In certain years the Doctor and Susan recorded the total number of asparagus spears, or, as they called them, 'heads', cut per season, thus revealing that this delicacy was grown in great quantities at The Mount. In 1842 there were '2,000 head cut' and in 1843 '2,853 cut altogether'. The score went down slightly in 1844 (2,652) and was down again in 1845 (2,150), but it rose to a magnificent 3,145 heads in 1850. On 4 April 1849, a first cut of seventy heads was made for a dinner party with 'Young Potatoes'.

The first asparagus was obviously a great treat. As we have seen, on 11 April 1851 Susan wrote '1st Asparagus cut for me, as I was ill with influenza'. There are no records of it being sent to any of their friends or family, which is remarkable as the Darwins were otherwise very generous with gifts of fruits and vegetables from their garden. However, on 5 May 1853 Susan writes: 'Asparagus sent to London 3 times.' The first cut had been made only ten days before, on 26 April, but she herself had gone to London on 12 April, which would explain the reason for its dispatch.[5]

The beds received occasional dressings of salt and a variety of manures, ranging from crushed bones, 'peat soil', nitrate of soda, 'stable draining', the contents of the 'Black Hole' and, in 1843, 'Guano Manure'. The latter had been introduced to Britain as a commercial fertiliser by Lord Derby only three years previously.

Beans

Broad beans, French beans and runner beans, as well as the less well-known cranberry beans, were grown in the field and the kitchen gardens.

Cranberry beans are a type of shelling bean similar to the flageolet bean or the Italian cannellini bean, so called because of the colour of the pod, which is a pinkish red like that of a cranberry, streaked with pale blue. They are South American (Chilean) in origin. The Doctor refers twice to cranberry beans, first on 12 October 1838: 'a small dish of cranberry beans. Those from Mr. H. Williams sowed on the 19th of June'.[6] A month later, on 12 November, when the beans have fully ripened, he writes: 'cranberry Beans gathered for seed'. They were obviously quite special as none of the contemporary vegetable lists consulted contains 'cranberry beans'. The identity of Mr H. Williams is also unknown.

Apart from the cranberry, only one other variety of kidney bean, the 'Dwarf Negro', is named, and that only once. This is an early bean with dark brown to blackish seeds; it was sown at The Mount in April 1850.

Beets (red and white)

Red beets, which we now call beetroots, were usually eaten hot and, also, pickled at this period, but no mention of pickling them is made in the Diary. Nor is there any mention of any particular variety, though the kind grown here does seem to be very large; in October 1841 one root weighing '8 pound & half' was dug up. They were available only in the winter months and were usually baked or boiled, although Susan does remark, as if this were an exception to the rule, '1 Beet root used for Boiled Salad' (8 October 1852).

Broccoli

This was grown on a huge scale – 300 plants were put out in August 1849 – and raised mainly in the kitchen garden, though there is one reference to its being grown in the field garden.

Sowing took place at The Mount in succession, sometimes as early as March, and sometimes as late as July, but on the whole the later varieties were sown in April and the early faster-growing sprouting kinds were sown on seed beds on a warm border in May. The seedlings were planted out in their final positions in summer or early autumn.

The practice of earthing up is mentioned once, in December 1839. The stems were covered in order to minimise injury by frost.

Dwarf

Early Purple/Purple [possibly means the tall, branching Purple Sprouting]: a late kind sown May, planted out August

Grange's, Granger's Early/Granger's Early White: a white-headed variety, the best for autumn and mid-winter supplies

Knight's/Knight's Protecting: so-called because the leaves fold themselves over the head as it forms, protecting it from frost. Late, sown April, May, planted out September

Miller's: sown May

Walcheren: an intermediate between cauliflowers and broccoli with a large white head, comes in early, at the very end of the cauliflower season

Brussels sprouts

As advocated by all gardening authorities, The Mount's Brussels sprouts were sown in spring (March–April) planted out around midsummer and eaten throughout the winter.

Cabbages

These were grown on the east, west and south borders of the kitchen garden and in the field garden. A glut in July 1857 led to a bracketed and underlined entry from Susan: '(<u>sold</u> Cabbages)'. The sowing and planting out of early, mid-season and late cabbages at The Mount was continuous from February to September, which would have made this vegetable available almost all the year round. Both early and late sorts were sown at the same time, beginning in March and going on into August. The slower-growing main crops were sown last, standing over winter and taking up to a year to reach full size, the faster ones taking perhaps only six months. Savoys were grown for winter and red cabbages for pickling.

Early unnamed varieties: sown August, planted June, September

Early Dwarf: the earliest and smallest cabbage; sown August for early summer crop the following year

Early Emperor: third earliest; sown March for eating the same year, planted August

Early York: very popular second earliest; sown April, May, July; planted out June, July; spring sowing hearts quickly for early winter

Jacob: not found in contemporary lists, may be a local sort; sown August; also planted August, September

Matchless: popular in the 1850s, early, sown April, hearts quickly for early winter

Red: large, red and round, grown as an early cabbage for pickling; sown August, pickled in October (also planted February, in 1843)

Savoy: green, wrinkled leaf, round head, for winter to spring use; planted August

Winter: for winter use; planted September

Carrots

Both red and white varieties were grown in the field and kitchen gardens, mostly as a main crop for the winter. There is a mention by the Doctor (26 September 1842) of six carrots from the kitchen garden weighing 10 lbs between them. White carrots are mentioned three times; they were grown in the field garden, harvested in September, October and December, and eaten by the family.

Altringham: this carrot had a very long, slender, horizontally ribbed root, which sometimes grew up to 20-in long. A considerable amount of its top portion characteristically projected 1 or 2 in above ground and was a bronze or violet colour, the rest of the root being red. By the end of the nineteenth century seedsmen were offering a thicker, shorter, smoother 'Altringham', as the extreme length and slenderness of the older variety tended to make it break as it was being pulled. (William Robinson, *Vegetable Garden*, 1905, p. 200)

White: grown in the field garden, got up September, October, December. Could be the Long White, recommended by Neill for its delicate flavour, though he says it does not keep well (p. 226).

Early Horn: sowed 1 Feb 1842, 13 April 1849, smallest of the Horn type; short cylindrical roots, recommended for early sowing.

Large Orange: sown 1 April 1843. Given by Patrick Neill, *Fruit, Flower and Kitchen Garden* (1849), p. 226 as another name for the Altringham

Cauliflowers

The second half of August (as near as possible to 21 August) was the traditional time for sowing the spring crop of cauliflowers. This the Darwins did very nearly every year during the period covered by the Diary.

Another sowing was made at intervals between February and May, to supply cauliflowers in autumn. The seedlings from the autumn sowing would need some protection during winter; these were transplanted in October and November to overwinter in a frame – some were even sown in the frame.

Likewise, the first of the spring sowings was either started off in a frame or inside the stove-house. No varieties are named, other than the spring-sown 'Walcheren', which elsewhere in the Diary (24 July 1849) is referred to as a kind of broccoli

Celery

Considering that the cultivation of celery is relatively straightforward, this vegetable receives a noticeably high number of entries in the Diary. Its sowing, transplanting, planting out, earthing up and first use are recorded in almost every autumn from 1838 to 1856, when the diary-keeping begins to tail off. It was grown solely for eating as a winter vegetable. One reason for the numerous entries in the Diary (which is after all a working diary) may be due to the need to record the formation of each successive trench, in order for the gardener to calculate when to begin earthing up. Every earthing-up operation is not recorded, but it is mentioned at intervals of anything from seven to ten days or so, beginning in August and continuing until December. It was a necessary process, carried out in order to obtain tender, white rather than tough, green stems.

A red variety was grown one year, in 1843, '3 sorts from Mr Dovaston' (a local nurseryman) were grown in 1840 and celery 'from Woodhouse' (home of the Owen family) was grown in 1843.

'3 sorts from Mr Dovaston'	Seymour/Ceymour white
Early white	Red
Giant	'celery from Woodhouse'

Couve tronchuda

A winter vegetable, also known as Portugal cabbage, Portuguese kale, large-ribbed borecole or Braganza cabbage, it was introduced to English gardens in 1821 by Portuguese wine merchants, and was the subject of an article the following year by John Wedgwood, who considered it 'an excellent substitute' for seakale.[7]

It was still so much a novelty in 1838 that the Doctor confused it with kohl-rabi and had difficulty with its spelling. He called it variously 'cove tronjudia', 'cove transhandra', 'kala Raba', 'cole transshanda' and 'cove transhard'. Even by the end of the nineteenth century it was considered 'not so well-known in British gardens as its merits warrant'.[8]

Cucumbers

As mentioned above, cucumbers were among the vegetables forced on hot-beds and in the melon frame. They were also grown outdoors in summer, on ridges. The family was thus supplied with cucumbers for nine months of the year, from April onwards. They were also pickled. Owing to 'their natural proneness to impregnate each other when grown together',[9] they are difficult to identify as varieties.

Endives

This autumnal salad plant was sown from May to August and planted out in late summer and autumn. It was hardy enough to withstand all but the most severe frosts and was blanched *in situ* when a good heart had formed, by tying the leaves and lightly earthing up. Alternatively, the mature plants could be dug up and stacked in dry mould in a shed or outhouse. A stack of this kind was made behind the stove-house on 23 December 1845. Only one variety is named and is described as the 'Green Curld Endive' (15 August 1839 and 11 August 1840).

'Greens' (also known as Open Kale, Borecole or Coleworts)

A fairly general term for what the Diary refers to as 'curley greens', 'Manchester greens' and 'winter greens'. These would be frost-resistant, non-hearting, mostly curly-leaved varieties of cabbage, sown in spring, planted out in mid-summer and eaten during the winter months and early spring when other vegetables are less plentiful. 'Winter greens', according to Lindley, include borecoles, savoys, kales, kohl-rabi and Brussels sprouts.[10]

Asparagus	Purple
Best Green Curled	Tall Green
Jerusalem	Kohl-rabi
Lapland	

Kales

A very hardy and therefore useful winter and early spring vegetable. It was grown on both the north and south borders of the kitchen garden at The Mount and five varieties are mentioned, one of which is 'Asparagus kale'. However, according to contemporary authorities, this name refers to more than one variety, including Jerusalem kale, which is also known as 'curled' and 'Buda'[7]. At The Mount it was sown early, in March, transplanted in June and 'first cooked' on 2 November, the seed being a gift from a Miss Jenkins. The other named kales were less hardy and not as sweet, and were sown later, for later crops.

Kohl-Rabi

There are only two entries for this vegetable. The first, 'Planted out Kohl Rabi from Condover. Or Kala Raba or Cove tronjudia' was made in early September 1838 and suggests that the Doctor was as unfamiliar with this vegetable as he was with couve tronchuda. It does not appear to have been a great success as a vegetable for the Darwins' dinner table. The second entry, 'Cole Raby sown in K.G. for cows' was made by Susan in March 1852. This is probably a large and late variety of kohl-rabi that was grown for cattle.

Lettuces

As mentioned above, lettuce was sown and planted throughout the year, both Cos and cabbage kinds, making them available at all times. They were raised in frames, on the south border, the vinery border and the herb garden.

Cos types

Green Coss/Hardy Green Coss/ Hardy Green Winter Coss: the latter is an overwintering kind, confusingly referred to five times in the Diary by the Doctor as the 'Hammersmith Hardy Green Coss', when in fact the Hammersmith is a hardy cabbage lettuce

Golden Coss: also known as the Florence or Marseilles cos, for summer eating. Large, needs tying

Cabbage types

Early Brown Dutch/Brown Dutch: the latter, if sown in August or September, being suitable for winter, the Early useful for summer

Hammersmith Hardy Green: sown in August to stand the winter for eating in early spring

Malta/Maltese: light green, large, stands hot weather well

Tennis Ball: the smallest of the cabbage types, dark green and hardy. Well able to stand the winter for earing in early spring. Also good for summer cropping

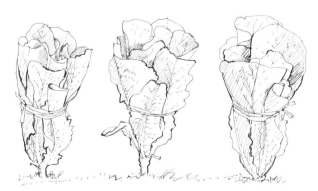

It was thought by gardeners at the time that lettuces actually enriched, rather than impoverished, the soil they grew in. A Diary entry for 'soil taken fresh to the peach trees and lettuce planted' (16 February 1839) could be taken as evidence of this belief.

Mangelwurzels

Variously called mangel, mangle or mangold, and wurzel, wurzle, wurtzel, wortzle or wortzel, this is a large, yellow form of the common beet (*Beta vulgaris macrorrhiza*). It was, and still is, grown mainly as cattle fodder for the winter, being eaten by humans only when times were hard. At The Mount in the Doctor's time it was grown with other roots (notably red beet) in the field garden, but Susan grew it in the kitchen garden as well (sown between the raspberries).

It was sown in late March and early April and harvested in November. It was stacked under cover over winter in the field hovel, in the garden house and, in 1855, in a shed specially made in the kitchen garden for it and the carrot crop. The green tops were trimmed off before the roots were stacked, given to the cows and, on one occasion, to the pigs (November 1857). One year (1843) two sowings were made, the first in April, the second six weeks later, as the first had clearly failed. The second sowing must have failed in part as well, as on 17 June 'Beet from Mr Haycock [was] planted in field to supply place of Mangel'. The last entry, 'bought a Ton of Mangold Wurzel for a Guinea', implies that Susan had ceased growing her own by 1861.

Mushrooms

There are two references to mushrooms in the Diary by the Doctor and two by Susan. The Doctor records '4 Mushrooms' in October 1838, and the making of a mushroom bed one year later. Susan mentions 'Mushrooms for Dinner' (11 January 1854) and 'Mushrooms gathered' (7 June 1855).

Mushrooms in January would need the assistance of a mushroom house, or at least a dark, heated shed. Mushrooms gathered in June might just possibly come from a mushroom bed or even a field, but this is too early in the year for field mushrooms. If they had been bought or were the gift of a neighbour who had cultivated them, both Susan and her father would, more likely than not, have recorded the fact. It may be that just for the odd season, Susan was growing them for herself.

Onions

Onions were grown on a fairly large scale at The Mount, with eight beds sown in 1840, and two or three beds the norm but, with the exception of the potato onion (see below), other members of the allium family are notably absent from both the Diary and, I assume, the Darwins' dinner table. There is no mention of garlic, spring onions, chives, shallots or even leeks.

The planting of onions from 'sets' was known to gardeners at this time, but The Mount's onions appear to have been grown, always, from seed.[11] There were two sowings, the first in mid-March, the second in mid-August. The only variety named in the earlier sowings is 'New Globe' or 'New White Globe'. The later crop, which was often named as the large variety known as 'Tripoli', would be transplanted a few months after sowing, in mid-winter. Cropping (i.e. pulling up) occurred in September. In November and December, when the onions were well dried, they would be strung up and stored either in the shed behind the hothouse, in the garden house or the apple room.

Potato Onions

This is so-called because it grows below soil level and develops clusters from each bulb. It is planted with the neck just showing and is earthed up as it grows. It is related to the *Allium cepa aggregatum* group, which includes shallots and the tree-onion. Dr Darwin may have been encouraged to grow it by John Wedgwood, who described its cultivation in full, but it appears only once in the Diary, on 25 January 1841.[12]

Parsnips

This useful winter root was grown both in the field garden and the kitchen garden at The Mount. It was usually sown in mid-March (occasionally in April), lifted in October or November, then stored in the garden house.

Peas

Successive sowings of peas, from November to July the following year, ensured that the Darwin family had peas on the dinner table from June to the end of October; a recent gardening tradition had it that the first dish of peas should be available on 4 June, George IV's birthday. A week or two later was the best that the gardeners at The Mount could manage, from sowings made of the early sorts in the previous winter. On two occasions (in 1852 and 1854) the first dish of peas coincided with Susan's return in mid-June from her annual early summer visits to London. The Diary makes no mention of the request, in 1841, from Charles to Abberley regarding the crossing of peas (see Chapter Three).

The first dish of Woodford's Marrowfat peas would appear a month later, in July. These were semi-dwarf peas; the latest peas, 'British Queen' and 'Knight's Tall Marrow', in contrast to these, were exceedingly tall by today's standards – climbing up to over 6 ft 6 ins. Rodding or 'sticking' the peas was begun in March and April. Sticks, rails, poles and rods were bought from various parts of the neighbourhood; from Eaton Mascott, Shelton (brought by cart in 1852, at a cost of £3 15s), Berwick (two cartloads sent in 1853) and

Bissall (brought down the river by boat in 1854). There is only one entry showing that pea rods were available from home and that was when they were cut from the bank below the mansion (March 1857).

Blue Imperial/ Imperial: summer pea, very late, excellent quality

Blue Symmetry presumably **Scimitar**: half-dwarf, 2½–3 ft height, very green pea, pods scimitar-shaped

British Queen: late pea, wrinkled white marrow, about 6-ft tall

Champion: height 6–7 ft, wrinkled blue marrow, good for general use

Cormacks Early: double-blossomed early frame

Early Charlton: early pea, tall, prolific, best for overwintering, open air

Early Emperor: early pea, very hardy, 3: ft high

Early Frame: tall, prolific, the earliest early pea; for forcing

Early Kent: early pea

Early Warwick: early pea

Knights Marrow/Knights Tall Marrow[fat]: latest crop, 6 ft 6 ins tall, very sweet, long pods

Miller's Dwarf

Race Horse

Superb

Victoria

Woodfords Green Marrow/ Marrowfat: 3 to 3 ft 6 ins high

Potatoes

Potatoes were grown in sufficient quantities at The Mount to provide the household with a year-round supply. The first earlies were forced, as described above.

The second earlies were planted outdoors on the sunny border beneath the south-facing wall of the kitchen garden, usually in March, but sometimes in February or April (Good Friday being the traditional day). The east border was also used for early potatoes in some years. The first of these would be dug up in June or July. The main crop was planted in March, April and even May, and was grown in the field garden. It was lifted in October and carted home, for eating and storing over winter. This crop averaged 50 'strike' (100 bushels) a year and might take anything up to five days' labour to plant and to dig up. Seed potatoes for the following year were selected in August, from the crops grown in the kitchen and field gardens.

One entry, for 14 November 1838, refers to covering asparagus, 'artichoke, rhubarb and everlasting potatoes'. Covering plants already in the ground with litter is a form of protection against frost, light and damp. When applied to any late-planted variety, they can be taken up as young potatoes during winter whenever wanted. This procedure may not have been a success; it was not repeated.

There is no mention of the potato blight that caused such devastation in Britain in the mid-nineteenth century, nor of any other disease that attacks potatoes. The only setback appears to have occurred in 1848, on 29 April when the thermometer went down to 28° F (-2°C) and a hard frost caught the potatoes in the field garden.

Ash leaved/Ash leaved kidney: a very old, early white variety, so-called because its leaves resemble those of an ash tree, and with kidney-shaped tubers; one of the best and good for forcing, also a good second early or mid-season potato, grown in the kitchen garden, south border

Fluke's, also known as **Ash-top Fluke, Yorkshire Hero** and **Lapstone**: pale yellow, long-keeping, kidney-shaped and grown in the kitchen garden

'from Lord Hill': Lord Hill of Hardwicke, grown in the kitchen garden

'from Ryton': winter potatoes

'from Worcester': grown in the field
'from Mr Instone': Henry Instone,

nurseryman of Shrewsbury; planted in pots for forcing

'from Sundorne': Sundorne Castle, home of Dryden Robert Corbet, grown in the kitchen garden, south border

kidney: late variety, grown in the field and kitchen garden
Lapstones: (see above)

Fluke's: (see above)

South American (Mr C. Darwin's): (see Chapter 3, pp.50-51

Wriotsley/Wrotchley: presumably Wriothsley, grown in the field

Radishes

This useful salad crop was sown two or three times a year at The Mount, making it available at all times. The winter sowings would have been in a frame or on a warm border. Although numerous varieties of radish are listed in contemporary gardening books, no particular kind is mentioned in the Diary, other than the 'Turnip raddish', which was round, rather than spindle-shaped, and sown in late summer for storing over winter. The seed pods are used on one occasion (August 1843) for pickle.

Rhubarb

Although usually eaten as a dessert, rhubarb has been cultivated since the early nineteenth century in vegetable gardens in a similar way to seakale. It was grown at first in the open, without blanching, to be picked for eating in summer. The stems of this rhubarb tended to be thin, coarse, stringy and acidic. It became a much more popular edible plant, when it was discovered (in 1820, by T.A. Knight) that it could be blanched and forced. The pale, sweet, tender shoots made a useful filling for fruit tarts while summer fruits such as gooseberries or apples were scarce or not yet in season.

For winter forcing the mature, dormant roots were taken into a warm, dark place indoors, in succession, to provide a refreshing fruit dessert from mid- to late winter. At The Mount, roots lifted in November and put in pots in the hothouse had stems ready for eating within a month. Plants forced and blanched outdoors were ready to follow on for eating in early spring. The outdoor crop would be covered with pots and 'leaf manure' from November onwards, or with fresh manure in February. It was ready for eating from late March.

The Diary makes frequent mention of the first rhubarb tart of the year, usually in late March. Later in the season, when the covers were removed, it was gathered for a preserve and, later still in the summer, for vinegar.

On 23 May 1845, the Doctor mentions eating 'English rhubarb for myself. Not so good as the other kind.' This was probably *Rheum palmatum*, the original, unimproved eighteenth-century kitchen garden variety. Charles Darwin's *Notes on Pollination*, 1840–43 (kindly sent to the author by David Kohn), include observations on rhubarb at The Mount, made probably in June 1841. Charles says that his father formerly planted Turkey or palmated and English rhubarb within a few yards of each other, which actually produced hybrids. His father 'when in the gardens, he knew there was none but English – the Palmated was introduced about 65 years ago [i.e. in 1776] – and soon after mules [i.e. hybrids] abounded so that Palmated has now nearly disappeared, and old English. But these mules in our garden show no trace of palmation!!?' 'Turkey' rhubarb would be *R. rhaponticum*, grown for the medicinal use of its roots. Possibly as a result of these notes, 'green or undulatum rhubarb' was planted in front of the stove-house later that year, on 13 November.

Dr Darwin also mentions 'French rhubarb', which is possibly a euphemism for 'foreign', as the French did not then grow culinary rhubarb (1 October 1840). The rhubarb bed was in front of the stove in the kitchen garden. Propagation was by seed, as well as by root division.

Salsify

This plant, with its long, slender, sweet, fleshy white root (also known as the vegetable oyster) was much better known in the Darwins' time than it is now. The seed was usually sown in April or May, though there is one late sowing in July 1840. It was dug up for eating in October and November, though there is one earlier gathering, late in August.

Seakale

Another relatively unknown vegetable in today's kitchen gardens. It grows wild on the seashores of Britain and northwest Europe and is not easy to grow inland. Salt was therefore applied to the beds at The Mount in late May. It is the blanched or forced shoots of the mature plants that are eaten. For a welcome mid-winter crop, forcing would begin in November or December. The roots or 'thongs' would be dug up and placed in pots, which were then kept in a warm, dark place. The delicate white shoots, which are in fact leaf-stalks, would be ready for cutting in three or four weeks. Rhubarb was forced in a similar way.

Outdoor crops were covered for forcing in the New Year, to be ready for eating in early spring. I grow it myself, as I have a seaside garden. It is usually on our dinner table by 31 March. The mature plant is very ornamental, with silver-grey leaves and fragrant white flowers; like Susan we grow it in the flower garden as well as the kitchen garden. There are three references in the Diary to Susan sending gifts of seakale to her sister Marianne, who lived at Overton, some 22 miles north of Shrewsbury (15 April 1852, with rhubarb; 17 December 1856 and 8 January 1857).

Spinach

Monthly sowings were made at The Mount from March to August for a succession of spinach in the summer. In order to have it over winter and into spring the prickly seeded variety would have been sown in September; this seems rarely to have been the case, though it was obviously worth one special entry, spinach being had for dinner on Sunday 11 March 1860. It was grown in the kitchen and field gardens. No varieties are named other than 'round-leaved' and 'prickly-seeded'.

Tomatoes

Tomato, or (as the Doctor twice calls it) the love apple, was rarely seen in the kitchen gardens of the mid-nineteenth century, being regarded as an acquired taste even as late as 1885.[13] However, it was grown annually by the Darwins. Usually sown in the stove-house in late March or early April, and occasionally in February, tomatoes do not appear to have been grown under glass thereafter, save once, in June 1855 ('potting tomatoes in Hothouse'). They were more usually planted out and grown on under the south-facing wall of the kitchen garden in May. The custom was to grow tomatoes on vacant spaces between the wall fruit trees, nailing them to the wall when

large enough (27 July 1852). The fruits ripened from late August to October. If they were still green by autumn, they were gathered for pickling and preserving or placed in the hothouse to ripen.

Turnips

There is not much, even for a Darwin, to say about the useful, fast-growing but humble turnip. They were grown in the field garden and around the haystack enclosure as well as in the kitchen garden, where they were grown in alternate years on the south- or north-facing borders, and once on the east border, as well as by the stove-house. Sowing began sometimes as early as February and continued until mid-August. In the years up to 1844 three or four successive sowings are recorded, with the crop dug up in September, October and November. They merit only one 'first for dinner' entry (29 July 1849). Only one variety is named: 'Six Weeks', or 'Early Six Weeks' turnip.

Vegetable Marrows

A novelty in early Victorian kitchen gardens, they were regarded as delicacies and were raised with as much care and in the same way as outdoor cucumbers. The first mention, in the Diary, on 8 May 1840, is of sowing the seeds of the 'Courge à la Moelle (Vegetable Marrow) ... from J. Wedgwood who had them from Paris'. They were planted out in the vine border, and the first 'Vegetable Marrow from Paris' was cut three months later, on 11 August. They continued to be grown by the Darwins until 1850, after which there are no more references.

C: HERBS

There are four references at the very beginning of the Diary to a herb garden, all in 1839. Three refer to mint, one to thyme and one to sage. Thereafter herbs are mentioned in separate beds for each variety, each one presumably situated in the kitchen garden.

Given the Doctor's profession, there is a noticeable lack of medicinal herbs; the selection consists mostly of the herbs a plain cook would use, but here too there are some notable omissions (like that of garlic), namely rosemary, chervil, savory and borage. Bay leaves too, get short shrift, the only reference here being Susan's, on 23 July 1855, 'cut down bay tree dead'.

Angelica

Only one entry, a bed planted in February 1840, but since it is a perennial no further attention would be needed.

Basil

Regularly sown and, on one occasion, 'sweet basil gathered for drying'.

Burnet

Another perennial, mentioned only once, in a bed in front of the stove-house.

Horehound

A perennial, this one is more useful as a cough-cure than a seasoning.

Horseradish

Another perennial, regenerating itself from the roots.

Marjoram /sweet marjoram

A perennial, although it can also be grown as an annual, which was the case at The Mount. There is one entry in which it is 'gathered to dry in a cake' (1 August 1839).

Mint

Forced in the hothouse on two occasions by Susan but otherwise grown outside in beds. Preserved by drying. 'A new kind of mint from Hardwicke' appears in 1839. This would have been sent by the great hero of Shrewsbury, General Lord Hill (1772–1842), who gave Dr Darwin many different plants from his garden.

Parsley

Sown at intervals; throughout the Diary.

Sage

Propagated by cuttings in 1842.

Tarragon

Also planted by cuttings and used to flavour vinegar.

Thyme

A perennial but replanted at least four times between 1839 and 1855. Preserved by drying. A 'thyme from Sundorne' planted in 1839. This is yet another example of the exchange of plants between the Doctor and his neighbours (or patients).

D: PRESERVING METHODS, AND PLANTS TO WHICH THEY APPLY

Bottled: cherries (Morello), currants (Naples), gooseberries
Dried: artichokes, greengages, marjoram, mint, onions, sweet basil, thyme
Jam: apricots, blackcurrants, raspberries, strawberries
Jelly: redcurrants
Pickled: beans (dwarf and French), cabbage (red), cayenne pods, cucumbers, kale seeds, radish pods, tomatoes (red? green), walnuts
'Preserved': apricots, artichokes, beans, blackcurrants, gooseberries, greengages, quinces, raspberries, rhubarb, shaddocks (green), strawberries, tomatoes
Syrup: cayenne pods
Vinegar: crab apples (Siberian and red), gooseberries, rhubarb, tarragon

[1] Thomas Botfield was a magistrate and the Deputy Lieutenant of Shropshire. He died on 17 January 1843, only a few weeks before the Doctor records 'capsicum seed from Hopton Court sowed'. Botfield was possibly one of the Doctor's patients (although the Doctor had 'given up business' ten years before) and was certainly one of his debtors. Botfield and his son, Beriah, had taken out mortgages of £12,000 and £19,000, respectively, with Dr Darwin; Cambridge University Library, DAR 265:9.

[2] Charles M'Intosh, *The Practical Gardener* (London, 1828), pp. 614–15.

[3] Martha Bradley, *The British Housewife* (1756), Vol. III (Prospect, facsimile edn, 1997), pp. 459–60.

[4] *Ibid.*

[5] Susan's visits to London were often made at this time of year and lasted for a month at least. She was probably staying at 57 Queen Anne Street, off Cavendish Square, with her brother Erasmus, who was the only close member of the family then living in town.

[6] The reference to 19 June 1838 is evidence of a previous Garden Diary kept by the Doctor, as the present diary begins only on 1 September 1838.

[7] John Wedgwood, 'Blanching the Portugal or Buda [*sic*] kale', *Horticultural Transactions*, 4 (1822), p. 570.

[8] George Nicholson, *Century Supplement to the Dictionary of Gardening* (London: L. Upcott Gill, 1901), p. 263.

[9] M'Intosh, *Book of the Garden*, II (Edinburgh and London: William Blackwood and Sons, 1855), p. 667.

[10] George Lindley, *A Guide to the Orchard and Kitchen Garden* (London: Longman, Rees, Orme, Brown and Green, 1831), pp. 529–30, 585.

[11] As recommended by T.A. Knight, 'On the management of the onion', *Horticultural Transactions*, 1 (1820), p. 158.

[12] John Wedgwood, 'On the cultivation of the underground, and some other onions', *Horticultural Transactions*, 2 (1822), p. 403.

[13] D.T. Fish (ed.), *Cassell's Popular Gardening*, Vol. 2 (London: Cassell & Co., 1885), p. 106.

PART 3:4

Forced Fruit, Soft Fruit and
Top Fruit

Incorporating lists of named varieties, times of gathering and positions where known

A: FORCED FRUIT

B: SOFT FRUIT

C: TOP FRUIT

A: FORCED FRUIT

The kitchen garden hothouse, the stove and the hothouse/vinery provided the necessary heat for raising exotics, as well as citrus fruits.

Grapes

Skilful forcing and a deliberate choice of varieties ensured that there were grapes for dessert at The Mount for nearly six months of the year. The earliest picking of grapes usually occurred in June or July, although on 30 May 1842 an unnamed variety from the 'Stove in K.G.' was cut. In 1856 the last hothouse grapes (also unnamed) were gathered on 5 December. (However, in December 1838 grapes were bought from Berwick, just upstream on the River Severn, at '4 pound at 2s 6d a pound'.) One variety, a 'Sweetwater' (also known as 'Dutch Water' or 'Dutch Sweetwater'), was planted outdoors against the front wall of the mansion beside the Doctor's closet window. Its fruit ripened late, in November, and in 1839 it supplied 'a large plate of grapes' for Christmas Day. All the other vines at The Mount were grown in the kitchen garden hothouse and in the large vinery which stood at the eastern side of the mansion, above the terrace. Eight varieties are named by the diarists. (See page275 for a list of named varieties, times of gathering and positions where known.)

Many of The Mount's vines were grown entirely indoors, in pots, but others were planted outside the vinery with their roots in a wide border. They entered the house through slots in the front wall, to be trained up the rafters within. This method involved pruning and cutting down the year's growth in late autumn, pulling the remaining stems or rods out of the house through the slots, and leaving them to stand the winter until late February or early spring, when they would be reintroduced to the house for forcing. This is the method first introduced by William Speechly in 1789 for training vines in a pinery, above the pine-beds. It was still used well into the nineteenth century and was preferred by many horticulturalists to the custom of planting vines within the house and allowing their roots to enter the external vinery border through subterranean arches in the front wall of the building.

Pruning and tying the branches to wires and thinning the infant grapes took place throughout the summer months. More pruning was done in the winter, and the cuttings would be potted up.

Rotted turf, cesspit cleanings and manure were put on the vinery borders, which were planted in summer with shallow-rooted plants such as mignonettes, stocks, vegetable marrows, lettuce and celery seedlings. The Doctor may well have been encouraged in this department by his late father-in-law, Josiah Wedgwood, who had 'obligingly informed' Speechly 'that some vines he planted in the ashes of his potteries, had grown with a degree of luxuriancy beyond any he ever saw'.[1]

Grapes all grown in the vinery, except for the Sweetwater.

The names in the Diary are confusing: the first three can all be classified as 'Muscats', as can 'Tokay' and 'Champion', but 'Champion' might also be a Hamburg.

Canon Hall: a seedling of the Muscat of Alexandria, but not as rich in flavour. September and October.

Muscat/Golden Muscat: could be the Muscat of Alexandria. September and October.

Sweetwater/Dutch Water/Dutch Sweetwater: white fruit, grown outdoors as well as indoors. November.

Tokay: fruit white, becoming amber when ripe. August and September.

Champion: could be a Muscat or Golden Champion, or Black Champion (a Hamburg). Mid-September.

Hamburg: late July to mid-September.

Lombardy: red or flame-coloured fruit. Late August to early September

Guavas

This is another exotic fruit in which the Doctor specialised, which grows on a smallish tree, making it more suitable for the hothouse than many other tropical or subtropical species. The Doctor grew both a purple or scarlet guava (possibly *Psidium cattleyanum*) and the white guava (*P. pyriferum*), obtaining the white variety from Condover Hall in November 1838. The trees were probably grown in pots, as on occasion (presumably after flowering) they were transferred from the ornamental collection of plants in the greenhouse attached to the mansion to the more practical stove-house in the kitchen garden.

The scarlet guava, also known as Cattley's guava, was introduced from China in 1820. It has claret-coloured, nearly round fruit, with the consistency of a strawberry, making not only an enjoyable preserve but also, according to Charles M'Intosh, 'a very desirable addition to the dessert during winter; and trees of only four feet in height have been loaded with not less than ten dozen of fruit'.[2] The Doctor's scarlet guava ripened in July, and showed its flowers in April, which casts doubt on its identity. The smaller fruit of the white or wild guava is described by M'Intosh as 'of a roundish, oblong form, and rather larger than a hen's egg. Its flavour is sweet, aromatic, and pleasant.'[3]

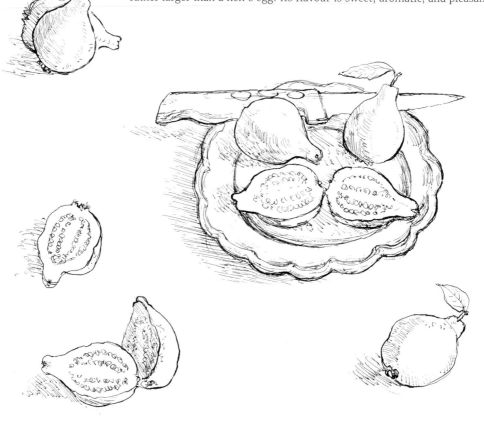

Maracujas (Passiflora quadrangularis)

A tropical American passionflower, with very large fruits. Also known as the granadilla, the fruit is described in the *RHS Dictionary* as 'ovoid, 8 in. or more long; juice purple, sweetly acid, edible'[4]; Charles M'Intosh describes the fruit as 'of an oblong form, about six inches in diameter and fifteen in circumference'. He adds that 'The flavour is sweet and slightly acid, and extremely refreshing in a hot climate, where it is usually eaten with wine and sugar.' M'Intosh quotes another authority,[6] who says that 'a strong plant will produce forty fruit in a season in regular succession, from the end of June till Christmas'. The Diary mentions them only three times, all in 1838, all for fruits picked in the autumn. There is no record of any others being grown or harvested. However, being a true Darwin, the Doctor weighed them. The first was picked on 1 September 1838 and weighed 4 lb 5 oz. The second, picked on 30 September, weighed 4 lb 12 oz and was sent to his friends the Corbets at Sundorne Castle. The third, picked on 22 October, weighed 5 lb 1 oz; it was sent to the Smythe Owens at nearby Condover Hall. Like the passion fruit, the maracuja seems not to have been grown after 1845.

Melons

Fifty years before the Diary began, the cultivation of melons in Britain was, according to John Lindley: 'so general, and their management so well understood, that it would appear unnecessary to treat particularly, and in detail, of what may be looked upon as an almost every day practice, not only in the gardens of the opulent but in those of their more humble neighbours'.[7] This 'everyday practice' involved the making of a fairly substantial hot-bed (a bed of fermenting dung) to retain its heat for a minimum of twelve to fourteen weeks, that being the time taken from the sowing of the seed to the ripening of the fruit. The depth of the bed depended on the size of melon grown; the smaller sorts needed beds 4-ft deep; larger needed 5 ft. The dung base would extend some 2–3 ft beyond the frame covering the melon plants, which were grown in a bed of soil or 'mould', some 15–18 in thick, on top of the dung.

Melons were grown on hot-beds of fermenting manure at The Mount until 1843, seeds sown in March providing the first fruits in July. Then, early in 1844, a 15 x 5 ft melon frame or pit was built (presumably of brick, since its construction took a whole month), to be heated by tanners' bark rather than manure.This would have been a great improvement on the old hot-bed system which was, as M'Intosh observed, 'a process attended with vast labour, care, expense, and waste of manure'.[8] Melons, like passion fruits, were clearly another of the Doctor's favourites, but they are mentioned only once – in 1849 – after he died. This was the year following his death; they are never mentioned again.

Seven varieties are named in the Diary, including one which is referred to as 'Sir John Seabright's melon', seeds of which (along with a Manchester cucumber from the same source) were sown on Saturday 19 March 1842. Charles Darwin had been staying at The Mount from 7–17 March and it is possible that he had brought these seeds with him. No evidence has been found to show that Charles actually met Sebright (1767–1846), politician, agriculturalist and creator of the Sebright bantam, but it is not unlikely, as he admired the man for his acute observations and insight regarding the improvement of domestic animals by selective breeding. A letter written later in 1842 by Charles Darwin to his zoologist friend William Yarrell indicates that Yarrell was well acquainted with Sebright, and indeed that the three men had much in common.[9]

Melons grown in melon frame in kitchen garden.

Beech Wood /Beechwood: an oval fruit with a netted, yellow-green skin and pale green flesh.

Cuthills: not identified.

Hardy: could be 'Hardy Ridge', small, ribbed and warty fruit, well flavoured.

Large Rock: Rock melons belong to the

Cantaloupe group, of which there are many varieties. The chief characteristic of the rock melons is their ribbed appearance, with flattened ends and knobbly, wrinkled, warty skin. Orange flesh.

Neils green-fleshed: not identified; green-fleshed as the name implies.

Pine apple: a small melon, can be either a red- or pale green-fleshed variety; slightly marked ribs; slightly netted green skin with darker green patches.

Sir John Seabright's Melon: see Chapter Three.

Passion fruit

'Passion trees' as the Diary calls them, were grown as much for their flowers as their fruit, in perforated pots or boxes set into tan beds, with their shoots and stems trained up the rafters, like grapevines. The newest shoots would be pruned in the autumn, and the following spring, before growth recommenced, the plant would be repotted in fresh compost, having had the root ball reduced. The 'purple passion flower' (*Passiflora edulis*) does not appear to have fruited very prolifically; the gathering of its fruits is recorded only twice, on 20 October 1839 and on 31 August 1845.[10] A scarlet passionflower is also mentioned, possibly *P. rubra*, which has red fruit.

Mr Salt, the Darwins' family lawyer, was the recipient of a scarlet passionflower plant. It was potted for him on 29 January 1839. The date is significant, as it was the day of Charles Darwin's wedding to Emma Wedgwood. Charles was at The Mount himself from 25–28 January and Mr Salt was doubtless involved at the time in drawing up the marriage settlement. Perhaps he received the gift of a passionflower plant at the same time. There are no mentions of the Doctor's passion fruit or flowers after 1845.

Pineapples

Pineapples were grown at The Mount six years before the Diary begins, as has been shown in a letter from Susan dated 15 August 1832 to her brother Charles, then on his voyage with the *Beagle* (see Chapter One). However, pineapples do not appear to have been grown by the Darwins any later than 1840. This may well be because their cultivation is an even more skilled and lengthy business than that needed for other tropical fruits, requiring hothouses equipped with deep beds of fermenting tanners' bark and flues or hot-water pipes capable of creating a constant temperature of 70°–100° F if the fruit is to ripen. In the first year the suckers or young plants are cultivated in small pots in the moist gentle heat supplied by the beds; in the second year, they are given larger pots and greater heat. Their flowers then appear and fruiting occurs shortly afterwards.

There are sparse accounts in the Diary of pineapple plants being potted and plunged into tan in the hothouse, but the only record of a fruit being cut is for Sunday 13 January 1839. This event coincides with a four-day visit by Charles to The Mount and was, perhaps, a celebration of his impending marriage to Emma Wedgwood, which was to take place some two weeks later.

Strawberries

Forced only in the Doctor's day, by potting strawberry plants in January and growing them in the hothouse, in a manner similar to the forced French beans (see Part 3:3). They would flower within a month and be ready for eating within another month. (For varieties see pages 285-6).

B: SOFT FRUIT

Currants

Both red– and blackcurrants were grown at The Mount, and although there are references to a 'white black currant' in the Diary, it is not at all clear that this is what we would think of as a white-currant. It could be a variety of blackcurrant, known as 'White Bud', which is referred to by Bunyard (1903).[11] Unfortunately, he also gives this as a synonym for the 'Black Naples' currant, which adds to the confusion over the 'white black currant's' true identity. Further confusion occurs with the Doctor's reference, on 28 December 1838, to '3 suckers of the Naples Currant taken from one of the Wilmot trees'. 'Naples' is a blackcurrant, but the nurseryman Wilmot's name is attached only to two varieties of a redcurrant and one of white ('Wilmot's Pale Red', 'Wilmot's Long Bunched Red' and 'Wilmot's Large White').

As with other soft fruits, the peak of the currant season is in July. At The Mount they were turned into preserves, jams and jelly (blackcurrants for jam, redcurrants for jelly). They were also bottled, and in June the unripe green fruits were put into tarts. Tarts were also made with the ripe fruits later, in July.

Currants can be grown as bushes, standards or espaliers against walls, but there is no reference in the Diary as to any specific form other than bushes. They were grown in the kitchen garden, but there is no reference other than to 'Naples currants planted in north border' and 'behind Frame', as to any other part in which they might have been grown. On one occasion mats were put over three of the bushes (31 August 1852). This was a common practice, done in order to retard the ripening of the fruit. Pruning took place from October to December, and cuttings were made from November to January. As in most gardens (including mine), the cultivation of currants at The Mount went hand in hand with that of gooseberries.

Currants all grown in the kitchen garden. Ripe in June and July.

Blackcurrant: no named varieties other than 'Common Black Currant', 'Naples' and 'White Black Currant'.

Naples: also known as Black Naples; according to Scott it is 'the largest and best of Black Currants for general cultivation, but at the same time it is more tender than the other varieties and should not be entirely depended upon for a general crop'.

Redcurrant: no named variety other than 'Wilmot'.

White blackcurrant: could be 'White Bud', given as a synonym for Black Naples (see above).

Wilmot: could be Wilmot's Long-bunched Red, Wilmot's Pale Red or Wilmot's Large White.

Gooseberries

Gooseberries were cultivated, as was the usual practice, in much the same way as currants and grown in the same parts of the kitchen garden. The first gooseberries of the season to be gathered were the tiny, unripe or under-ripe thinnings. They were picked in mid- to late May and made into tarts. Susan seems to have been very fond of gooseberry tarts, noting regretfully on 29 May 1859 that they had had only one that year. The riper fruit was gathered for bottling, preserving and jam in June and July, and in August the last gooseberries were used to make a flavoured vinegar. No specific varieties are mentioned, other than 'Mr Knight's' (30 July 1842); this could be a red variety listed in *Scott's Orchardist* as 'Knight's Marquis of Stafford'.

Raspberries

The Darwins grew only summer-fruiting raspberries at The Mount, and only one variety is mentioned by name, 'Fastolf', also known as 'Filby'. This rarely appears in varietal lists, but when it does so it is highly recommended, having fruit that is 'large, roundish, conical; bright purplish red, and of excellent flavour'.[12] It is 'an English variety of high reputation', according to the author of an American book on soft fruits, which 'derived its name from having originated near the ruins of an old castle so called, in Great Yarmouth'.[13]

Cultivation followed the usual routine for raspberries: pruning or cutting back and planting new canes (or 'trees' as the Doctor sometimes called them) in autumn and winter, manuring in winter or early spring and gathering them in July for preserves, jam and tarts.

They were grown in the kitchen garden by one of the 'Magnum Bonum' plum trees and trained on wires 'in arches' (17 March 1837). Wood ashes,

'Soumach manure' and leaf soil were used as dressings or manures for the beds. In 1843 the Doctor appears to be carrying out some sort of experiment with manures. The space between the beds was trenched. It is not usual to grow anything between raspberry beds, but in April 1854 mangelwurzel was sown between the rows.

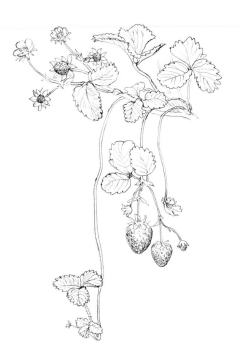

Strawberries

The Doctor recorded the appearance of the first flowers and the first fruits of his strawberry crop at The Mount almost every year between 1838 and 1846; the earliest flowering on the outdoor crop is 31 March 1841, and his earliest fruit appears on 15 June 1844. Susan mentions the first strawberries six times, including '1st strawberries for breakfast' (in 1852, 1855 and 1856). She is equally interested in the dates of their gathering for jam and preserves. Due to a glut in one particular year (1858), she mentions that three lots (of 15, 56 and 20 quarts) were sold on 25 and 30 June and 29 July, at 4d a quart.

The season was prolonged by growing late varieties, such as the Elton Pine, on the north-facing border of the kitchen garden, by the garden house. Earlier varieties were grown on the east and west borders, with some behind the frame of the small hothouse, also known as the kitchen garden stove-house.

In the Doctor's day they were also forced in the hothouse/vinery, a process that started by potting the plants in January, to have them flowering by mid-February. They presumably produced ripe fruit three weeks later. However, the Doctor does not record this event.

Thanks to a selection of early, mid-season and late varieties, the outdoor strawberry season began in mid-June and continued into late September. The Darwins obtained several varieties from their neighbours, among them some unnamed strawberries from Onslow; 'Elton Pine', a 'Hilton' seedling and 'Scarlet strawberries' from Sundorne, and 'British Queen' and 'Myatt's Pine' from Hardwick Grange. Other references are made to 'Ellesmere' and 'Thorn Grove' strawberries, neither of which are known varieties and so presumably mean the places from which they came. There is also a reference to the 'British Queen strawberry from 'the Duke of Bedford's' (21 August 1843).

The beds were manured with pigsty cleanings after fruiting, and cow manure in early spring. They were prepared with 'Bog soil from Roughton, Bones and Cow Manure' (1843) before planting or renewing in September.

Strawberries grown mainly on the north border as well as other borders in the kitchen garden. Also forced in the hothouse.

Black Prince: described in Cassell's[14] as 'dark red, glossy, as if varnished, very early, and enormously prolific', but according to *Scott's Orchardist*[15] was 'supplanted by Cuthill's Black Prince and is now no more'.

British Queen: described by Cassell's (1885) as 'fruit large, highly flavoured, and greatly esteemed, but requires good cultivation'.

Ellesmere: unknown, probably from Ellesmere.

Elton Pine: described by Cassell's as raised in 1850; 'still about the very best late strawberry in cultivation, large, crimson, sub-acid', and by Scott as 'A valuable late variety, and an excellent bearer of the British Queen tribe.'

Hautbois: variety not given, but the fruit is generally greenish-white, with a purple tinge and a musky flavour.

Hilton/Hilton Seedling: either a misspelling of 'Elton' or the place from which it came.

Hooker's/Hooper's Seedling: according to Scott 'a good bearer and an excellent variety for general purposes'.

Myatt's Pine: unidentified, could be Myatt's Deptford Pine.

'Nicaise': presumably Auguste Nicaise or Dr Necaisse which, according to Scott, is 'rich, sweet, and handsome, a great bearer'.

Thorn Grove: unidentified.

C: TOP FRUIT

Almonds

This is usually grown in England as an ornamental tree, rather than for its fruit. The Doctor records the gathering of thirty-one almonds from 'the tree in front' on 12 December 1838. 'In front' presumably means the south-facing front of the mansion but given the latitude of Shrewsbury, this is the only time the fruit is mentioned. The opening of its first flowers is recorded only three times: 19 April 1838, 14 April 1839 and 28 March 1841. Thereafter it is not mentioned again.

Apples

Sixteen varieties of apple, including crab and cider apples, are mentioned in the Diary. The trees grew in the kitchen garden, in borders, in the orchard and against north and south walls.

The fruit was stored in a room above the coach house and in a cellar under the hothouse. Susan twice sent baskets of apples to Charles in 1849, and once in 1852. She also sent a basket to John Wedgwood in 1849. The first baskets were sent in January, of apples and pears that had been stored over winter. The others were sent in October. The basket for Charles in 1852 contained five dozen 'Ribston Pippins', six dozen 'Ross Nonpareils', twelve dozen 'Astontown' pears, six dozen 'Beurre Rose' pears and four dozen 'Belmont' pears.

Some of The Mount's apples appear in Lindley's *Guide to the Orchard and Kitchen Garden*. As a co-founder of the London Horticultural Society, he would have known T.A. Knight and quotes often from his *Pomona Herefordiensis*.[16] Knight was also acquainted with Dr Darwin; a letter from Knight to the Doctor dated 17 February 1803 refers to four new varieties of apple which Knight had raised and was sending to the Doctor for his (then) new garden.[17] The first apple was a pollinated cross between 'Golden Pippin' and a cider apple, 'Loan Pearmain', and named 'Grange Apple'.[18] The second apple is 'of the same parentage', unnamed, 'tolerably good' when fresh, but considered inferior to the 'Grange'. Apple number three is also unnamed, but 'it promises to be an abundant bearer'. The fourth apple, 'middle aged and excellent', is 'Golden Harvey', another cider apple according to Lindley.[19] 'Golden Pippin' is another of Knight's progeny and is also known as 'Downton Pippin' and 'Elton Pippin'.

Apples

Baking Apple: early October. Tree by hothouse and Susan's 'own' in orchard.

Beaufin also known as Beefing: a culinary apple. Mid-October to early November.

Burr: early August to late October. Rich and juicy. Tree in sea-kale bed.

Crofton Pippin: late October, dessert apple.

Crab/Siberian/Red/Yellow: late September. Fruit used to make vinegar. Ornamental as well as useful. Yellow crab on lawn.

Duke of Wellington: a long-keeping culinary apple. Mid-October. In orchard.

Franklin's Pippin: late September. By garden house. Dessert apple, introduced from America *c.* 1819.

Hawthornden: late September. Tree in orchard. Culinary apple.

Knight's Golden Pippin/Golden Pippin: late September to mid-October. Two trees by the frame in kitchen garden 1838, by stove-house and/or hothouse. One moved to orchard in 1850. Dessert apple.

Nonpareil/Ross Nonpareil: mid-October to early November. Tree on lawn, also by kitchen garden door and/or in kitchen garden. Fennel-flavoured dessert apple.

Peach Apple: late September to early

November. Dessert apple.

Pearmain/Orange Pearmain: late September to early October. 'Tree from Harwood'[20] planted north border kitchen garden 1839. Could be any one of the many different 'Pearmains'.

Red Lane/Red Stock/Red Apple: late September. Planted in orchard. Unidentified.

Ribston Pippin: late September to mid-October. In kitchen garden and orchard. One of the most popular dessert apples of the day.

Russet: late October. Planted by garden house and in orchard. Could be any one of the many different 'russets'.

Scarlet Costor: early October. Tree by the hothouse. Culinary apple.

Apricots

These grow mainly in southern England, but the Darwins grew them at The Mount, and most years they did well. They had four varieties: 'Moor Park' (considered the best of all apricots), 'Brussels', 'Breda' and 'Orange'. The 'Moor Parks' grew in the orchard (as a standard), and on the south, west and east walls of the kitchen garden. There was also an 'Orange' on the east wall, a 'Breda' on the west wall and a standard 'Brussels' in the orchard. Unnamed apricots were grown on the west wall outside the kitchen garden, 'by the pump at the bottom of the garden' and against the wall of Abberley's house

– gable ends being particularly favoured by apricot-growers, as can be seen in the village of Aynhoe, in Northamptonshire. Dr Darwin obtained a 'Moor Park' and a 'Breda' as grafted stocks from his nephew Harry Wedgwood in April 1840. To avoid damage to the blossom by frost the wall-trees were sheltered with pea-rods, boards, cedar or fir tree branches in early March.

The Doctor and Susan recorded the first flowering almost every year, which in the case of the 'Moor Parks' was usually three weeks later than the other sorts. However, in 1859 they flowered as early as 16 February, with dire consequences, as on 1 April, 'Snow and cold weather killed all the fruit on the apricot trees' and there were no apricots of any kind that summer.

The crop was very variable but in a good year there would be 'sufficient without buying'. One wonders who did the counting, as twenty-one dozen apricots were picked in 1854, and 214 from one tree in 1840. The fruit was thinned out between April and early August when it was about the size of a nutmeg. The little green fruits were made into tarts. The fruit ripened in August and September. In 1848 an apricot was ripe enough for Susan's birthday (3 August). The fruit was also made into jam and preserves by the housekeeper.

Apricots ripened between early August and late September. They were grown in the orchard, on Abberley's house, and on the west, east and south walls of the kitchen garden.

Breda: flesh 'deep orange, rich, highly flavoured and free' (Scott).

Brussels: flesh 'yellow, firm, brisk flavoured' (Scott).
Moor Park: according to Scott, the flesh is 'bright orange, firm, juicy, and of rich luscious flavour'.

Orange: deep orange flesh, succulent and well-flavoured.

Berberries

There are numerous varieties of this prickly evergreen shrub, called berberry and barberry by both diarists. All have brightly coloured fruits and flowers and are grown in gardens both for ornament and for fruit. The bright red fruits of the common barberry (*Berberis vulgaris*), which grows wild in Britain, vary in acidity, and although the berries of all the varieties are considered to be edible, it is the stoneless *B. vulgaris asperna* that is considered best for culinary use. Only two specific varieties are mentioned: the '*holy leaved berberry*' (*B. aquifolium*), the seeds of which 'from Eaton' were sown in a pot in 1841, and, more significantly, '2 Berberry Darwinii', which were planted in Susan's 'own bed' in April 1854. *B. darwinii*, or Darwin's berberis, was collected by Charles during the voyage of the *Beagle*, in Tierra del Fuego, and was named in his honour by J.D. Hooker.[21] Charles was interested in the pollination mechanism of the berberis, and it is possible that he had asked his sister to grow these two specimens specially for him.

The Doctor does not describe the variety used for eating; he records that three pints of barberries were gathered in September 1839, although in 1841 there were 'but few' for picking. These, if grown at The Mount, would have been from bushes planted in the shrubberies rather than the kitchen garden.

Berberries were also 'got' in November 1858 from nearby Copthorne. There is no way of knowing if this refers to the berries, which usually fruit in September, or to bushes, but they presumably came from the hedges bounding the Darwins' fields beside the Copthorne Road (now the B4386). According to the Reverend William Leighton, who wrote *The Flora of Shropshire*, these hedges, like many others in the neighbourhood, were a rich source of barberries.[22]

There are further references in the Diary, in 1849, to a barberry tree being moved from the terrace to 'below the wall', which is presumably the wall at the top of the flower garden. Four years later a barberry (possibly the same tree?) is moved from the bog bed (which was under said wall) to 'the Glade'.

Cherries

Morellos predominate, grown behind the stove-house, on the west wall of the kitchen garden, and on every available north wall, including the wall in the drying yard. 'Mr Knight's Eagle', also known as 'Knight's Black Eagle' and 'The Florence Cherry', are the only other two varieties mentioned. In 1843, a morello cherry tree 'from B. Smith' was planted by the hothouse. This was probably the Benjamin Smith who came to help nail and prune the wall fruit trees in the 1850s. Standard cherries were grown in the orchard. They grow to a considerable size; this would explain the felling of 'the large cherry tree in the Orchard' on 23 August 1844, 'to open the view of the Castle'. The fruit was made into tarts and bottled, as well as eaten for dessert.

Cherries

Florence: grown on west wall and in orchard, gathered in July and August.

Knight's Black Eagle: grown on west wall and in orchard, gathered late June and mid-July. Said to be 'rich and delicious' (Cassell's *Popular Gardening*). 'Knight' is presumably T.A. Knight.

Morella, also called Morello: a kitchen cherry, grown on every available north-facing wall, gathered in July, used for bottling, 1850, 1851.

Figs

With their fruiting ability improved by a limited root run, fig trees were not grown in the orchard or against a garden wall at The Mount, but in the yard behind the kitchen, presumably against the south-facing wall which also housed the dairy room and the laundry (once the boyhood laboratory of Charles and Erasmus). Pruning and nailing are recorded at various times throughout the year, apparently without any beneficial effect; there was more than one tree, but the crops were never prolific. They were sent as presents only in threes and fours, once to Josiah Wedgwood II, but mostly to Overton (home of the Parkers). 1851, though, was a bumper year, when as many as ten figs were sent to the Parkers.

Medlars

Late flowering (May or early June) and late to ripen (early November), only fifteen medlars were picked in 1838, but there is a record number of 220 picked in 1844. (Again, one wonders, who did the counting?) At first there appears to be only one tree at The Mount (in front of the hothouse in 1840) but a medlar was 'layed [layered] in the orchard' in 1841. There may well have been another tree in the orchard bearing fruit in 1845, when medlars were 'gathered in the orchard', and thereafter there are records, first of how many medlars were gathered from one tree and then, of how many from 'the' tree. They grew into fair-sized fruits, the Doctor proudly recording in November 1842 that '11 of them was rather more than one pound'.

Mulberries

Mulberries as an edible fruit are not mentioned, but one mulberry tree at The Mount was assiduously measured by the Doctor. The Diary for 16 March 1839 mentions its width as having been '8 inches girth 2 inches below fork' in 1835. This had increased to 15 in by 1838 and to 28 in by 1845. The remains of a very old mulberry tree can still be seen on the lawn at The Mount today. One tree grew in front of the hothouse, another in the orchard. The fruit was gathered in late November.

Peaches and nectarines

Hardy varieties of both fruits were grown outdoors at The Mount on the south wall of the kitchen garden. They appear to have done perfectly well without any protection (although Susan makes one mention of 'mildew' on a peach tree in 1852). It was not until the latter part of the nineteenth century, when this blight (now known as peach-leaf curl) was made easier to control by growing peaches and nectarines with the protection of glass copings.

Disbudding (the removal of young budding shoots which would overcrowd the bearing wood later on, if left in place) was done between late April and mid-June. If this was properly done, little or no winter pruning would be necessary, but in January and February the branches would need to be detached from the wall and re-nailed so that the new growth of the previous year could be realigned. There are a few mentions of pruning and re-nailing in July and August. The first blossoms appeared in March, and in spite of being protected with boughs of spruce they were, in 1856, damaged by frost. The fruits were thinned in May and the mature fruit was gathered from mid-August onwards.

The crops were good enough in some years for them to be sent to neighbours; in September 1852 Susan sent peaches and nectarines to Mr Woodward, a neighbour and local seed merchant, and in September 1853 she sent 'peaches &c' to Mr and Mrs Harding (the incumbent of the local St George's Church, and his wife), to Mr Blunt (the Shrewsbury apothecary with a shop at Wyle Cop) and to Mr St Aubyn (whose family had been patients of Dr Darwin) – '3 baskets'. The delicate fruit would not travel far.

Peaches and nectarines ripe late August to late September.

Double Peach: possibly Double Montauban/Montagne, ripens before the Noblesse.

Knight nectarine: (Mr Knight's tree) not otherwise identifiable.

Noblesse: one of the best hardy peaches. Ripens end of August.

Royal George: peach, ripens mid-September.

Pears

Pears were grown on various kitchen garden walls, in the orchard and 'by the Hothouse'. Twenty varieties are mentioned, though 'baking' could be any of the kitchen kinds, for instance 'Catillac' or 'St Germain'. There was also a 'family tree' bearing four different sorts of unnamed pear (11 October 1844). 'Chaumontelles' were taken to market in 1855 and were for sale in 1852 at 4s a strike.[23] These and 'Aston Towns' were the most prolific.

Susan sent a small basket of 'Aston Towns' in October 1856 to 'the Rugby boys'. These would have been her two eighteen-year-old nephews, then at school there. One was Charles Darwin's eldest child William and the other was William's cousin, Ernest Hensleigh Wedgwood. Other baskets of pears, with apples, were sent as gifts to Charles himself (1849, 1851) and Jos Wedgwood III. (1849).

Pears were stored in the cellar behind the hothouse, and with apples in the fruit storeroom over the coach house. Nailing was done mid-January; pruning in mid-January, mid-February, October, November and December; root-pruning in July. The trees were trenched round, and stocks planted in December; gathering was done mostly in October.

Pears

Aston Town/Asin Town/Acton: in orchard, gathered October. Hardy and free-bearing. Good market variety.

'Baking': grown on west wall by garden door, on tree by hothouse and 'on other side of the Orchard' – may mean the Catillac; '48 baking pears broke the branch … 21 pounds in weight', 23.ix.1842.

Belmont: tree in orchard, dessert pear, eaten November.

Bergamot/small/large/autumn/Gansel
Bergamots: tall tree, large Bergamot/Gansel Bergamot in the kitchen garden by the stove and frame, gathered early October. Positions not specified, but Bergamots are supposed to do best on a wall.

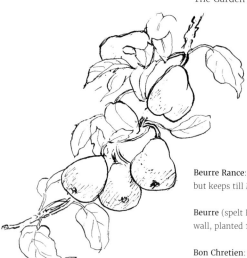

Beurre Rance: dessert pear, eaten November, but keeps till May; does best on a wall.

Beurre (spelt Bearre) **Rose**: does best on a wall, planted 1858 in kitchen garden.

Bon Chretien: grown by hothouse; the best early pear, large and abundant, gathered early September and put into hothouse to ripen, 1842.

Burgundy: mentioned only once, 'small Burgundy pears gathered' 30 September 1840.

Cardilac, more correctly known as Catillac: two trees, one 'tree below hothouse' and in one in orchard, gathered October. For baking; bears exceptionally large fruit – 12 weighed 7 lbs 11 oz, another 12, 8 lbs 14 oz (1841).

Chaumontelle/Charmontelle: in orchard; 'tree at bottom of orchard', gathered early October. 'Old tree top of lawn' gathered late October, one pear weighed 12 oz (1839). Basket put in stove-house to ripen, December 1841.

Choiseul: in orchard, cut down in 1843.

D'Arenberg, also known as Beurre D'Arenberg: planted in kitchen garden 1858, does best on a wall. Good market variety.

Flemish: in orchard, 'trees that came from Mr Lacelle'.

French: not identified.

Green St Germain: 'by/below stove in Kitchen Garden', gathered mid-October.

Hancornes (Hacon's Incomparable?): planted in the orchard, 1842.

Jargonelle: does best on a wall, large fruit, very old variety, early but does not keep. Early flowerings are noted in the Diary, 'tree by the pump', but there are no records of any gatherings and in 1853 the Jargonelle is cut down.

Marie Louise: in orchard. One of the best sorts, can be left on the tree till mid-November. Does not appear to have been very prolific at The Mount but was picked early November.

Swan Egg: one planted in the orchard, 1851, one planted in the kitchen garden, 1858. Good market variety.

'Tree with 4 sorts': presumably the 'family tree'.

Plums and Gages

The Doctor and Susan usually refer to a plant by the name of its variety or sub-family, but they often describe it simply by colour, size, position in the garden, or the name of the person or place of its origin. This occurs most frequently with their plums. A damson comes 'from Millingtons garden', namely, the almshouses at Millington's Hospital, across the road from The Mount. Lord Powis (a neighbour, friend and patient) gives the Doctor 'the Lord Powis plums' which are also called 'nectarine plums'; they grew on the coach house and in the orchard. Harry Wedgwood, the Doctor's nephew, gives him a 'yellow plum', as well as two 'Winesours' and a blue gage.

Some varieties were grown for the kitchen, others for dessert. Greengages served both purposes; they were dried, made into jam or otherwise preserved; other culinary kinds, such as 'Winesours', 'Damsons', 'Imperials', the very early 'Lammas' and any unripe plums were baked or made into tarts. 'Golden Drops' were the favourite dessert plums, protected from the birds by a net of black crepe and scrupulously counted. Only once is there a record of unripe 'Golden Drops' being baked, but twice the treatment for them was to put them in the hothouse to ripen – eighteen large ones were taken there in mid-October 1838 and three dozen in late September 1840.

The propagation of their own plum trees for friends and family occurs throughout the Diary. A 'Winesour' and a 'Golden Drop' were 'engrafted for Mr Charles Darwin' in March 1843. He had moved to Downe, in Kent, in 1842. One of 'Harry Wedgwood's plums' was inarched for 'M' (the Doctor's eldest daughter, Marianne Parker) in April 1851 and a 'small golden drop plum' was 'budded for Mr Parker' in September 1839. The 'Irish kind' of 'Winesour' plum from Preston and Ford[24] was ingrafted on a sucker in February 1839 and budded in July 1839.

Plums and gages

Blue Gage (Gage family): planted against north wall.

Blue Plum: grown on west wall.

Damson: grown in the orchard.

Golden Drop/Coe Golden Drop/large/small or yellow plum/large /small (Imperial family): ripens September to October; 'Large Golden Drops' referred to as 'outside', 'tree on walk by pump' and 'by pump in kitchen garden'. Small Golden Drops, referred to as 'outside garden', 'west wall outside garden' and 'east wall in garden'. Yellow plum 'outside near door'. Small yellow plum also referred to as 'from H. Wedgwood' and 'in orchard'. Probably 'Golden Drop' and Yellow Plum' are one and the same kind. 'Tree by the pump' referred to as 'Coe Golden Drop' by the Doctor in October 1839. Coe's Golden Drop was raised from the stone of a greengage pollinated by a white magnum bonum, by Jervaise Coe in 1800. It is regarded as one of the best dessert plums.

Greengage (Gage): ripens late August to late October. Grown on the east and west (outside) walls. Very often dried, preserved or made into jam.

Imperatrice/Downton Imperatrice (Imperial and/or Prune families): ripens October to early November. No indication of where grown or what variety a Downton Imperatrice might be, but 'Downton' indicates that it would have come from T.A. Knight's nursery.

Imperial/Red Imperial (family name): ripens September; an 'Imperial Plum' was planted in the orchard 'below the hothouse' in 1848. No specific variety other than 'red' named. Red Imperial plums are named by Evelyn and Parkinson (seventeenth century).

Lammas: ripens end of July to early August; so named because of its time of ripening. Grown in the orchard.

Magnum Bonum/Red Magnum Bonum (Prune): ripens August to September. Grown on wall below flower garden, in kitchen garden and in orchard. Bulbs planted under one of these trees on New Year's Day 1844.

Nectarine Plum (family name): ripens August, September, October; one on the coach house, by the doors, and one in the orchard. No specific variety named, but referred to as 'Lord Powis', who presumably gave the trees to the Doctor. Sweet peas were sown round the tree (orchard or coach house?) in April 1843; they flowered in July.

Orleans (Orleans): planted in the orchard, 1850.

Red Plum: outside west wall.

Victoria: September planting recorded in Diary, but not picking. Planted in 1852 on west wall. The Victoria is a chance seedling which originated in Alderton, Sussex. It was sold to a nurseryman in Brixton (Denyer/ Danyer) and introduced by him in 1840. Prolific and mainly used as a cooking plum.

Violet Plum/Violet Gage: ripens September. Grown on east wall.

Winesour/Irish Winesour (Perdrigon family): September; 'against north wall' and 'wall below flower garden'. 'Tree near garden door in orchard'. Standard (in orchard?). 'Irish kind' came from Preston and Ford.

Yorkshire: grafted 1856.

Pomegranates

On 9 January 1839, the Doctor sowed seeds of a pomegranate given to him by Arthur Hill. By 1848 a pomegranate was growing on the front of the mansion and was pruned on 20 December. Pomegranates were a favourite of the mid-nineteenth-century gardener, and although they require 'a considerable length as well as heat of summer', they were often grown outdoors in England, and trained 'as a sort of pilaster, on each side of the entrance-door of a mansion'.[25]

Quinces

There were probably three quince trees at The Mount. It may be that one of these was a tree planted when the Darwins first came there. On 24 April 1845, the Doctor records that 'The old quince tree' was 'pruned & manure put under it'. This may be the quince 'by [the] Green House', by which the Darwins usually meant the conservatory attached to the mansion; another grew 'by [the] Hothouse', which could be the stove-house close to the

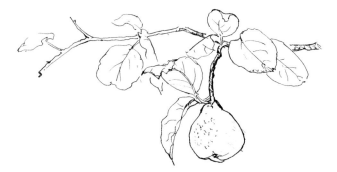

conservatory, just above the terrace. In 1843 there is mention of another quince tree 'by the garden door at the bottom of the Orchard', which would have been near the garden sheds in the kitchen garden. Susan's entry in the diary for 5 November 1849 clarifies these positions somewhat; it reads: '50 Quinces gathered from large Tree by Hothouse. 20 fr tree by Garden shed. 18 fr Terrace tree.'

The fruit was gathered between mid-October and mid-November and counted in dozens. Baskets were sent to several members of the family and friends, notably to the Wedgwoods (Jos II and Bessy) at Maer, Francis at Barlaston and Harry at Seabridge. Among their neighbours in Shrewsbury, three dozen were sent to Edward Haycock, three dozen to W. Wynne and two and a half dozen to Mr Kinaston (26 October 1838). The Darwins preserved their quinces and also roasted them.

Walnuts

The first walnut tree to be mentioned (in October 1839) grows 'by outside gate at entrance'. Another tree is cut down on the north side of the mansion in October 1840; there is a third walnut at the end of the terrace, which in 1841 yields 300 nuts in August and another 300 in September the following year. In other years nuts are gathered green for pickling in late July or early August, and ripe for eating as they are, in October.

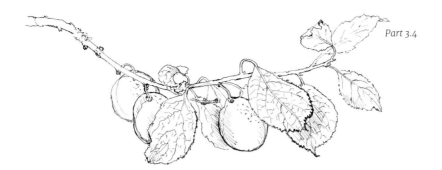

1 William Speechly, *A Treatise on the Culture of the Vine* (London: Longman, Hurst, Rees & Orme, 1805), p. 45n.

2 Charles M'Intosh, *The Greenhouse* (London: William Orr & Co., 1838), p. 375.

3 *Ibid.*

4 Fred J. Chittenden (ed.), *Royal Horticultural Society Dictionary of Gardening. A Practical and Scientific Encyclopaedia of Horticulture Dictionary* (Oxford: Clarendon, 1951).

5 M'Intosh, *Greenhouse, op. cit.*, p. 379.

6 William Micheson, 'On the Cultivation of the Passiflora Quadrangularis', *Gardener's Magazine*, 2 (1827), p. 203.

7 John Lindley, *A Guide to the Orchard and Kitchen Garden* (London: Longman, Rees, Orme, Brown & Green, 1831), pp. 237–8.

8 Charles M'Intosh, *The Book of the Garden* (Edinburgh: William Blackwood & Sons, 1855), II, p. 668.

9 CCD vol. 2, p. 331.

10 'Purple' refers to the colour of the fruit of *P. edulis* when ripe; it bears fruit between August and January and needs 65°–70° F (18°–21° C) to ripen.

11 Edward Bunyard and Owen Thomas, *The Fruit Garden* (London: George Newnes, 1904), p. 49.

12 J. Scott, *Scott's Orchardist*, 2nd edn (London: H.M. Pollett, 1872), p. 529.

13 Edward P. Roe, *Success with Small Fruits* (London: Seeley, Jackson & Halliday, 1880), p. 301.

14 D.T. Fish in *Cassell's Popular Gardening*, vol. iv (London: Cassell & Co., 1885), p. 250.

15 Scott, *op. cit.*, p. 542.

16 T.A. Knight, *Pomona Herefordiensis* (London, 1811).

17 Darwin Archive; Cambridge University Library, DAR 227.6.94.

18 Lindley, *op. cit.*, p. 106, describes the 'Grange' apple's parentage as 'raised at Wormsley Grange by Mr. Knight, from a seed of the Orange Pippin, which had been fertilised by the pollen of the Golden Pippin, in 1791. It is a very excellent cider fruit, and obtained the premium given by the Agricultural Society of Herefordshire, in 1802, for the best cider apple recently raised from seed.'

19 *Ibid.* 'Golden Harvey' produces cider of 'very great strength'; it is also known as the brandy apple. It makes 'a most excellent and beautiful dessert apple too, ripening in December, and keeping till May or June [...] not a large grower, but very hardy; a great and constant bearer, and no garden, capable of containing ten trees, ought to be without one of it.'

20 The tithe map of 1849 shows a John Philip Harwood as the owner/occupier of a small house and garden (TM238) near The Mount.

21 CCD vol. 2, p. 422, n. 8.

22 W.A. Leighton, *The Flora of Shropshire* (London: Van Voorst, and Shrewsbury, John Davies, 1841). Leighton (1805–99) was a local clergyman, botanist and early schoolfellow of Charles Darwin.

23 The Darwins measured crops such as apples, pears and potatoes in strikes or pecks. A strike is two bushels or eight pecks. A peck is eight gallons.

24 Preston is a village 31/4 miles east of The Mount; Ford was a hamlet nearby, on the Severn.

25 Edward Bunyard and Owen Thomas, *The Fruit Garden* (London: George Newnes, 1904), p. 49.

Bibliography

The Account Books of Robert Waring Darwin, Darwin Manuscript Collection, Cambridge University Library

Aydon, Cyril, *Charles Darwin* (London: Constable & Robinson Ltd, 2002)

Bagshaw, Samuel, *Gazetteer of Shropshire* (Sheffield: Samuel Harrison, 1851)

Beales, Peter, *Classic Roses*, 2nd edn (London: Harvill, 1997)

Bettany, G.T., *Life of Charles Darwin* (London: Walter Scott, 1887)

Bingham, Paul and Kris Swiger, *Charles Darwin's Associations with the Isle of Wight* (Proceedings of the Isle of Wight Natural History Archaeological Society, 24, 2009)

Bradley, Martha, *The British Housewife (1756)*, vol. III (Prospect Books, facsimile edn, 1997).

Browne, Janet, *Charles Darwin: Voyaging* (London: Jonathan Cape, 1995)

Bunyard, Edward and Owen Thomas, *The Fruit Garden* (London: George Newnes, 1904)

Campbell, Susan, *A History of Kitchen Gardening* (London: Frances Lincoln, 2005)

Campbell, Susan, '*Sowed for Mr C.D...*', a paper contributed to *Garden History*, Journal of the Garden History Society 37:2 (Lavenham: The Lavenham Press, 2009)

Campbell, Susan, '*Its Situation was exquisite in the Extreme...*', a paper contributed to *Garden History*, Journal of the Garden History Society 40:2 (Lavenham: The Lavenham Press, 2012)

Campbell, Susan, '*The Darwin Family's Kitchen Garden at The Mount...*', a paper contributed to *Garden History*, Journal of the Gardens Trust 47:1 (Lavenham: The Lavenham Press, 2019)

Cassell's Household Guide (London: Cassell, Petter and Galpin, *c.* 1880)

Cassell's Popular Gardening, ed. D.T. Fish (London: Cassell & Co., 1885)

Chittenden, Fred J. (ed.), *Royal Horticultural Society Dictionary of Gardening. A Practical and Scientific Encyclopaedia of Horticulture Dictionary* (Oxford: Clarendon, 1951)

Correll, D.S., *The Potato and Its Wild Relatives* (Renner, 1962)

The Correspondence of Charles Darwin, vols 1–14: 1821–36, eds Frederick Burkhardt and Sydney Smith, with David Kohn, et al. (Cambridge: Cambridge University Press, 1985–2004)

Darwin, Charles, *Charles Darwin's Notebooks, 1836–1844*: transcr. and ed. Paul H. Barrett, Peter J. Gautrey, Sandra Herbert, David Kohn and Sydney Smith (British Museum [Natural History], Cambridge University Press, 1987)

Darwin, Charles, *Journal of Researches*, vol. III (London: Henry Colburn, 1839)

Darwin, Charles, *The Variation of Animals and Plants Under Domestication*, vol. 1 (London: John Murray, 1868)

Darwin, Charles: his life told in an autobiographical chapter, and in a selected series of his published letters, edited by his son, Francis Darwin (London: John Murray, 2nd edn, 1902)

Darwin, Charles, *Darwin's Journal*, ed. Sir Gavin de Beer (Bulletin of the British Museum [Natural History] Historical Series, vol. 2 no. 1, London, 1959)

Darwin, Charles and Thomas Henry Huxley, *Autobiographies*, ed. Gavin de Beer (Oxford: Oxford University Press, 1983)

Darwin, Charles, *Charles Darwin's Notes on the Fertilization of Flowers, 1840–1843*, ed. David Kohn (draft transcription, n.d.)

Darwin, Emma, *A Century of Family Letters, 1792–1896*, ed. Henrietta Litchfield (London: John Murray, 1915)

Darwin, Emma, *Recipe Book*. darwin-online.org.uk

Darwin, Emma, *Diary*. darwin-online.org.uk

Darwin, Robert Waring, *The Account Books*, Darwin Manuscript Collection, Cambridge University Library

Dealamer, E.S., *The Kitchen and Flower Garden* (London: George Routledge & Sons, *c.* 1855)

de Salles, Mary, *The Story of Shrewsbury* (Herefordshire: Logaston Press, 2012)

Eddowe's Shrewsbury Journal

Harris, Donald F., *The Story of the Darwin House & other Darwin Property in Shrewsbury 1796–2008* (privately printed, 2008)

Healey, Edna, *Emma Darwin* (London: Headline, 2001)

Herbert, Rev. William, *Amaryllidaceae: Preceded by an Attempt to Arrange the Monocotyledonous Orders and Followed by a Treatise on Cross-bred Vegetables, and Supplement* (London: Ridgeway, 1837)

Humboldt, Alexander von, *Personal Narrative of Travels to the Equinoctial Regions of The New Continent 1799–1804*, trans. Helen M. Williams, 7 vols (London); facs. repr., 6 vols (New York: Ams Press, 1966)

The Illustrated Dictionary of Gardening, ed. George Nicholson, vol. II (London: Upcott Gill, n.d.)

Keith, Arthur, *Darwin Revalued* (London: Watts & Co., 1955)

Knight, T.A., *Pomona Herefordiensis* (London, 1811)

Law's *Grocer's Manual* (London: William Clowes & Sons, n.d.)

Leighton, W.A., *The Flora of Shropshire* (London: Van Voorst, and Shrewsbury: John Davies, 1841)

Lindley, George, *A Guide to the Orchard and Kitchen Garden*, ed. John Lindley (London: Longman, Rees, Orme, Brown and Green, 1831)

Loudon, Jane, *Practical Instructions in Gardening for Ladies* (London, 1841)

Loudon, John Claudius, *An Encyclopaedia of Gardening* (London: Longman, Rees, Orme, Brown and Green, 1825)

Loudon, John Claudius, *The Suburban Horticulturalist* (London, 1842)

Loudon, John Claudius, *The Villa Gardener* (London, Wm. S. Orr & Co., 1850)

Meteyard, Eliza, *A Group of Englishmen 1795–1815, being records of the younger Wedgwoods and their Friends* (London: Longman, Green, & Co., 1871)

Micheson, William, 'On the Cultivation of the Passiflora Quadrangularis', *Gardener's Magazine*, 2 (London: Longman, Green, & Co., 1827)

M'Intosh, Charles, *The Greenhouse* (London: William Orr & Co., 1838)

M'Intosh, Charles, *Practical Gardener* (London: Thomas Kelly, 1847)

M'Intosh, Charles, *The New and Improved Practical Gardener* (London: Thomas Kelly, 1847)

M'Intosh, Charles, *The Book of the Garden*, vol. II (Edinburgh: William Blackwood and Sons, 1855)

Nicholson, George, *Century Supplement to the Dictionary of Gardening* (London, L. Upcott Gill, 1901)

Quinn, Henri, *Charles Darwin, Shrewsbury's Man of the Millennium* (Shrewsbury: Redverse Ltd, 1999)

Parish Register, St Chad's, Shrewsbury

Parish Register, St George's, Frankwell, Shrewsbury

Paul and Sons, *Rose Catalogue* for 1856–7

Paul, William, *The Rose Garden* (London: Sherwood, Gilbert & Piper, 1848)

Roe, Edward P., *Success with Small Fruits* (London: Seeley, Jackson & Halliday, 1880)

Sale Particulars of The Mount, 1866, Shrewsbury Archives

The Salop Fire Office Policy Book, 1797

Scott, John, *Scott's Orchardist*, 2nd edn (London: H.M. Pollett, 1873)

The Shrewsbury Chronicle, 1810

The Shropshire Star, 2019

Speechly, William, *A Treatise on the Culture of the Vine* (London: Longman, Hurst, Rees and Orme, 1805)

Stamper, Paul, *Historic Parks and Gardens of Shropshire* (Shrewsbury: Shropshire Books, 1996)

Stone, Irving, *The Origin* (Doubleday, 1980)

Symes, Michael, *A Glossary of Garden History* (Princes Risborough: Shire, 1993)

Transactions of the Society (Hort. Trans.), vol. vi (Horticultural Society, London, 1819)

Uglow, Jenny, *The Lunar Men, the Friends who made the Future, 1730–1810* (London, Faber & Faber, 2002)

Wedgwood, Barbara and Hensleigh, *The Wedgwood Circle* (London: Studio Vista, 1980)

Wedgwood, John, *Blanching the Portugal or Buda kale*, Hort. Trans. iv (London: 1822)

Wedgwood, John, *On the cultivation of the Underground, and some other Onions*, Hort. Trans. ii (London, 1822)

Woodall, Edward, *Charles Darwin, a paper contributed to the Transactions of the Shropshire Archaeological Society* (London: Trubner, & Co., 1888)

Index

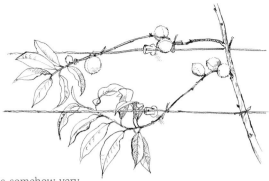

ACKNOWLEDGEMENTS

I always enjoy reading an author's acknowledgements. It is somehow very satisfying to read the names, sometimes familiar and quite often not, of people who have helped a book to finally make it into print. However, when it comes to making my own list I am in a quandary. In what order should my thanks be given? This book took thirty-five years to appear, and I am a historian of sorts, so it seems suitable to give my thanks in a roughly chronological order.

First, therefore, I owe thanks to my eldest son, William Campbell, who first spotted, in 1986, that the Garden Diary of Doctor Robert Darwin was being offered for sale. Next comes the late Willy Mostyn-Owen, who not only led me to the Diary's owner, the natural history historian and conchologist S. Peter Dance, but also took me on a splendid Shropshire tour of the many places mentioned in the Diary. Peter himself was crucial in helping this book to get off the ground, having generously collaborated in the early days and, finally, sold the Diary to me.

Peter also led me to a meeting with Dr. David Kohn, Director of the Darwin Manuscripts Project at the American Museum of Natural History in New York, whose help with Darwin's hitherto unpublished Notebooks and experiments at The Mount was invaluable. Professor Kohn led me first to another great helper, Randal Keynes, a great-great grandson of Charles Darwin and a vital link to Darwin's house at Downe, in Kent, and secondly to the helpful folk at the Manuscripts Department of Cambridge University Library. This led inevitably to my reading of Charles Darwin's Correspondence, which has supplied a constant source of collateral information.

In 1988 I made the first of many visits to Shrewsbury, where I was given a tour of what is left of The Mount's gardens by its inhabitant, the District Valuation Officer and his then neighbours, Sharon Leach and Daphne Capps. This was followed by useful meetings in later years with various members of Shrewsbury's Darwin Research Society, including Peter Boyd and the late Deirdre Haxton. Deirdre proved to be an indefatigable researcher, as was her colleague, Joyce Butt. Other significant helpers in Shrewsbury were Andrew

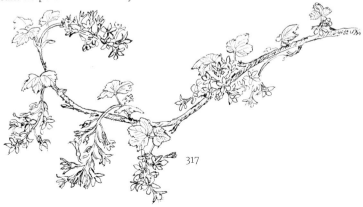

317

Arrol and Christopher Gallagher of the Shropshire Parks and Gardens Trust, Karen Young at Shropshire Archives and my dearest, late friend, Fiona Grant.

I received, too, throughout this time, the most welcome support from my many friends in the Garden History Society (now the Gardens Trust), most notably Keith Goodway, Kate Feluś, Paul Stamper, Sally Miller, David Jacques and Barbara Simms.

The late Neville Hoskins and Dr. Richard Gaunt of the History Department, University of Nottingham, were generous with information about the drawing of the Terrace Walk by Ellen Wilmot. Christopher Proudfoot of the Old Lawnmower Club helped with information about donkey-powered lawn mowers. Grant Muter helped me with John Wedgwood's Garden Diary in the Lindley Library.

In 2016, John Hughes, the development manager of the Shropshire Wildlife Trust and his then colleague, Sara Lanyon,' gave me a useful tour of their newly acquired bank site at The Mount. Both of them, with Councillor Jane McKenzie, have kept me up to date with recent developments at The Mount.

More recent help has come from Lucy Lead, at the Wedgwood Museum; Graham Deacon of the Historic England Archive; Clare Broomfield and Dr. Olivia Fryman, of English Heritage, Down House; Rachel Morrison of Marble Hill and Dawn Culmer of Pope's Grotto, with information about white poplars; Glynis Shaw at Wynnstay, on banana houses; Vicky Basford of the Isle of Wight Gardens Trust, on Charles Darwin's holiday on the Isle of Wight in 1858, and http://darwin-online.org.uk for all sorts of details. Numerous local gardening friends have given me plants for the drawings, among them Richard Channel, Jane Bateman and Victoria Bonham-Carter. Thanks, too, to Fiona Brooke who persuaded her guinea fowl to pose for me, and to Victoria and Peter Roper-Curzon who allowed me to draw their pigs.

Meanwhile, during the actual writing of the book, I was encouraged and helped by the most generous and relentless of researchers, my friend Hugo Vickers, by the kindness of Nicholas Baring and his introduction to three of his friends, the editor Eleo Carson, Professor James (Jim) Secord, the writer of the Foreword to this book, and the garden designer and writer Mary Keen, who generously looked at the manuscript with a critical eye.

I owe endless thanks to copy-editors Elisabeth Ingles and Ramona Lamport, and to Lucy Pitman, for her help with botanic Latin. The excellence of the design of the book is entirely due to Emily Jagger (who also acted as photographer) and my very old friend Stafford Cliff. It also seems proper to thank Ian Strathcarron, the chairman of the Unicorn Publishing Group, for letting us get on with it without any restrictions, except Time.

I also have to thank a doctor, Professor Christian Ottensmeier. He is the pioneer in immuno-oncology who treated me at Southampton's University Hospital. It was his interest in my work, and his miraculous medicine, as well as his splendid team, that has enabled me to live long enough to write the book. And one more important figure in my life, to whom I can never give enough thanks, is my long-suffering, darling husband, Mike Kleyn.

FOOTNOTE

It must look as if I have been extremely selfish in keeping the contents of the Diary to myself for so long, but now that the book on which it is based is finished, I intend to donate it to the place to which I feel it really belongs, and where it will be available for all to see, namely the University Library at Cambridge.

IMAGE CREDITS: Cover and photos on frontispiece and pages 2, 4–5, 14, 158 and 204 by Emily Jagger, Styling and Art Direction by Stafford Cliff. Ellen Sharples Images reproduced with kind permission of Historic England. Line drawings in the text and on cover by Susan Campbell. Some have already appeared in two of her previous books, *Cottesbrooke* and *A History of Kitchen Gardening.*

Published in 2021 by
Unicorn, an imprint of Unicorn Publishing Group
5 Newburgh Street
London
W1F 7RG
www.unicornpublishing.org

Text © Susan Campbell 2021

ISBN 978-1-913491-78-9

Printed by Fine Tone Ltd

Designed by Emily Jagger, Jaggerdesign Creative Services.